INTERMEDIATE TENNIS

Robert Gensemer
University of Denver

Morton Publishing Company
925 W. Kenyon Ave., Unit 12
Englewood, Colorado 80110

Copyright © 1985 by Morton Publishing Company.

All rights reserved. No part of this publication may be reproduced, stored in a retrieval system, or transmitted, in any form or by any means, electronic, mechanical, photocopying, recording, or otherwise, without the prior written permission of the Publisher.

Printed in the United States of America

ISBN: 0-89582-130-3

Preface

It has been rumored that there are people who do not play tennis. This book is not for them. Nor is it for those who play but have little desire to improve. Rather, this book is for players with experience, however varied, who want to become good — even excellent!

It is presumed that you, the reader, are no longer preoccupied with merely coaxing the ball over the net. You can prolong a rally, hit to an opponent's weaker side, angle the ball cross-court, and serve with respectable pace. At the very least, your blisters have turned to calluses, and perhaps now you play often enough to wear out a couple pair of shoes a year. You have had your apprenticeship and are ready to become a complete player.

The discussions which follow should help. They focus on techniques that will allow better levels of play. In fact, there is little difference in techniques of professional players and what all other experienced players should try as well. This makes for an agreeable situation: skills that were once thought to be elusive are now seen as attainable.

There are four major considerations within this book. The first is hitting the ball, discussed in chapters one through eight. The dialogue, though directed toward the experienced player, is not excessively detailed, for one of the palatable features of tennis is that even at its highest level, the formulas for successful performance remain uncomplicated.

Next, attention is given to the strategy of playing, both for singles and doubles. This is technique in application and is vital ammunition for all who would test their skills in competitive play.

The third consideration is a threefold preparation for play: how to practice intelligently, how to be physically ready, and how to be mentally equipped for playing at top form all the time.

Finally, there are amenities: a discussion of misunderstood rules, guidelines for equipment selection, routines for conditioning, even how to choose a tennis camp, and others.

Most chapters include condensed "reminders" about the techniques of play, a "problem-solving" section designed for quick reference about how to correct a flaw, and an "on-the-court" discussion of how to practice given aspects of the game. In all, this book is intended to help you become a better, more perceptive, and more self-appraising player. It is not a substitute for practice, but rather a compliment to it. These pages simply contain helpful information. So do books on brain surgery. But neither is enough, without practice and guided instruction, to assure a successful performance.

Acknowledgments

The author extends his gratitude to the many people who gave willingly of their time and talents to assist in this book. Special thanks go to Ed Doyle and Ellen Yeiser who are the players in most of the photographs. Nancy Kuhl contributed the photographic work for these pictures, and the Holly Tennis Center provided the setting. Darryl Wisnia was the artist for the illustrations.

Table of Contents

Chapter 1.   A Concept of Successful Tennis   1
Chapter 2.   Effective Technique   5
Chapter 3.   Hitting Decisive Groundstrokes 19
Chapter 4.   Spin and Power For The Serve 47
Chapter 5.   Returning The Serve 67
Chapter 6.   Playing The Forecourt 77
Chapter 7.   Tactics For The Lob 91
Chapter 8.   Making Extraordinary Shots Ordinary 101
Chapter 9.   Strategy For Singles 113
Chapter 10. Strategy For Doubles 129
Chapter 11. The Mental Game 143
Chapter 12. Realistic Practice 159
Chapter 13. Aerobic Conditioning For Tennis 165
Chapter 14. The Equipment Revolution 177
Chapter 15. Rule Interpretations 183
Appendix A. The National Tennis Rating Scale 189
Appendix B. A Self-Appraisal Checklist of Skill 193
Appendix C. Rules of Tennis and Cases and Decisions ... 197
Glossary 211
Index 215

CHAPTER ONE

A Concept of Successful Tennis

As all who play the game know, there is something magnetic, totally captivating, about tennis. It excites and it pleases. It challenges and it exhilarates. It wins our allegiance easily, often for a lifetime, to a degree that few other sports can. To take long, purposeful strides across the backcourt, arriving at the right millisecond to plunge racket into ball and feel the reassuring "thwack" of the strings — this is a game that fascinates. To be good at tennis — no, to be **excellent** — is a desire shared by all who play with any measure of spirit.

However, excellent playing ability does not happen overnight. It evolves. Watching accomplished players hit with elegant grace and pinpoint accuracy belies the countless hours it took to develop those skills. They, too, had to evolve. Every stroke was learned through progression, in logical sequence. And, even after having acquired a skill, they continued to rehearse it. Their ability came from having mastered the **basics** of the game — the same skills that we all routinely practice. Any special strengths of accomplished players are simply variations of themes — adaptations of well-rehearsed fundamentals.

Vince Lombardi once said it about football: "Extraordinary teams do not do extraordinary things; they do ordinary things extraordinarily well." In tennis, extraordinary players excel in the ordinary skills of the game. They make fewer mistakes in fundamentals, giving them the privilege of being more flamboyant and daring in their play.

It's All Predetermined By Physics

The most basic of all truths about tennis come from physics. The sustaining factor that grants excellence to any player is how well that player can conform to the dictates of physical law. Whenever a racket strikes a ball, the response of the ball is entirely ordered and predestined by the laws of matter and motion. It is the same for professional and beginner alike.

In this regard, the techniques of skilled play are reduced to a common denominator. There are no gimmicks, no mysteries, no esoteric methods. Instead, the factors of successful hitting can be found in the absolute, definable, and comprehendable laws of physics. This means that regardless of how contradictory different players' styles appear to be, at the critical microsecond when racket and ball are in contact, everyone must impart the same force to achieve the same end. Consequently, it becomes possible to describe the irreducible ultimate of what it takes to make a tennis ball behave in prescribed ways.

There Are No Secrets

This also means that the components of effective hitting are public domain. Nothing is confidential or classified — not even for top-level play. No one person knows something that no one else knows. Nor are any secret techniques used by professional players. Rather, everything about the game is unreservedly available for anyone to observe, analyze, draw conclusions about, and apply on the courts.

K.I.S.S.

Real estate salespeople are often taught to avoid overloading customers with too much information about a property, thus clouding the decision of whether to buy or not. It's called the K.I.S.S. principle: "Keep It Simple, Stupid." A bit indignant, perhaps, but in substance it also applies to tennis.

It's easy to become overloaded with instructional facts about each stroke. But the brain has only a given amount of thinking room. At some point it can no longer handle all the information while simultaneously organizing commands about what the muscles should do. When the brain experiences too much excitement, it tries to rid itself of the excess energy by sending it randomly throughout the entire muscular system. The result is tension — tight muscles and hampered movements.

Furthermore, whenever a stroke is analytically overcomplicated, unnecessary extraneous motions may be added in practice. For instance, a beginner first learning to serve will try to execute a stylistic swing by cranking the body into a pretzel-like contortion which only produces stilted, puppet-on-a-string movements. It would be less confounding to merely take the racket back over the shoulder, then swing straight forward.

Often the best method is the simplest. Pro players do not try to make their game complex, nor should anyone else. As verification, the critical eye of physics has actually **minimized** the number of performance factors that are now recognized as essential for effective performance. In reality, the more tennis is analyzed and subsequently understood, the less complicated it becomes.

Beyond Physics

However, there **are** certain characteristic on-court behaviors common to better players which **cannot** necessarily be described by physics and which are not playing "technique" in the standard performance sense. Yet these mannerisms seem to be part of every competent player's game, whether at Wimbledon or at the local community courts. For example:

- Better players **look** different — they appear more relaxed, yet alive and energetic.
- They are **poised**, in full command of their physical responses.
- They are confident and self-assured. They believe that they can play well. They think **positively**, not negatively, about their game.
- The racket seems to be a part of them — a literal extension of their hitting arm.
- Every stroke is **fluid** — not segmented into parts, but a continuous, rhythmical, flowing motion.
- They hit the ball with their **entire body**, not just with the arm.
- Their style is often free-lanced, not incessantly bound by a compulsion to always have perfect, picturebook form.
- They focus their attention on the **ball**, without agonizing over their opponent, the net, the baseline, or a previous errant shot.
- They play dynamic, aggressive, spontaneous tennis.
- They **enjoy** the game and want to be challenged. They optimistically relish every chance to hit the ball.
- They are mentally, as well as physically, stimulated by the game.

In total perspective, excellent tennis requires an agreeable harmony of physical aptitude and mental readiness. It is mind and body together, each providing its important part for the whole of quality play.

A Feel For The Game

Tennis is a game that for splendid performance requires certain **feelings,** both mental and physical. It asks first of all for the right **attitude** — openmindedness, willingness to experiment, readiness to hit with flair, and even some recklessness. Cultivated tennis cannot evolve from a persistently conservative approach of push-the-ball-over-the-net-to-keep-the-point-alive. Instead, if your full potential is to become actualized, the mental component must be **permissive,** giving full sanction to the body to experience new techniques, to profit from mistakes, and to become unconstrained.

There is also an essential **physical** feeling. To become flamboyant at tennis, you cannot play with machine-like insensitivity. It simply isn't that kind of a game. In fact, it's actually possible to be too "perfect" in form. Players who are compulsive about being stylistic might have flawless style. But their strokes, which appear so esthetic to an unknowing observer, are often very mechanical and inert. As a result, these players have difficulty getting caught up with the **flow** of a match. They never seem to become free hitters and never truly play with spontaneous enthusiasm.

This is usually because such players have programmed their strokes by watching and listening to others, but not by **feeling.** Their source of information is mostly **outside** of them. Yet the more natural, seemingly instinctive way to acquire artful physical skills is to sense, experience, and learn from the **inside** information — from the muscles, tendons, and joints. To become a crafty tennis player, you must be alert to the biofeedback of your own nervous system. You must be sensitive to your inner self — to literally get inside the muscles, monitor their activity, and more effectively control their movements. As a result, you'll perceive the racket as part of you, and the ball will jump off the strings with a new liveliness. Best of all, you will have opened your mind and body for spirited play and genuinely personified refinements of talent.

CHAPTER 2

Effective Technique

Quality tennis, like a sturdy building, requires a solid foundation. Sometimes, however, when a player becomes impatient to learn advanced techniques, the fundamentals take on secondary importance and are perhaps no longer practiced — potentially allowing the foundation to crumble. Even world-class players continue to polish up on the basics, not because they forget them, but because they want their fundamentals to remain finely honed. This, in turn, provides the dependable framework for better, more artistic, levels of play.

What follows in this chapter is foundational tennis — not beginner's basics, but a series of substantive reminders about what should be automatic court behavior. They are the building blocks of excellent performance.

Stay Relaxed

Tense muscles produce rigid shots — nervous shots that are scattered and faulty. The first requisite for smooth, coordinated hitting is to remain relaxed — not lethargic, but calm.

It is often believed that better tennis comes from concentrating more intently and hitting harder. So we might inadvertently overtry: squeeze the racket with a vice-tight grip, firm up the shoulders, take a fighting stance, perhaps even sneer at the ball. But by concentrating too ferociously, we tie ourselves up into a constraining knot.

Instead, relax your body. Consciously untie your muscles. Go limber — not to where you're unresponsive, but rather relaxed and ready. Stay loose, yet alive and energetic. Keep that feeling no matter what kind of shot you are about to hit. Slacken your body; it will help you not only to hit more imaginative shots, but also to enjoy the game more.

Think Rhythm and Timing

Generate a sense of rhythm and timing. Tennis isn't weight lifting — it's more like a dance. Create an image in your mind of gliding through your strokes, then hit with spontaneous flowing. Give each swing a fluid motion with an unhurried start, a solid middle, and an unrestrained finish — especially the finish. You'll get greater depth and accuracy when you complete your stroke with a follow-through that lets the head of the racket continue into the direction of the shot.

Relaxation, rhythm, and timing. They will **allow** you to hit more dynamic serves, more decisive groundstrokes, and more freewheeling overheads.

Be Ready to Respond

Whether waiting for a return shot at the baseline or at the net, you need a flexed body position that prepares you for springing into action. You need to be able to **move** — to pivot, or accelerate, or change directions, or get out of the way of the ball.

A lot of players think that the ready position is a static stance. They cement themselves to the court: thunk — lead feet, straight legs, body leaning forward at the waist like peering over a wall. In this stiff stance their muscles rebel, leaving the body unresponsive.

The ready-to-react position is more alive and spring-like, yet not tense. Have a low center of gravity: feet shoulder-width apart, knees bent, weight mostly on the toes, buttocks down. It's the same cat-like, poised-to-pounce position you would use when guarding an opponent in basketball, or playing shortstop in softball. Keep your racket forward, elbows held in front of your hips. Relax your shoulders, and ease your grip on the racket.

Try adding "bounce" to your readiness. Instead of keeping your weight at rest, energize it by bouncing rhythmically on your toes. Feel the alertness go from your toes up through your legs and hips, all the way into your shoulders. Use your thighs to give you the lift, like you did when speed-skipping a rope. It will give your whole body more voltage and your reactions more quickness.

Effective Technique 7

This stiff-legged, lead-footed stance being demonstrated here leaves the body unresponsive.

Here's a more alert ready position, albeit posed.

And here's the same player actually playing a point. There's plenty of life and spring-like energy in this ready-to-respond position.

Pivot the Whole Body

A classic tennis admonition is: "Get the racket back early." It means to initiate the backswing in preparation for a groundstroke or volley as soon as possible to avoid having to rush the swing or risk a late hit. It's a valid suggestion, but what is usually ignored is **how** to get the racket back.

To execute a backswing, the **whole body** should pivot. If you bring the racket into a backswing with just your arm, then you have only your arm to use for power. But if you prepare for the hit by pivoting your entire body, then you can use your whole self to explode into the ball.

From the ready-to-respond position, as soon as you sight the oncoming ball, begin to rotate your upper body. Do not take the racket back by extending the arm and sweeping it around behind you like a door on hinges, but rather by turning shoulders, arms, hips, all together. In this way, as the shoulders pivot they bring the arms and racket with them in a neat, packaged backswing that coils the body ready for uncoiling into the foreswing.

This pivoting windup can be facilitated by the nondominant hand. If you keep both hands on the racket between exchanges of a rally, you can use your nondominant hand to literally push the racket into the backswing for a forehand, or pull it into the backswing for a backhand.

Using such a rotating, whole-body-coiling backswing will eliminate any tendency to slap at the ball with an arm-only swing. This is especially critical for a backhand, where the shoulders play an important power role. It also reduces the potential for lifting the hitting elbow when preparing for a backhand (which from its high position produces a chopping, powerless foreswing).

Furthermore, this whole-body pivot should precede every stroke, including the serve. Relatedly, if you need to chase down a ball hit to the side of the court, the upper body should first rotate to "pull" you into the direction of your run. And, when you're at

The whole-body coiling precedes every stroke. It's a unit turn of shoulders, hips, and arms, with the spare hand helping the pivot, as the body winds up for a groundstroke . . .

... or prepares to hit an easy volley (left) or respond to a crashing shot hit directly at the body (right) ...

... or begins the windup for a serve.

the net and your opponent crashes a shot directly at you, a quick pivot of the shoulders will help get you away from the onrushing ball and give your arm enough freedom to operate for a retaliatory stroke.

Circle Around Behind the Ball

Most opponents have a nasty habit of hitting the ball away from you. So you spend a lot of time running for it. The natural inclination is to go directly to the ball, on a straight line. But it's better, when you have the time, to go **behind** the ball and then move **forward** into it.

This path will add more power to your stroke and will help you to judge the bounce of the ball so that you can meet it at an ideal, waist-high contact point. It also lessens the chance of arriving too close to the ball, where you would need to cringe your arm instead of swinging with a naturally extended, fluid motion.

As soon as you know that you must run for a ball, pivot your upper body, get your feet moving, and circle around to approach the ball from behind.

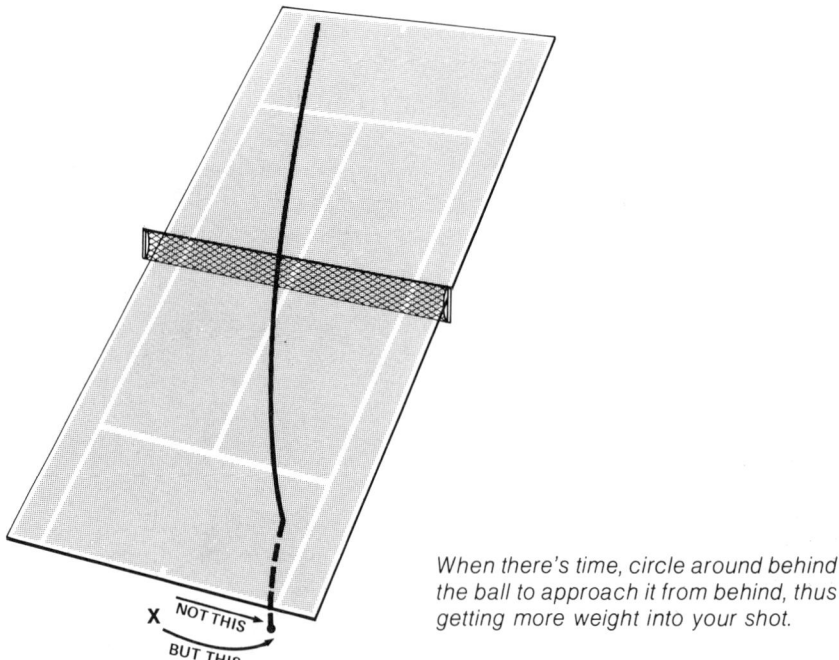

When there's time, circle around behind the ball to approach it from behind, thus getting more weight into your shot.

Go Forward at Impact

If you've done your homework for a groundstroke by circling around behind the ball, then during the contact you should be able to have your weight going **forward** — toward the direction of the intended shot. Commonly, its suggested that you should step **into** the ball. But this is too often translated into a response of stepping **at** the ball, with your weight leaning toward the sideline at contact. Unfortunately, this leaves you with an arm-only foreswing.

Bring everything — racket, arm, shoulders, hips, knees — toward the target as you uncoil into the swing. Reach out and **forward** with the stroke. Feel the energy of your body driving to where you want the ball to go. Even when you must chase down a ball on the run, try to get into position to make your last step directly toward the net.

Even when on the move to chase down a ball hit to the side of the court, try to circle your approach so that you can swing your weight around into the ball while moving forward at impact.

Suppose you're caught backing up and can't get your weight into the shot! You can still generate a **sense** of forward motion by using your upper body and arm to drive the racket head out and straight through the ball. At least try to get your shoulders turned sideways to give yourself more hitting freedom and leverage for the swing.

Make this forward-impulse-at-contact part of every shot you hit. It's important not only for groundstrokes, but also for serves, overheads, and volleys. When you put your weight into your stroke, you will produce a more affirmative shot, and the ball will feel heavier on the strings of your opponent's racket.

Hit the Ball at Ideal Contact Points

Hitting late is a common flaw in ineffective groundstrokes and volleys. It usually comes from a too-slow racket or too-late preparation, coupled with weight that stays back and a ball contact that is too far behind the ideal point.

Perfect contact points vary somewhat from player to player and from shot to shot, but the general key is to meet the ball diagonally **in front** rather than alongside or behind your body. On forehands, the ball should be met a bit more forward than your front foot, and about 12 to 15 inches ahead of your front foot on backhands (at least for players who use conventional Eastern grips). Both these points will find you stepping toward the target with good weight transfer and racket momentum at contact.

When you must hit from up around shoulder height bring the racket into the backswing on a higher plane, and . . .

. . . make sure to bend your knees for low shots. In all instances make contact diagonally out in front of your body.

For a volley, intercepting the ball early in its flight is one of the prime requisites for solid, dependable strokes. And if you habitually hit too long on overheads, it might be from letting the ball come too far above you instead of making contact more out in front.

For groundstrokes, another contact consideration is how **high** off its bounce a ball should be struck. Other things being equal, the best place would be at the peak of the bounce, since the net is then relatively less of an obstacle. But it's anatomically difficult to hit a ball that arrives at, say, shoulder height. Consequently, it's more economical and reliable to try to hit at belt height, or perhaps even a bit lower.

When to hit? As a beginner, you were probably taught to be patient, stay behind the ball, and wait for it to descend from its bounce. While this is ideal for steady groundstrokes, as an advance player it is also advisable to acquire an aptitude for hitting the ball earlier — on the rise — **before** it has reached the peak of its bounce. This ability will: (1) let you hit from further inside the court, where you're closer to your point of aim; (2) allow you to cut off angled shots before they have dragged you outside the court; and (3) permit you to return the ball earlier and give your rival less time to recover for the next shot.

The technique for taking the ball on the rise is to prepare the racket early, take a shortened backswing, keep a steady wrist throughout, and tilt the racket face over slightly to hold the rising ball down. And, hit the ball **in front**.

Hit Through the Ball

It's one of the most commonly used phrases in sports: "Hit through the ball!" It means, for tennis, to make sure that the racket is not quitting its forward speed as it meets the ball. If it does, the ball is unresponsive and lifeless and feels like a rock on the strings. On off-center hits it may twist the racket in your hand, and you'll tell everyone you have weak wrists. To compensate, you'll probably tighten your grip and make your swing too stiff instead of fluid.

To give more direction to the ball, it's essential to feel like you're carrying the ball on the strings for as long as possible. To do this, you must hit forward and **through** the ball. Keep your racket active in the hitting zone — do not let it slow down by holding back on your swing. Let it come to a gradual rest only after you complete a solid, flowing hit.

Check your follow-through on groundstrokes. Hold your finish position for a second to see where the racket head is at the end of the swing. It should have come around your hitting shoulder (but not "wrapped around your neck" in the forehand). It should also be higher than your contact point, indicating that you lifted the ball over the net, not into it.

It's difficult to drive the racket through the ball with good force if the weight is not going forward at impact. Here's a demonstration of an often-seen finishing position where the weight is leaning too much toward the sideline.

This leaning back, "wrap-around" finishing position is the end of a swing that lacked power and whole-body rhythm. It's usually the result of trying to give strength to the swing using the arm only.

When the weight has gone forward at impact it finishes on the front foot, with the racket completing an unrestricted follow-through that ends higher than the contact point.

On serves, your follow-through should be unconstrained, with the racket head finishing down toward the court, indicating that you swung freely at the ball instead of pushing it passively.

On a volley, a lazy racket head is a disaster. The ball will overpower the racket, and the stroke will be punchless.

Watch other players hit overheads. Those who do not have a lively racket at contact will slap at the ball, shoulder hunched up, with hesitancy in their swing. The racket quits — and the ball is listless.

Even on a lob, when you need to hit a soft shot, the racket must come up and through the ball, with its head following the lifted flight of the ball.

Always keep your racket alive, actively moving through the hitting zone — on **all** shots.

Bend Your Knees; Keep Your Eye on the Ball

There are two other timeworn suggestions, standardly stated but universally valid.

(1) "Bend your knees." It's difficult to play the ball well when hitting with stilted legs. Planting a stiff forward knee on a groundstroke will jar the whole body and deny a proper weight transfer. Flexed knees (especially the forward leg) will allow a smooth shift of weight from back to front and will provide a uniform, rhythmical swing. You'll rotate around your front knee rather than having to climb up over it.

Never lock your knees. Not when hitting; not when waiting to hit; not when serving; not when receiving the serve; especially not at the net. Stiff knees make for stiff shots and an unresponsive body.

(2) "Keep your eye on the ball." This means to follow the ball right up to the point of contact on a groundstroke. You don't really need to see the actual hit, but you **do** need to fix your attention on the approaching ball and visually track it into the hitting zone. This will keep your head steady and prevent you from looking up prematurely to find out where the ball is going.

Focus on the ball as it leaves your opponent's racket, then refocus again after the bounce. Notice how much the ball slows down from its bounce, giving you time to clearly set your sights and organize the coordination of your swing.

Don't subconsciously tilt your head to visually track the ball. Groundstrokes are best hit when the upper body stays relatively vertical and the eyes horizontal. Tilting the head interrupts **the** normal perceptual position of the eyes. This minor distortion in your visual readout might be just enough to produce occasional off-center hits.

Keeping your eye on the ball is especially critical on two strokes: volley and serve. If there's any time you need to follow the ball as close to racket impact as you can, it's for a volley. This will help you to meet the ball in the center of the strings and get more solid returns. On the serve, keep your chin up and see the actual contact. Even see the spot **after** the hit. Say to yourself, "See space!" — and you will almost be able to watch the air coming in to fill the space where the ball was before you hit it. That way you'll not drag down your hitting shoulder and lose power.

It's especially vital to keep your eye on the ball during the serve, not only watching it hang in the air waiting for you to crash into it, but also seeing the impact of the racket on the ball and the spot from where it was hit.

Coil and Uncoil

Every hitting sport — golf, baseball, badminton, racketball, tennis — involves a windup and an unwind. The body coils in preparation for the hit, then uncoils with rhythm and power. If there is a single dimension which underlies effective play in tennis, it is the fluid, continuous motion of wind and unwind. Coil and uncoil. Everything back together — then forward together. It's a compact maneuver for a volley, more sweeping for a groundstroke, freely expressive for a serve. No matter how intense the swing, the movement should be flowing — effortless energy in motion. It makes you a human being, not a machine. It makes tennis a game, not work. And it makes the game a pleasure, not a stressor.

Reminders

1. Relax. Stay limber, yet alert and responsive.
2. Stay lively on your toes. Between exchanges in a rally, keep your feet active. Be loose and bouncy.
3. To prepare for any stroke, pivot the whole body as a unit. Coil and uncoil; back together — forward together.
4. Get the whole body into the stroke — racket, shoulders, fanny — all moving on-line toward the target at impact.
5. Give rhythm to every hit. Produce smooth strokes. Flow through every swing.
6. Hit every ball in front, with unlocked knees.
7. Keep the racket active through the hitting zone.
8. Let your swing be dynamic, spontaneous, expressive.

Problem Solving

Problem	Probable Cause	Solution
Sluggish responses	Tense, static, unready starting position	Be an athlete, prepared in a ready-to-*move* position
Tight, jerky shots	Body too stiff	Relax grip; slacken body
	Overtrying or Overhitting	Think rhythm and timing
Improper weight transfer	Stiff front leg	Keep legs springy; bend and flex between points
	Not going forward at contact	Drive whole body toward target during foreswing
Lifeless shots	Racket quitting in hitting zone	Exaggerate the follow-through
Hitting too far behind ideal contact point	Preparing racket too late	Bring racket back before ball crosses net
No power	Arm-only swing	Coil and uncoil with whole body; everything into swing

On the Court

Next time out, give attention to the sensation of rhythm and timing in your swing, emphasizing coiling and uncoiling and the position of your body relative to the ball. During practice hitting, it's easy to be careless — not paying much mind to the design of your strokes. So the ball might get casually struck, perhaps at poor contact points, with inadequate weight transfer, or with stiff knees, whatever. The hazard is that some ineffective habits, not being of much consequence during a practice knockabout, might filter into becoming part of your regular routine. Every time you hit a ball, your body remembers, to some degree, the swing that it took. Make it remember your **best** style.

Emphasize footwork. Try the "bounce step," where you **unweight** just as your practice partner is about to hit the ball. Take a hopscotch skip-step into a ready-to-respond position, timing it so that you have split your feet wide and taken the weight off your heels just as the ball is about to be struck. Try it not only for groundstrokes, but also at the net. You'll be less likely to get caught flatfooted on any ball. And you'll notice, especially when receiving serve, that you no longer get stuck in a frozen position as the ball is on its way.

In particular, use the practice session to give rhythm to every stroke. Make it form and function together. Think of the **art** of tennis. Try to "look good" as you hit. Talk yourself into it. Say "smooooth" as you bring your racket into and through the ball. **Float** through your strokes. Then when it feels right, think of **why** it feels right. Let the sensation linger in your muscles, and grant them the freedom to have the same swing for the next ball. Soon, when it's right, you'll **know** it's right.

CHAPTER 3

Hitting Decisive Groundstrokes

At all levels of play, from novice to professional, the groundstrokes are the nucleus of tennis. Forehands and backhands — they support every other aspect of the game. They are the framework upon which advanced skills are built.

In match play, the groundstrokes have two basic values. One is to keep the ball perpetually alive to give an opponent repeated chances to make a mistake, and the other is to win points outright through pace and placement.

This chapter tells how to hit affirmative groundstrokes — shots from either side of the body that give the ball compelling velocity and coerce opponents into defensive returns, or no returns at all. Discussion is included on how to give the ball spin, this being an important tactical difference between a weekend backboard-type player and a versatile, all-court competitor.

When Racket and Ball Meet

When a racket intercepts a ball, both racket and ball are deformed, the degree of the deformation being related to the force of the impact. On a strong return of a rapidly approaching ball, at impact the racket will bow backward like a springboard absorbing the weight of a diver. The strings will stretch like a trampoline receiving a jumper, and the ball will flatten out on the strings to half its normal diameter. Then in an instant everything reverses: the racket recoils, the strings rebound, and the ball kicks into acceleration by quickly regaining its shape.

Isaac Newton explained it: "For every action there is an equal and opposite reaction." In tennis, it means that the more the racket and ball are misshapened on contact, the greater will be the magnitude of their response. Consequently, the more velocity the ball will enjoy in its resulting travel. Thus, the faster the racket head is moving at impact, the greater will be the speed of the struck ball. How, then, can you generate good racket head speed for strong shots?

Ease the Grip

It might seem that it's possible to have too much of a good thing — too much racket head speed could result in a loss of control. However, a lack of control generally does **not** come from too much velocity on the racket head at impact, but more commonly from the manner in which the racket is swung. Power and control are not mutually exclusive; you can have both simultaneously. The first requisite for this happy combination is to hold the racket loosely.

Loosely? That's contradictory to what you've probably always been told. "Keep the wrist firm" is a standard admonition. It was good advice when you were a beginner and needed a constant, steadying grasp of the racket because your swing was unsure. And it still is correct to have a solid wrist at the moment of impact with the ball, but **not before.** The moral, therefore, is: "Loose grip to start — firm grip at contact."

If you lock your wrist for the early part of your swing, you will reduce the feel of the racket in your hand. The racket becomes too much of a club, and it becomes more difficult to be versatile for hitting a strong drive on one shot and a softly touched drop shot on the next. You need a direct line of **sensitivity** from brain to racket head, and the nerve endings that supply the link are in your hand. A too-tight grip shuts them down.

Next time out, ease your grip — not to where you have a floppy, lifeless wrist, but a relaxed grip, holding the racket without strain. This will loosen your arm and your whole body for a livelier, flowing swing. You'll automatically squeeze the racket harder as it approaches the ball, but what you do not want is to start the swing with an arm-restricting, hammerlock grip. Between points, consciously open your fingers to take any stress out of your hand. And between shots of a continuous rally, keep your grip loose, unbound. Cradle the racket in your opposite hand to take some of its weight out of your hitting arm. During practice, say to yourself, "Loose to start — firm to hit." Eventually you'll develop so much feel for the racket that you'll think you have strings between your fingers.

Accelerate the Racket

It's another physical law: a racket head that is accelerating at impact will impart more force to the ball than if the racket has the same forward speed, but no acceleration.

Take a positive, convincing swing — a good coil and uncoil — and stay tenaciously active through the hitting zone. Make the racket gather momentum so that it comes into the ball while still gaining speed. It is a primary requisite for power on the groundstrokes.

You can tell if you're accelerating the racket by how the ball feels on the strings. If the racket is not gaining speed at contact, the ball will feel heavy, like a hunk of lead. Off-center hits produce a "twang" — your hand vibrates, and the racket may twist from your grasp. By contrast, with an accelerating racket, the ball will feel like it has virtually no weight. Your feedback will tell you that the racket head has overpowered the moving mass of the ball, rather than vice-versa, and the ball will spring into noticeably livelier flight. It even **sounds** different — a higher pitched "thwack" instead of the dull "thud" that comes from a lazy racket head.

Sources of Power

How do you get the racket into optimal acceleration? In two ways:

1. Linear momentum, resulting from the transfer of weight from back to front foot.
2. Rotary momentum, coming from the unwinding — rotation — of the body during the foreswing.

Both work together in a sequential chain of events which, when coordinated correctly, has the following order:

1. With the completion of the windup, push off the back foot so that your weight begins to transfer forward.
2. Hips move forward and begin to rotate, opening up toward the target.
3. Trunk picks up the rotation.
4. Shoulders rotate.
5. Arm and racket come forward and around the shoulder.

The end product of these integrated forces is more than the sum of the parts. But to maximize their effect, they must be

Linear momentum originates from a forward stride and transfer of weight, while . . .   *. . . rotary momentum results from an unwinding of the shoulders in the swing.*

performed **sequentially.** Optimal power will not be generated if, for example, the forward swing does not start with a weight transfer. If the weight stays on the back foot, linear momentum is minimized, and the hitter will be left with only the rotary component to deliver the power. Thus it should be: (1) step, then (2) swing.

Open Versus Closed Hitting Stance

Curiously, many players who fail to transfer their weight forward will, when trying to hit with power, subconsciously swing their front foot completely around to where it finishes opposite of their hitting side. This is apparently a compensating act which, since it produces no linear momentum, will instead try to generate the power with extra rotary motion. But it makes for a circular, wraparound swing, with inferior control potential. Nonetheless, it does illustrate the mechanical fact that, for rotary momentum to gather its optimal force, the body literally needs to get out of the way of the hitting arm.

Often, beginning players will either be taught, or will quite naturally, hit their forehands from out of a closed stance. When power is an objective, this closed stance will place a sort of "governor" on the swing, restricting a free-flowing motion since the left side is now in the way of the follow-through. It also impedes the rotation of the hips; thus, racket acceleration at contact is unlikely.

Observe the professional players. Given enough time to collect themselves for a forehand (that is, not being forced to hit on the run), they will generally hit from a variable **open** stance. The reason is to allow the hips and shoulders to add unrestricted rotary momentum to the swing. It also is easier to hit topspin from an open stance (to be discussed later in this chapter).

So there's a medium somewhere. The forehand should not be hit from a closed stance, nor from an exaggerated "spun-around" open stance. It should be opened enough to permit freedom for rotary movement in the swing, but not so open as to hinder the transfer of weight onto the front foot.

For a backhand, an open stance is not vital because the swing moves out and away from the body. In fact, an open stance will tend to restrict the **backswing** for a backhand. Consequently, a somewhat closed hitting stance is more economical for a clean

The conception of "stepping into the ball" is sometimes misinterpreted to mean . . .

. . . stepping at the ball, resulting in too much of a closed stance that can hinder weight transfer . . .

. . . and reduce the free flow of the swing and follow through.

When the stride is more forward . . .

. . . linear momentum is greater, and the unrestricted rotation from the hips allows for . . .

. . . a free swing and clean follow through.

On the backhand side, more rotary momentum is necessary from the shoulders, thus . . .

. . . a closed hitting position permits a bigger backswing . . .

. . . without restricting linear momentum and a free follow through.

backhand. Make sure, however, that this closed stance does not pull your weight to the side during the hit.

The Inside-Out, Flattened-Arc Swing

Think of what it's like to paddle a canoe. To get maximum pull, you take as long a stroke as possible and paddle flat against the direction of the pull. It's the same for a groundstroke. To increase effective hitting length, the swing should flatten out and lengthen as it approaches the ball, racket face staying square-on to the target.

This flattened arc comes from an inside-out swing. The racket starts from close in, then moves out and forward through the hitting zone. The elbow unbends, giving a hint of a "push" to the effect. It is in contrast to the often seen circular swing of a novice, or to the player who initiates a forehand with an arm-extending backswing followed by a foreswing that pulls the racket back into the body again.

Properly executed, the inside-out swing may first give the hitter an impression that the ball will be driven off to the side of the court. It starts with the elbow flexed, about the same as it is when held in the ready-to-move position. Then the arm **extends** into the hitting zone. It is the natural, centrifugal response of your arm anyhow, and its effect is to lengthen the radius of the swing, thus adding whip to the stroke and power to the ball. As the swing flattens out, the distance during which the ball can be accurately hit also increases, since the racket head stays on course toward the target longer.

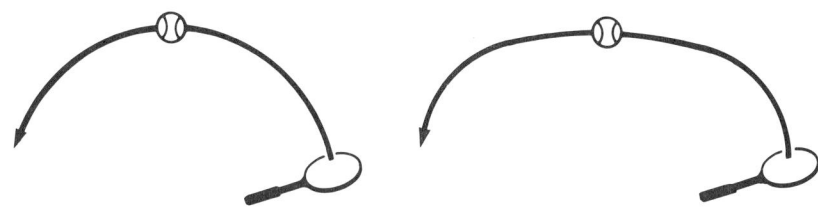

Linear momentum can be increased through an inside-out swing which produces the flattened arc shown on the right, compared to a static-arm swing which results in the circular path shown on the left.

That Troublesome Backhand

Some people suggest that the backhand is the more natural of the groundstrokes because the swing moves away from the body. But for too many players, the backhand is an exemplification of Murphy's Law.

The major obstacle to a fluid backhand is a failure to rotate the shoulders. This is less of a problem for a forehand, where a functional shot can still be produced with minimal shoulder rotation. But the backhand is hit with a weaker set of muscles; thus, more shoulder involvement is necessary to generate the rotary momentum for an authoritative stroke.

Emphasize the unit turn of your upper body from out of the ready-to-respond position. Rotate your shoulders around so much that your opponent can see the logo on the back of your shirt (or your shoulder blades, if you don't have a logo). Think of

If your backhand shots lack depth and accuracy, try to increase the rotation of your windup, looking over your lead shoulder at the oncoming ball . . .

. . . then hitting with a firm wrist, while freely unwinding your shoulders . . .

. . . and emphasizing a high follow-through to eliminate the common tendency to chop the swing.

what the word says: **back**hand. Show your **back** to hit the shot. Turn so that you must look over your lead shoulder to see the approaching ball.

Often, it's likened to throwing a frisbee. Turn sideways to the target, draw the arm back close to the body, then fling forward and outward, letting the arm straighten naturally, toward the target. The analogy should help to keep your elbow close to your body for the windup and to bring the racket out and through the ball.

Another menace is a "flying elbow." This is when the elbow leads the foreswing, racket trailing behind, usually accompanied by little or no weight transfer, and the racket is yanked across the body to "slap" at the ball. Try this little trick. Take a spare ball and tuck it under your armpit. Hold the ball there in the backswing and through the hitting zone. It should then drop to the court in the follow-through, well after the shot is on its way. It will provide some assurance that your swing went out and away from you, with a high finish.

Still having trouble with the backhand? Here is a checklist of ingredients for successful execution.

- Use your cradling hand to help guide the racket into the proper backswing position.
- Do not roll your hitting elbow up as you bring the racket back.
- Get both feet turned to point toward the alley for the backswing.
- Let the handle of the racket point in the direction you want to hit the ball during the backswing.
- Elbow points down at the end of the backswing.
- Point your lead shoulder at the oncoming ball during the windup. Feel your shoulder come under your chin.
- As you begin to uncoil, step toward the net.
- Don't crowd the ball. Hit the ball firmly with an extending arm in the foreswing.
- Meet the ball in front. Lean your body weight toward the net as you hit.
- Stay down on the ball, eyes following its path, and shoulders level at contact.
- Hit through the ball, trying to keep it on the strings as long as possible.
- Hold a firm wrist through the hitting zone.
- Use a full follow-through, racket finishing forward and high.

- The lower the ball, the more you must drop your shoulder and point it at the ball to keep from the racket head from drooping. Don't forget to bend your knees.
- On a high-bounding ball, lift your arm and shoulder to go up for the ball without changing the angle between forearm and racket handle. Don't attempt to lift your elbow up to the height of the racket.

Ode to the Two-Fisted Backhand

Why are there so many two-handed backhand hitters in this game? The standard reason given is because many youngsters pick up a racket about the same time they are learning to walk, and since they don't have adequate strength to swing it with one hand, they naturally grab it with two. A more complete answer would be that the double-handed backhand actually makes good sense. Overall, it's a mechanically efficient way to hit the ball.

Using two hands adds power to the stroke. A one-handed backhand requires more strength to slug the ball hard. Players who lack the necessary strength often try to compensate by slashing their arm across in front of their body, or by dragging the racket forward with elbow leading in an attempt to sling it into the ball. With the benefit of an extra hand, much of this power deficit can be made up.

In a regard, the two-fisted backhand is two forehands in one. There is no need to change to a backhand grip; two Eastern forehand grips can be used (although some players do prefer to slip their dominant hand into a Continental grip). Generally, this leaves the hitter with a feeling that the two-hander is more like a forehand on the opposite side of the body than a backhand.

If you are a two-handed hitter, or are experimenting with it, make sure that you keep your two hands close together. This will help you to capitalize on the extra leverage given to the racket. The two hands, reinforcing each other, will also prevent the elbow from leading the swing and will assure firm wrist control of the racket at contact.

Give an emphatic shoulder turn to the two-hander. A convincing pivot and proper weight shift are necessary to generate the full power of the stroke. Help your shoulder rotation by rolling your back knee in and forward as you start the weight shift. This will open your hips, allowing your shoulders to come through unrestricted.

Hit the ball out in front, but not so far as for a one-hander. Make the contact just ahead of your forward foot.

On the follow-through you have two choices. One is to keep both hands on the racket to the end, finishing with the lead arm bent, trailing arm extended. Don't let the spare hand push the racket too much and override the lead arm. At the finish of the stroke, you should be able to watch the flight of the ball by looking over your trailing elbow.

The other choice is to let go with your second hand after the ball has been sent on its way. By that time the spare hand will

A principle advantage of the two-handed backhand is the power it generates...

...by more effectively transferring the rotary momentum of the shoulders to the racket. But make sure there's also good linear momentum...

...by hitting the ball out in front, with definite weight transfer...

...and a determined swing which accelerates the racket into a high finish.

have done its work — providing impetus and strength to the stroke — and then it can be released from further duty. Be sure to let the hand come off the racket only after it has guaranteed acceleration through the impact with the ball.

If your two-handed backhand feels constrained . . .

. . . try making contact with both hands on the racket . . .

. . . then releasing your trail hand . . .

. . . to permit a disengaged follow-through.

Groundstroke Reminders

1. Keep the grip loose to start, firm to hit.
2. Get a good shoulder turn for the windup, especially for backhands, and emphatically for the two-hander.
3. When coiling for a backhand, look over the forward shoulder to sight the approaching ball. Pretend that an arrow extended through both shoulders would point at

the ball. Bring the front shoulder down low for a low ball, high for a high-bounding ball.
4. Watch the ball all the way into the hitting zone.
5. Unweight your front foot as you coil into the backswing so that you can step toward the net as you move your weight forward into the shot.
6. Point the handle of the racket at the target in the backswing.
7. Get all your weight into the shot. Accelerate the racket. Explode into the ball.
8. On two-handers, keep the trailing arm directly behind the handle at contact.
9. Extend fully through the ball. Bring the racket head toward the target, inside-out, as far as you can before allowing it to arc around in front of you.
10. Try to carry the ball on the strings as long as you can. Imagine that each ball has three other balls behind it. Try to thread the racket through all four as you swing.

Problem Solving

Problem	Probable Cause	Solution
Erratic shots	Not watching ball	Keep head down, following ball into hitting zone
Ball goes dead on racket	No acceleration	Drive racket into ball; do not be tentative
Poor accuracy from high- or low-bounding ball	Racket coming into backswing always in same plane	Bring racket into backswing at same level as anticipated contact
Unstable wrist at contact	Listless, drooping racket head	Maintain constant 45-degree angle between forearm and racket, regardless of height of swing
Poor balance	Poor position relative to ball	Take small shuffle steps when nearing ball
	Not stepping toward net at contact	Make last step toward the target

(Continued)

Problem	Probable Cause	Solution
Minimal rotary momentum	Hips restricted from complete turn	Hit from open stance on forehand, only slightly closed on backhand
Minimal linear momentum	No weight shift	Get head out in front; lean toward net during hit
Slashing, wraparound swing	Stance too closed	Drive weight toward target
	No linear momentum	Swing inside-out

The Advantage of Spin

When you can intentionally spin the ball from your groundstrokes, you automatically move up one level in tennis. The favorite is topspin, where the rotation of the ball will send it curving downward toward the court. With topspin you can clear the net with a greater margin of safety, or rip a crushing crosscourt forehand that will dip into the court out of reach of your helpless opponent.

The opposite is backspin, which allows you to drop a soft shot just over the net and have it "sit down" in front of your scrambling rival. Or you can send a backspinning ball to a corner and watch the low hop force your opponent to hesitate on the swing.

Spin helps any player to produce more effect with their shots. Topspin grants the freedom to hit with extra pace and with confidence that the ball will arc into the court. Backspin can be used to take the sting out of an opponent's strong shots.

Spin makes your game more versatile, more opportunistic. You can be an offensive dynamo when the moments are right and suddenly switch to a defensive perfectionist when you need to. All the while, you'll have more influence on the pace of a match and more control over the outcome. Eventually, you'll be so delighted with the results of spin that you'll want to give it to every shot you hit.

The Effects of Spin

It was a renaissance man of physics, Daniel Bernoulli, who first described what happens to a rotating object in flight. His explanation became appropriately known as the Bernoulli principle, and it accounts for not only why a tennis ball can be made to curve, but also a baseball, golf ball, volleyball, or any other spherical object.

The influential factor is not what the air does to the ball, but what the ball does to the air. As it spins, the ball grabs a layer of surrounding air molecules and spins them around with it. In flight, this has the effect of changing air pressure around the ball. If the ball has topspin (where the top surface of the ball is spinning into the direction of its flight), it will be pulling air up over its top surface. As the ball moves forward, this air is flung into a headlong crash with the stationary atmospheric air. This friction creates a crowding of air molecules on the upper surface of the ball, thereby increasing pressure.

But underneath the ball, the effect is the opposite. The rotating ball is, in flight, pushing air molecules out of the way much in the fashion that a car tire, when accelerating on a dirt road, will kick gravel out behind it. Consequently, there is less crowding of the air underneath the ball and therefore less pressure. And by decree of physics, the ball will always move away from high pressure, toward low pressure. Thus, a spinning ball will, during its flight, curve in the same direction as the rotation of its forward surface. For topspin, this means that the ball will inherit a downward arc in its travel.

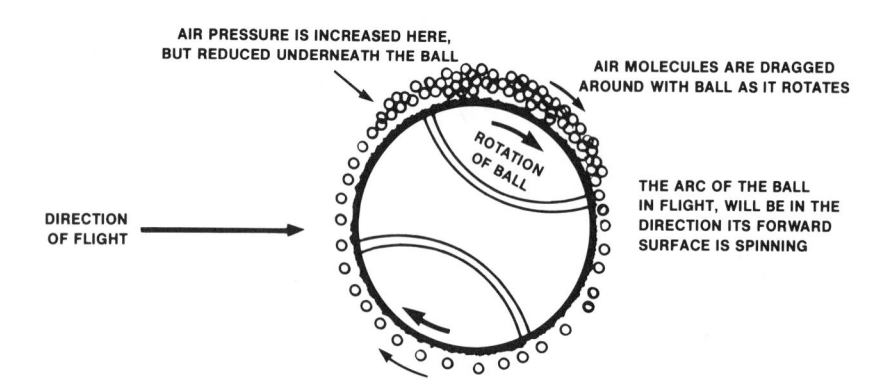

The effect is greatly magnified by the felt cover of a tennis ball. The fuzz of the ball creates more friction with the air — with better "grabbing" capability — and thus the spinning ball will pull a greater volume of boundary air around with it. Conversely, a ball that has lost its nap will not have nearly as dramatic a curving path in flight because it will not drag as much boundary air around with it while it spins. This is the reason for the introduction of new tennis balls after the first seven and every nine games thereafter in professional tournament play.

The advantage of topspin becomes obvious. Since the ball will arc downward in its flight — much more so than by the effect of gravity along — it allows a player to hit stronger shots and still have them find the opponent's court. Additionally, the downward bend of the ball will drive it into the court at a more vertical approach angle than a ball hit with no spin. Thus, when the ball hits the court, its spin and steep entry angle will cause it to "kick" from its bounce in an apparent accleration that results in a higher and deeper rebound. Consequently, it forces opposing players to stay further back in their own court to play the ball and to frequently receive the ball at a more uncomfortable shoulder-level height.

The effect of a backspinning ball is the opposite. In the ball's flight, the greatest friction and higher air pressure will be built up underneath the ball; therefore, the ball will want to stay airborne longer than if it had no spin. Ordinarily this would be considered a disadvantage, for a backspinning ball will "float" during its travel and have a better chance of carrying over the baseline. However, backspin can effectively be used to land a shallow shot that will "grab" the court and seemingly "back up" in its rebound, thus staying further away from a too-deep opponent. Or, if the ball is hit with good pace and low trajectory, it will tend to skid and remain low from its bounce, thereby coercing an opponent into hitting lunging, off-balance returns.

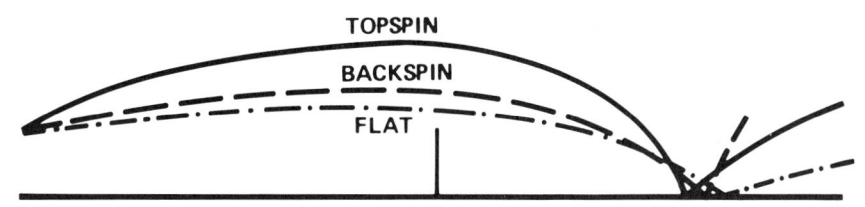

A topspinning ball can be hit to clear the net with a higher margin of safety, and its kick will compel opponents into staying deeper in their own court. A ball hit with backspin will "back up" after its bounce, making the timing for a return more unsure for opponents.

How the Racket Produces Spin

Every ball that leaves your racket will have some spin, however slight. The direction and magnitude of this spin will be determined by the direction in which the racket head is traveling at the moment of impact. If the racket head is on an upward path, the ball will leave with topspin. If the racket head is moving downward at impact, the ball will be given backspin. The more emphatic the upward or downward racket path, the greater will be the spin given to the ball.

It's physics again. When a racket crashes into a ball, the ball sits flattened on the strings for a millisecond, without rotating. Then, as it regains its shape and leaves the strings, the ball will inherit a spin that is a reaction to the acceleration and direction of travel of the racket during contact.

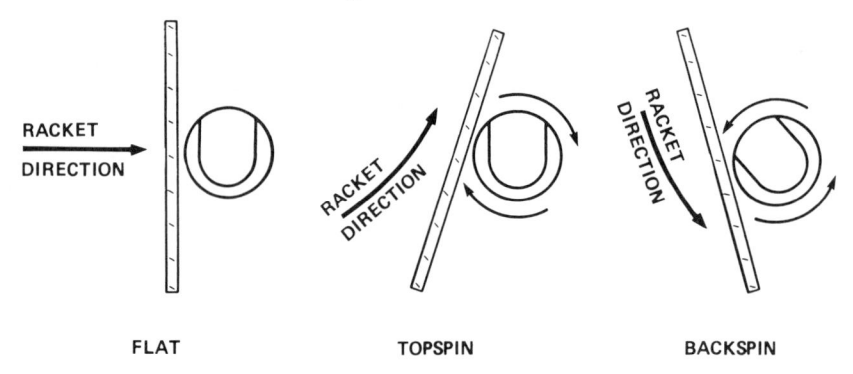

FLAT   TOPSPIN   BACKSPIN

There's a widespread belief that the tilt of the racket face at impact will also have a significant effect on the spin given to the ball. In truth, the effect is minimal. The angle of the racket face will primarily determine the direction of flight the ball takes from the racket, while the ball's spin will be a product of the upward or downward **path** of the racket at impact.

Giving Topspin to the Ball

Low to high. The only way a ball can be given topspin is to swing upward — low to high — so that the racket head is traveling an uphill path **before** and **during** contact with the ball. The steeper the incline of this swing, the more RPM's the ball will acquire. It is the law of effect: the greater the impulse, the greater will be the result.

Overall, the quality of topspin production depends on (1) the nature of the swing, (2) an appropriate weight transfer, and perhaps most critically, (3) a ready state of mind to hit with the freedom of motion which is essential.

1. **The swing.** To achieve the upward swing necessary for imparting topspin, the racket must start its foreswing

from **at least a foot below the point where the ball will be contacted.** It is **not** possible to come straight into the ball and then try to lift it while it's on the strings. The racket head must be moving upward **before** it strikes the ball.

This means that the racket must be brought into the backswing lower than for a more ordinary flat groundstroke. There are two ways to do this. Either (1) take a regular unit turn and drop the racket head down, or (2) use a loop backswing.

There was a long-held belief that a loop in the backswing would consume too much time and therefore increase the possibility of hitting late. But when Bjorn Borg showed the tennis world how successful a looped swing could be for hitting topspin forehands, he revolutionized the game. His style was to start his arm back by lifting his elbow, racket trailing, then whirl the racket head around in a long, sweeping rainbow arc that culminated in a dramatic upward path at contact.

Emulating this flamboyant technique requires, first of all, a loose forearm. Gripping the racket tightly will forbid it. Let your elbow lead the backswing, in spite of what you've always heard about not doing this. Take the racket through a long, continuous looping path, coming from high behind your shoulder to below waist level and then up into the ball. Make sure that at the bottom of this circular path your racket head has dropped at least a foot below the point of contact. Keep your wrist absolutely steady as you come up and through the ball. Make it feel that the whip of the swing has come mostly from your shoulder and forearm, not from a rolling wrist at impact.

Here's the looped swing for a topspin forehand. The racket starts back . . .

. . . and up as the elbow is lifted . . .

. . . to whirl the racket head around and . . .

. . . up into the ball . . .

. . . to finish high across the opposite shoulder.

A more conservative preparation is to simply drop the racket head in the backswing. Let your forearm sink as you bring the racket back, even permitting some droop in the wrist. The lower you drop the racket head, the more room you'll have for generating upward momentum for the ball contact.

Hitting topspin on a backhand is infinitely more difficult. Two-handers have an advantage here, for the trailing hand can provide the useful function of propelling the racket upward into the ball with an emphatic fling that is difficult to achieve with one hand alone.

There's no loop for a topspin backhand. Just drop the racket head down . . .

. . . and make sure there's plenty of shoulder rotation . . .

. . . then swing without restraint, racket finishing high.

Normally, there is no loop in the backswing for a topspin backhand. Just drop the racket head down as you prepare for the hit.
2. **Weight transfer.** The patented suggestion of "bend your knees" has added utility for hitting topspin. By bending your knees you can more readily get your racket below the point of contact. More important, with bent knees you can deliver a little extra lift to the swing. Start the motion with a sensation of upward impulse that comes from your legs through your backbone, shoulder, arm, and racket.

Do not drive your weight toward the target as much as for a flat groundstroke. If you do, it means that your weight will be going forward while your arm is trying to go upward. Make the two complimentary by giving **lift** to your whole body as you swing up to meet the ball.
3. **The right state of mind.** To impart topspin to a ball is not all that difficult, mechanically. The biggest obstacle might be psychological. An upward swing seems impractical, and if the first few attempts send the ball into the next county, you'll be convinced of the illogic. But send a couple of sharply descending forehands into the opposite court, and you'll be hooked.

Knowing **how** to hit topspin is the first part. The second is having a **willingness** to hit it. There can be no holding back. Your arm must be **flung** into the ball, with good acceleration, to produce the effect. Otherwise, the ball will simply not take the bite — it will not be compressed enough on the strings to pick up spin from the upward path of the racket. So hit topspin with a liberal mindset and a free-flowing swing. Give plenty of life to the motion, and the results will show.

The Technique for Backspin

Backspin, often called underspin, is for most people easier to hit than topspin but is not necessarily easier to control. The technique is simple: swing high to low. Bring the racket into the ball from above the point of contact. Have it moving downward at impact.

Actually, that's only two-thirds of the story. The complete swing is high to low to high. To hit a strong, driving backspin shot, the racket head should finish off **higher** than the point of contact. Why? To keep the racket driving **through** the ball. There's a common belief that to give effective backspin to the ball you must **chop** the racket with a dramatic downward swing. The result often is that so much impetus is taken out of the ball, the shot has little pace. In reality, the swing should be closer to a flat stroke. The important backspin-giving factor is a tilted-back racket face.

To hit backspin, it **is** necessary for the racket to be on a high-to-low path at contact. The tilted-back racket face compensates for this path (otherwise the ball would be driven into the net) and combines with the downward movement to send the ball on its proper course.

Thus, a direct relationship exists between the tilt of the racket face, the path of the racket at impact, and the resulting flight characteristics of the ball. To hit an affirmative backspin drive — one with good pace — the racket should be tilted only **slightly** back and the swing should have the racket traveling marginally downward into the ball. The natural finish of this stroke will find the racket coming back up again. If there's good acceleration at impact, the ball will have a skidding, low bounce that will be tormenting for an opponent.

However, there are times when it's feasible to float a backspinning ball just over the net and have it drop shallow in the opposite court. In such a case, the intent is to maximize the spin, so the racket should be tilted further back. Now the swing does take on somewhat the characteristics of a "chop." It's easy to

To deliver a backspinning drive, lift the racket head higher than the anticipated point of contact . . .

. . . and tilt the strings back . . .

... then slide the strings through the ball with a stroke ...

... that's like dragging the racket across a table top, finishing higher than the point of contact.

overdo it, however. Not much of a swing is required for productive results. Nor do you need to be too concerned with where your weight is for this shot. It can be on either foot, and you can still get good effects, but make sure that your wrist stays firm through the stroke.

Accordingly, the more you want to backspin the ball and have it drift weightlessly in flight, the more the swing must have a downward path with a tilt-back of the racket face. But when you want to add backspin to a normal groundstroke, the swing is only slightly downward, with less tilt of the racket face. This stroke gives the hitter a sense of **sliding through** the ball rather than one of drawing the racket downward.

Coming to Grips

When first learning tennis, the grips were an annoyance. Later they became automatic, no longer requiring conscious attention. Now, as you add spin to your game, they become a concern again.

Eastern grips are the standard. They have the most generic utility. On both forehand and backhand sides they provide stability and versatility for dealing with high and low balls. But to facilitate topspin on the forehand side, try experimenting with a Western grip. It's somewhat of an "underhand" grasp, where the hand is slipped more under the handle than for the Eastern. Some professional players exaggerate this grip, holding the racket with their palm completely under the handle.

40   *Intermediate Tennis*

An Eastern forehand    *A Continental grip*

The Western forehand

    The advantage of the Western forehand grip is that it tilts the racket face over, toward the court. If you hit with emphatic topspin, this tilted racket will compensate for the vigorous upward path of the swing by keeping the ball in the court. It's also an ideal grip for receiving a high-bounding ball, but it places a severe restriction on the swing when hitting a low ball.

Hitting Decisive Groundstrokes

Here's a forehand hit with a Western grip.

It's not a practical all-around grip for most players...

...but it does provide an added advantage for giving topspin to the ball...

...and therefore is worth experimenting with.

Occasionally it's suggested that experienced players use a Continental grip. This is halfway between an Eastern forehand and Eastern backhand. The advantage is that this single grip is used for both forehands and backhands, without any change. Thus, it is functional for play at the net, where the exchange of shots is often so rapid that there is little time for switching grips. On this basis it can also be useful for receiving strong serves. But it tilts the racket backward on both sides; consequently, it is antagonistic to hitting topspin on the groundstrokes.

There are other grips: semi-Western forehand; Western backhand; hammer. Which one to use? Most instructors still favor the Eastern grips, since they position the hand behind the handle. If you've been playing a long time, a change in your grip now could be a nuisance and not worth the trouble. However, some experimentation may produce better results for spin.

Interestingly, most professional players switch their grips in the middle of a point to suit the situation. For example, they'll change from an Eastern to a Western forehand to return a high ball, or switch to a forehand grip to hit a backhand smash. They often make these ongoing changes subconsciously. It seems that they are more sensitive to the position of the racket face relative to the ball than they are to the specific kind of grip they are using. This appears to suggest the importance of developing a **feel** of the racket in your hand — a sensory awareness of the relationship of the racket face to the position of your hand, rather than trying to keep a static, exact grip for each situation.

Using Spin in Match Play

Because there's a net in tennis, topspin makes sense. Its main advantage is the room it gives to all your shots. You can lift the ball over the net with plenty of margin and have it dip into the court. And you can whack your most powerful shot and watch the ball bend in-bounds instead of sailing over the baseline. Consequently, it encourages a more offensive game.

There are other merits to topspin. High-lofted topspin shots will be particularly distressing to an opponent who likes to hit aggressively, for the ball will not provide them with the pace they want. Moreover, the rainbow arc forces opponents to stay further back to receive the ball. And the bounce will usually put the ball in an awkward hitting position.

Additionally, topspin is effective against an opponent who has come to the net. To hit a flat passing shot, out of reach to their side, requires needle-threading accuracy. But topspin permits you to crash into the ball and have the advantage of its dipping action. Even if you hit a strong shot directly at a net player, the downward arc of the ball will make it more difficult to intercept, and the ball will feel heavy on the strings, all of which rob the net player of some offense.

Giving backspin to a ball, though its effect is less dramatic, is a good compliment to topspin. The player who can control both backspin and topspin will keep an opponent constantly off-balance. Topspin shots can force an opponent deep, and shallow backspin shots can then become surprise winners.

Backspin can also produce a deep ball without much effort, since the ball floats during its flight in apparent rebuttal to gravity. This is especially valuable when you are coerced into a defensive position, or caught on the run, or otherwise forced to hit without adequate time to prepare a normal swing.

Hitting down on the ball also has the effect of stabilizing your racket, thereby producing a more solid stroke that can take the sting out of a strong shot from an opponent. Consequently, serves are often returned with backspin, and volleys are more durable when hit with some downward motion.

Backspin is touch. Topspin is flair. Together they make for a well-rounded player.

Reminders

1. For both topspin and backspin, keep the wrist firm through the hitting zone.
2. Always accelerate the racket for topspin; accelerate for driving backspin shots, but use touch for shallow placements of backspin.
3. Hit low to high for topspin. Come up with the whole body. Finish high.
4. Use an open stance to help the rotation of hips and shoulders for topspin.
5. Give the topspin shot plenty of clearance over the net.
6. Hit high to low for backspin; emphatically for shallow placements, but only a slight downward path for shots hit with good pace.
7. Tilt the racket back slightly for backspin drives, more so for shallow shots.

Problem Solving

Problem	Probable Cause	Solution
Not able to produce topspin	Coming straight into ball	Drop head of racket below contact point in backswing. Hit low-to-high.
Ball flies too far	Racket face tilted back	Keep racket face vertical for topspin; only slight tilt for backspin.
Ball into net	Racket face tilted over	Keep racket face vertical for topspin; tilt back for backspin
	Too much chopping motion in backspin attempts	Make swing more like regular groundstroke.
Lifeless response on topspin attempts	Trying to roll wrist up and over ball to produce spin	Keep wrist steady throughout stroke; hit with shoulder and forearm, low to high.

On the Court

Stop running around your backhands. Get over any inferiority complex about that side. During practice sessions, hit backhands intentionally. Run around your **forehand** to compel yourself into practicing backhands. Get your racket back early. Get sideways to the net. Exaggerate the shoulder turn. Then get your weight into the shot.

Become accustomed to taking the ball early. Many intermediate players let the ball drop too low off the bounce. Move in and catch the ball earlier, before it has dropped below net height. In matches this will help you to keep your opponent on the defensive and will let you move into the court where you have better opportunities for angling the ball off to the side for winners.

Extend fully through the ball on all your shots. Try to hold your racket on course, carrying the ball on the strings as long as possible. Use your racket head to say to the ball, "Go there!"

Give extra attention to accelerating the racket. It's too easy to have a lazy racket head during practice. Don't worry about hitting too long. Hitting out is often a sign of good acceleration. To program the feeling of acceleration, you and your practice partner could stand several yards behind your respective courts, near the fence. Try to drive each ball from there to your partner's baseline. Stay back all the time, even if you must let the ball bounce several times before it gets to you.

Keep tension out of your forearm. Let your grip breathe in between shots by opening your hand. Remember: loose to start — firm to hit.

There is a common tendency to think that the wrist should be active when trying to give spin to the ball. Thus, backspin attempts get hit with a woodchopping wrist and topspin trials are given upward flicks of the wrist. As you gain in experience you'll discover that an active wrist **can** be of benefit for imparting spin. But for now, if you're just learning spin, let your forearm do most of the work in determining the racket path, with wrist held steady. In particular, keep from rolling your wrist over when hitting topspin forehands. The wrist does **not** need to roll, and the racket does **not** need to climb up and over the ball. This is a critical point. Check your follow-through. If you finish with the racket face down and your elbow up, you probably rolled your wrist. The ball will not respond. Take some practice balls, bounce one in front of you in hitting position, then drive your racket, low to high, into the **back** of the ball. Look at the ball in flight. Is it spinning end over end? Repeat with another ball, and another, until the spin of the ball tells you that your swing is coming into the ball with an unwavering wrist, forearm giving the spin rather than an attempt at a rollover wrist. Keep the feeling, then let a rallied ball get in front of that swing.

Experiment with an open stance for topspin forehands. It'll give you more freedom for the rotation of your body and the upward arc of the swing.

Give your spare hand something to do. Keep it on the handle (if you're not already a two-handed hitter) for backhand topspin shots. Use your spare hand to give lift to the racket as you come around, under and up through the ball. Feel uncomfortable? Releasing your spare hand before the follow-through might help, but let go only after ball contact has been made.

Here's a novel way to get the feel of the topspin backhand. Stand sideways at the net. Press a ball against the tape of the net with the strings, on your backhand side. Pull the racket up and out, as if actually hitting, and watch the ball go spiraling off with topspin. Then stand away from the net, bounce a ball net-high in front of you, and use the same motion, finishing with your racket high and your thumb pointing skyward.

Recognize when it's economical to give the ball spin, and when it does not make sense. For example, it's difficult to give topspin to a ball that comes to you below waist level. You simply can't get the racket down low enough. The best ones are the high "sitters" that come floating up with little pace to about chest height.

Most of all, use the practice sessions to clear your mind of any apprehension about trying topspin. Realize that the ball will not respond properly unless you let fly with a flamboyant, freewheeling swing. You cannot be tentative. Your arm must **fling** the racket into the ball. No holding back. Give your racket head enough speed to take it through the sound barrier. Soon you'll discover a fundamental truth: the more you accelerate the racket, the more the ball will spin; the more the ball spins, the more it will arc downward in its flight; the more it arcs downward, the better chance it has to find the opposing court. Keep that uppermost in your mind. Write it down and tape it to your racket. Hit ball after ball with a free-swinging stroke until you can produce it anytime you want without hesitation — and no fear. Then practice being humble, because the next time you play a match your opponent will keep saying to you, "Nice shot!"

CHAPTER 4

Spin and Power For The Serve

It is generously written that one is assumed to have an advantage over an opponent when serving. Not everyone can be readily convinced of this. The serve, for many players, is a source of frustration, or even panic. As evidence, an otherwise enthusiastic class of experienced players can suddenly shrink to only a few eager participants when the instructor innocently suggests, "Now let's hit some serves." Strange, that at a level where solid groundstrokes and lively net play are commonplace, the serve often seems to confirm the suspicion that "tennis is a game of mistakes." Perhaps in recognition of this, the rules thoughtfully adjust the odds by allowing the server not one, but two attempts to accomplish the objective.

Why should serving be troublesome? Maybe it's because there are two distinct movements involved: tossing a ball and hitting it. Or possibly serving is unique unto itself, not necessarily related to the other skills of the game. Perhaps it simply is an awkward maneuver to hit a ball from a point so high overhead.

Yet the act itself is hardly more difficult than throwing a ball. The mechanics of the skill are not as hopelessly complicated as they are often made out to be. Moreover, serving is a truly enthralling part of tennis. It's enlivening, arousing, and catalytic for the rest of one's game. Watch good servers: they **enjoy** it. They **want** to serve. They radiate **confidence** and hit each ball with an optimistic attitude that it will go in.

The target, that seemingly elusive service court, is 13½ feet wide and a full 21 feet in length. That's **a lot** of room. And the server even gets to select the specific point of aim beforehand, unhurried. So serving **should** be an advantage. Furthermore, for better levels of play, it **must** be an advantage. Here are some ways to make it so.

Liberate Both Mind and Body

Start with an attitude of freedom, both mental and physical. Serving is a dynamic act. It's explosive — a free expression of power. To sense its electric pulse you must have some reckless abandon. If you hold back, you tighten the tendons and chords of your whole body, and the swing has a cement-arm feeling. Symptoms are: letting the toss drop too far, then hitting with a hunched-over shoulder and bent-arm push, resulting in a too slow (and too low) racket.

To hit compelling serves you cannot be mentally cautious, nor conservative in style. Your swing must be unconstrained; free and flowing. It originates from a willing mind and a loose arm.

Release your psyche. Unlock your arm. Feel unbound; untied; fluid. Then **fling** the racket into the ball, pendulum-like, with all-out spontaneity. Enjoy the raw pleasure of crashing into the ball with a free-spirited liveliness.

Hit Up, Not Down

Relatedly, the swing must be upward and forward, but not down, for a strong serve. There is a common notion, albeit wrong, that you should hit **down** on the ball to drive it into the service court, and this deception can lead to those bent-arm, hunchbacked swings. Instead, the serve should extend the arm and racket **up** to meet the ball. Use the full pendular motion of your swing. It will allow for maximum speed in the racket head. Be as tall as you can when you serve.

Check your toss. Is it high enough to give your racket arm room to extend through the top of your swing? And does it give you enough time to go through an unhurried sequence? Serve a few times in slow motion to find out. Then try stopping your racket just as you are about to hit, and check this frozen-in-midswing position to see if (1) your hitting shoulder is elevated, (2) your hitting arm is extended, and (3) your racket head is vertically aligned above and in front of your forward foot.

Give the Ball Topspin

In a practical sense, there is only one type of serve that a better player needs: **topspin.** It can originate as a natural outcome of an upward swinging racket, and its principle advantage is the same as topspin on a groundstroke: the ball will bend through a descending path in its flight. As a result, it will have a much better chance to seek out the service court. And **that** is the first law of serving — to get the ball **in.**

Typically, a ball hit as a topspin serve will also inherit some sidespin. Thus, the served ball will have not only an earthbound arc, but also some sideward slip on its journey to the service court. Then, when it lands, the topspin-produced descending arc will yield a higher rebound, and the sidespin will ricochet the ball at an angle opposite from its original flight path. Because of this exaggerated rebound action, the topspin serve is sometimes called a "kicker," and its coercive action is, of course, quite disconcerting for a receiver.

Additionally, the definitive downward curve of a topspin serve allows for a higher net clearance. The ball can be aggressively hit to cross the net with as much as six feet of spare room and still find its plunging way into the service court. In contrast, with a more everyday flat serve (which is hit without any attempt to spin the ball), the margin for error is small indeed.

By varying the speed and spin of the ball, topspin is suitable for both first and second serves. It can be a lethal, overpowering

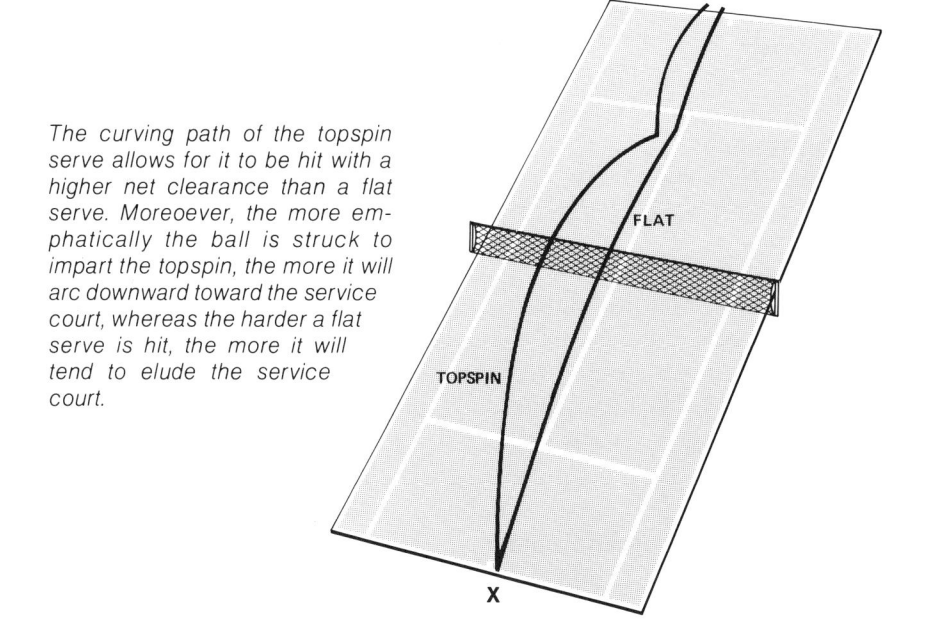

The curving path of the topspin serve allows for it to be hit with a higher net clearance than a flat serve. Moreoever, the more emphatically the ball is struck to impart the topspin, the more it will arc downward toward the service court, whereas the harder a flat serve is hit, the more it will tend to elude the service court.

offensive weapon, yet at the same time a decisively accurate staple of control. As confirmation of its value, witness that professional players rarely hit flat serves, but rely almost exclusively on spin for effectiveness in serving.

What the Racket Must Do

To impart topspin to a served ball, the requirement is the same as for a topspin groundstroke: the racket must meet the ball while traveling upward — low to high. The back of the upper arm and the wrist do much of this work, flinging the racket up (and outward) to clip off the backside of the ball and send it tumbling on its way with overspin.

This is a departure from the technique for a flat serve, where the racket is brought straight into the back of the ball — **flat** into the back — with the strings square to the intended line of flight and the thrust of the racket head traveling directly on that line. It's like a baseball pitcher who, when releasing a fast, straight delivery, will have the throwing hand directly behind the ball to utilize the full force of arm and body. But when the pitcher elects to throw a curve ball, the wrist must be rotated, or "snapped," at release to roll the ball off the thumb side of the index finger and provide the proper spin. For a topspin serve, the racket becomes an extension of a similar wrist action. The "snap" of the wrist takes the racket through a curving path to strike the ball a glancing blow. Contrary to common opinion, the racket does **not** go up and **over** the ball at contact, but instead kicks into the **back** of the ball while still on the upward sweep of its arched pathway. Consequently, the ball is actually struck before the racket has reached the peak of the swing.

Use a Continental Grip

To hit topspin serves it is imperative to employ a **Continental grip.** It is one of the "universals" of tennis. If you were to try hitting topspin with a forehand grip (which is common for flat serves), the upward impulse of the racket at impact would send the ball flying off into the stratosphere. The Continental grip will compensate for the uphill nature of the topspin swing by tilting the racket face over, angled more toward the court at contact, and will thankfully keep the served ball from seeding the clouds.

Check your grip often — it's easy to forget about the Continental and slip back into a forehand grasp. Make it feel that you could, as you settle into your ready-to-serve stance, more easily dribble a ball on the court with the **edge** of the racket instead of the strings.

Close the Stance

Next, take up a serving stance that is decidedly closed. Pull your back foot around behind you, enough to make it feel you have turned too far away from the net, literally making it seem as if you must look over your forward shoulder to set your sight on the service court.

On the left is the standard preparatory stance for a flat serve: body turned toward the court and racket held with a forehand grip. On the right is the position for a topspin serve: body pulled around in more of a closed stance and racket held with a Continental grip.

Why such an awkward and suspiciously illogical starting position? To keep the racket head **behind** the ball at contact. If you stood in a more conventional "squared-off-to-the-net" position, it is likely that your hitting elbow would be pulled too far forward during the swing, and this, because of the Continental grip, would drag the racket around to meet the **outside** of the ball and send it off-target wide of the service court.

These two changes — the closed stance and Continental grip — will probably be disturbingly uncomfortable at first. As verification of their value, try a few topspin serves with a squared-off stance and forehand grip. Assuming you use the appropriate swing, the results of these trials will imprint two checkpoints in your mind before every topspin serve attempt: closed stance, Continental grip.

The Toss

The direct objective of the toss is to place the ball in front of the swing. It's a modest task, yet a plague for many players. If you are still having trouble with the toss, it could be a result of laboriously hefting the ball into the air. Instead, **lay** it up. A tennis ball weighs only two ounces. No need to throw it. Lift it up gently, without any flick of the wrist. Release the ball when your arm reaches unstrained extension, passively opening your thumb and fingers simultaneously to allow the ball to proceed on its way. Pretend you are trying to settle the ball onto a shelf, or maybe releasing a bird into the air.

It'll help to hold the ball lightly, cradling it in the pads of your thumb and fingers, not in the palm. Tilt your hand back, without straining, to raise the heel during the toss; this will discourage the ball from going too far behind you. **Use your thumb as a guide,** first pointing it then lifting it directly toward the final destination of the toss.

Where to toss? For a flat serve the ball is placed an arm's length out in front of your hitting shoulder, but for a topspin serve the ball is lifted further **back** to allow for the upward path of the racket. Make the toss so that the ball seems to be almost directly overhead, even though at first you'll think it's too far back.

The Windup

It is commonly said: to start the serving windup the arms go "down together .... up together." It suggests a synchronized start of both arms. In unison, they both drop to near the front thigh, then concurrently go their own ways, one to toss the ball, the other to crank the racket into hitting position.

The windup that follows this "down-up" beginning has been given wide varieties of description, often with excessive analysis. Suggestions range from a simple up-and-over-the-shoulder backswing to exotic double-helix patterns. The fact is, there is no classic or absolutely mandatory way to bring the racket back in preparation for its swing at the ball. However, all accomplished players do the following:

1. Both arms **do** start together, then continue into the windup rhythmically, without pause or hesitation.
2. There is no hurry at the start. Until the ball is in the air, everything is slow and deliberate.
3. The chin comes up as the toss is made, with the eyes focused on the eventual point of contact, even before the release of the ball.
4. Most, if not all, of the weight is on the back foot as the ball is tossed.

And to prime the windup for a topspin serve, the following are also essential:

5. There is an emphatic arching of the back.
6. Simultaneous to drawing the racket back, the shoulders rotate, much in the same "unit-turn" fashion as for a forehand groundstroke, and the hitting shoulder twists around and down, adding a spiral to the arched back.
7. There is extra knee bend.
8. The racket drops into the so-called "backscratching" position, with its **butt end pointed up at the tossed ball.**

It's a strange looking contortion, to say nothing of how it feels if you have never really tried it. Properly executed, it seems that your windup has literally corkscrewed you into the ground, with your skeleton having been wrung into the configuration of a question mark. But you also feel a great sense of multiplying **power** and kinetic **energy,** for you are now a coiled up spring about to be released — a cobra ready to strike out at the helpless ball. And then . . .

The Hit

. . . the racket inherits all your accumulated energy, and the ball becomes its victim. You've wound up your physical spring and then released its power into the ball.

This discharge of energy comes from the ground upward: knees rebound from their bend, the backbone uncoils, the hitting shoulder catapults toward the ball, and the arm thrashes up and over with the elbow unbending and the wrist adding a final vigorous snap that makes the racket feel like a whip. It's a continuous sequence of lever actions that start slowly, then finish explosively.

Remember that it's topspin you want out of this, so at the point of impact (1) the racket must strike the **back** of the ball, while (2) still traveling upward. Consequently, your swing must have both **upward** and **forward** impulse at contact. In this regard, the racket does **not** go up and over the ball to provide the topspin, but the **sensation** you get is that it **does**. It **feels** like you took the racket up to "jerk the ball down" from its hanging position.

The Finish

A topspin serve will not "drag" the hitter into the court as much as a flat serve. There is more of an "up-over-down" quality to the topspin motion, and it leaves you with an aftereffect of feeling like you've just landed from a descent of a flight of stairs.

Because of the emphatic wrist action, the racket will complete its path with a feedback sensation of being more out in front of the body than for a flat serve, with racket head down and elbow elevated and trailing into the follow-through.

Occasionally, pause in your finished position to let this frozen follow-through give you information about what went on during the swing. If your racket has not come around to narrowly miss a whack of your opposite knee, then you might not have accelerated it through the hitting zone, or you did not provide enough wrist snap. If your free arm is behind you, it's a sign that you rotated your shoulders around toward the net too quickly before ball contact. And if you are not one step into the court, you either tossed the ball too far back or failed to drive your weight from back to front foot.

Adding Power

At first, there may be a disappointing lack of power to your topspin serves. It can be discouraging — you take a big swing, give the ball lots of spin, and it climbs lethargically over the net. Your response might be to try serving harder by **swinging** harder. But contradictory as it might sound, the way to hit harder is to **swing easier.**

When you can't seem to hit a forcing serve, it's common to force the serve. But then the swing becomes tense; rigid in its motion. It's rather like trying to fall asleep by **forcing** yourself to fall asleep instead of relaxing and **allowing** sleep to occur.

Watch the pros. Before serving they relax. Some shake their arms loose. Or shrug their shoulders. Maybe take a deep breath or two. They want to **calm** their body — settling it down for the rhythm of the swing. They want a loose, live arm, and they know they can't get if their muscles are tense.

So **relax** before you start the swing. Let your body be flaccid — more so for serving than for any other part of the game. Hold the racket loosely. To help generate this feeling, hit some practice serves by holding the racket on the end of the handle with only your first two fingers and thumb.

Spin and Power For The Serve

Both arms start the motion simultaneously, for topspin serving as well as for any serve . . .

. . . but the toss for a topspin serve is further back than for a flat serve . . .

. . . making the ball seem almost overhead, and at the same time the weight begins to come up on the toes . . .

. . . while the body coils spring-like for its whip . . .

. . . upward and forward into the ball, racket snapping off the backside of the ball . . .

. . . with a vigorous fling of the arm and wrist.

Next, have your instructor or a friend watch to see if you are coordinating your weight transfer properly. Your weight should be coming forward and upward before the tossed ball reaches its highest point, and before the racket drops into the backscratching position.

Sense a sequence to the swing. Knees-hips-back-shoulders-arm-wrist; in that order, all uncoiling and adding their part to the whole. Use your body like a whip. **Fling** it into the ball.

But start slowly, deliberately. Consciously take your time at the beginning of the swing. The sequence is: slow start — fast finish.

Once underway, keep the swing going. No stops. No hesitations. The whole motion should be unbroken, without any disjointed parts. Build speed as you go. Feel like at the moment you crash into the ball your swing is still gaining momentum.

Make sure that in the swing the racket head drops down to the backscratching position, butt end pointing at the ball. Have someone watch to double-check. A powerful serve comes from good racket head speed at contact. By dropping the racket head down behind you, the arc of the swing is increased in length, providing more distance and time for building speed.

Make the wrist snap the final consummation of power. An otherwise well-coordinated swing will dissipate its strength if the wrist is stiff. Keep a loose wrist throughout the swing, but explode it boldly into the ball as your forearm comes up. The snap is upward, forward, and outward, bringing the racket head through a rainbow arc up over your hitting shoulder.

First and Second Serves

Watch the typical weekend players: they'll bash away at their first serve attempt and, having failed, will hit a punch-it-over-the-net-and-get-the-point-underway second serve. They have the false assumption that the motion for both serves is the same, while the energy expenditure is different. In truth, both serves should be hit with about the **same effort.** It's basically the **direction of the swing** which differentiates the two serves.

Speed is taken off the second ball not by slowing down the swing, but by tossing the ball further back and emphasizing the upward lift of the racket. This will magnify the rotation of the ball and give it more bend toward the court in flight, and the slower pace will allow gravity to have more effect.

Accordingly, for the first serve the ball is tossed out in front of your hitting shoulder, and the swing motion is forward and upward. For the second serve the ball is tossed further **back,** and the motion becomes more decidedly **upward.** It's even possible to toss the ball to where it seems to be **behind** you, then swing emphatically upward and watch the ball curl into the court as if pulled by magnetic influence.

A key element of the second serve is conviction. It must be hit with a sense of daring, without holding back in the swing. At first it will seem as if the ball can go only into the clouds, but soon you'll realize that a mathematical relationship exists: more upward swing — more spin; more spin — more arc; more arc —more serves **in.**

There's a subtle yet definite difference between first and second topspin serves which originates out of the toss. On the left is a first serve where the ball is tossed in front and the body attitude is one of preparation for going up and forward. For the second serve, shown on the right, the toss is further back and there's a bit more bend in the legs to prepare for a swing which is more upward than for the first serve, but with the same explosion of energy (use the light pole as a reference to compare the two serves)

Add a Slice for Versatility

The slice serve is a hybrid of the topspin. It's more easily learned **after** having grooved the swing for topspin.

The slice is hit with some sidespin, and consequently the airborne path of the ball is not only downward, but also sideward. The ball will swerve off to a right-handed server's left, and therefore it is more effective when hit into the far corner of the deuce court, where it will swing away from the receiver. As a result, it will pull the receiver far off the court and, if not an outright winner, will open up the entire court for the server to hit the next ball.

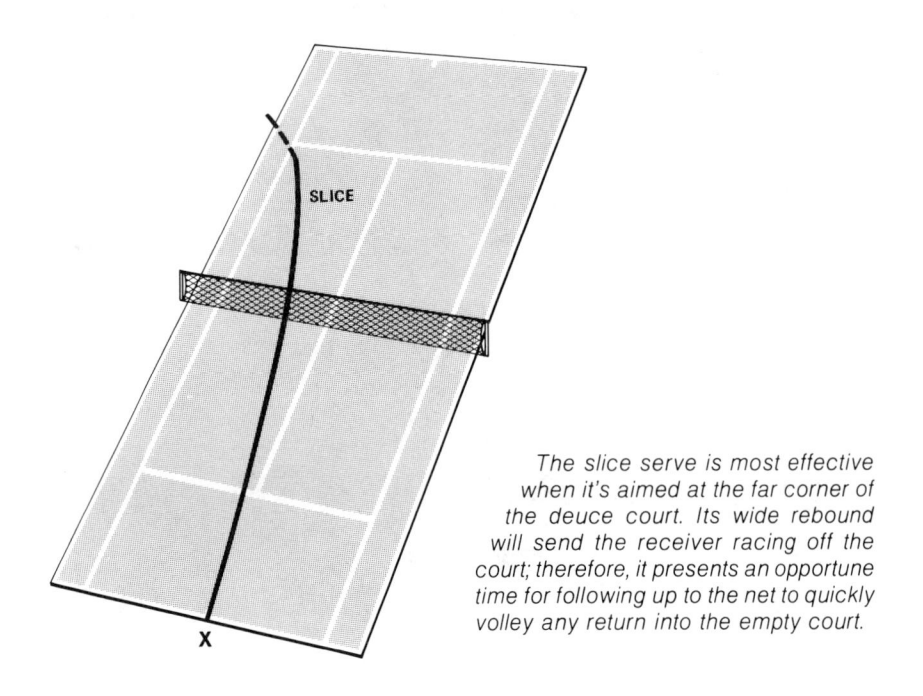

The slice serve is most effective when it's aimed at the far corner of the deuce court. Its wide rebound will send the receiver racing off the court; therefore, it presents an opportune time for following up to the net to quickly volley any return into the empty court.

The potential of this serve is also its shortcoming. It is best when hit wide in the deuce court, but that also means hitting the ball to the forehand side of a right-handed receiver. So, unless the slice can be made a lethal weapon, it could instead become a setup for the receiver's strength.

Left-handers, therefore, have a bonus. A left-handed server can swing the ball wide in the advantage court, not only pulling the receiver off the court but also attacking the presumably weaker side. It's the best time to follow the serve up to the net.

To hit a slice, toss the ball more out to the side. Swing the racket somewhat "out and around" the ball, but still with good upward impulse. Imagine hitting the lower outside corner of the ball.

You'll need to experiment with the toss and swing, but when you have a technique down, you'll find that it adds even more effect to your topspin serve, for now you have more arsenal in your serving repertoire. The receiver will be more off-balance, not being able to predict what you will do. You can choose: topspin up the middle, or slice to the outside, maybe even a flat serve, here and there. And the receiver will have nothing to do except collect the ball and toss it back so that you can serve your next point-winner.

One way to facilitate this (out and around) swing is to serve from a distinctly closed stance. Pull your back foot around behind you, even more than for a topspin serve. Then let your elbow be more of a lead in the swing, racket trailing behind, and this will emphasize the circular path of the racket head.

Reminders

1. Serving is a dynamic, explosive, whole-body act. Create a picture of it in your mind before starting.
2. Relax your whole self. Let your arm go limber. Make it feel like spaghetti.
3. Close the stance. Take a Continental grip.
4. Cradle the ball in your fingers. Lift it gently, using your thumb as a guide.
5. Spiral yourself into a coiled windup, racket head dropping behind you.
6. Make the whole motion continuous, rhythmical.
7. Fling the racket into the ball, with a whip-like motion.
8. Start slow — finish fast. Build speed throughout the swing.
9. Hit the back of the ball, racket still moving upward, for topspin.
10. Hit the lower outside corner, racket moving up and out, for slice serves.

62　　　　　　　　　　*Intermediate Tennis*

A-1

B-1

A-2

B-2

Spin and Power For The Serve   63

The nature of the slice serve is more emphatically seen when compared to a flat serve. Here, in Sequence A, the server delivers a flat serve. Note that the momentum of the swing is forward, with the racket head flat behind the ball at the moment of contact. A slice serve is demonstrated in Sequence B, starting with a more pronounced coiling and arching of the back for the swing. At contact the racket head is on its way around the lower outside corner of the ball, and this whip of the swing brings the racket into a follow-through which is more to the left of the server than for a flat serve.

Problem Solving

Problem	Probable Cause	Solution
Uncoordinated swing	Not synchronizing movement of the arms	Count **one** for arms to drop; **two** for arms to separate and lift; **three** for the hit
Hesitation in the swing	Ball toss too high	Lift ball only a bit higher than contact point
Lack of weight transfer	Weight stays on back foot during swing	Start with weight on front foot; keep it there, and swing back foot past it during swing
No power	Failure to rotate shoulders	Take racket back with a unit turn, as in preparation for forehand
	Failure to coil in windup	Crank body into a spring-like windup
Insufficient whip in racket	Wrist too firm at contact	Loosen forearm before windup; hit like a baseball pitcher throwing a curve ball
Serve too long	Ball tossed too far back	Lift heel of tossing hand, toss further out
	Pushing at ball	Emphasize whip of arm and snap of wrist
Serve into net	Ball tossed too far out in front	Toss further back; swing more up
	Failure to transfer weight	Emphasize push off back foot
Only minimal ball rotation	Not dropping racket into backscratching position	Drop racket to where butt end points at ball
	Not snapping wrist	Take racket "up and over" ball with wrist

(Continued)

Problem Solving — continued

Problem	Probable Cause	Solution
Ball goes wide of court on top-spin attempts	Squared-off stance	Use closed stance
	Elbow pulled forward in swing	Swing in rainbow arc, up and over, keeping elbow behind ball

On the Court

Watch a javelin thrower. The body uncoils dynamically, and the arm extends fully up and forward at the moment of release. You can almost **feel** the power.

For strong serves, you need to have the same explosive release of energy. During practice, let fly with your most exertive efforts. Give it all you have. Turn the throttle to full speed.

Give your practice serves lots of explosion. No holding back, CRUSH the ball on your strings.

Fling the racket, whip-like, into the ball with a free-wheeling abandon.

When practicing second serves, emphasize the dropping of the racket head into the back-scratching position.

There's a valid saying: "You're only as good as your second serve." Spend a lot of practice time hitting second serves. It'll be of direct benefit for honing these follow-up serves and will indirectly help the first serve by developing a free-swinging motion.

Now's the time to experiment. Pull your grip around toward a backhand. Hit some topspin serves. Pull it around even more. Keep turning it toward the backhand until you start hitting off the edge of the racket. The closer you can get to a backhand grip, while still hitting the ball solidly on the strings, the more spin the ball should acquire.

You must compliment this, however, by emphasizing the upward thrust of the racket. Try to drop the racket head as low as you can in the windup, arriving in the backscratching position with both its butt end and your **elbow** pointing skyward. Then feel like you're swinging up and into the ball by lifting your elbow, arm coming up and over. Think **up** as you swing.

Eventually you'll realize that the second serve is much like the first. You can hit all-out on both attempts. It's the direction of the swing, not the effort, that is different.

Experiment also with your stance. Second serves are often facilitated by a very closed stance, whereas slice serves need more of a square stance.

Keep exploring new ways to hit the ball. The serve is probably the most individualized part of the game. Everybody must find their own best style — within reason of physics, of course. But keep an open mind. Feel like you're responsible for those statements about the serve being too much of a dominating factor in tennis.

CHAPTER 5

Returning The Serve

There is no more neglected phase of tennis than the return of serve. Rarely is it ever practiced, or even **thought** about. Maybe it's subconsciously perceived to be just forehands and backhands, and therefore not needing special attention. Yet for some players the only thing that causes more anguish than serving is returning somebody else's.

No doubt about it, the service return does give you somewhat of a helpless feeling. The server has control of the moment and there's nothing to do, it seems, but wait until the ball is on its way. What happens too often is that the brain starts to fill the empty time with such as: "Oh no! Here comes another big serve — what can I do to keep from being embarrassed?"

Most of the time the problem is **psychological.** This is usually because the player does not have the **tactical know-how** to return the serve effectively. And the reason why the tactical know-how is absent is because the service return is **seldom practiced.** For example, a player might spend fifteen minutes of a practice session hitting overheads, yet only hit half a dozen in a typical match. And that same player might never practice service returns, even though in a match service returns will be required for half the points played.

Statistics compiled in professional matches show that the service return actually influences the outcome of more points than any other single stroke, including the serve itself. And in amateur play, if more players were capable of returning serves effectively, the serve would not exist as the dominating factor it so often is. Furthermore, the player who can return well has a great psychological advantage, for most big servers do not expect the ball to come back, and when it does it may be disconcerting for them. In turn, it provides the receiver with a heightened sense of confidence.

The return of serve is not the purely defensive affair it's often believed to be. It can in fact be used to develop offense. And here's the best part: the techniques for success in hitting back serves are surprisingly simple.

Where to Stand

The traditional answer of where to stand when receiving serve was probably originated by a geometry expert: "Bisect the angle of possibilities." It means to stand in the middle of the widest possible area into which the server can hit. But consider that most players will have more difficulty swinging the ball wide into the far corners than in hitting up the middle. Also, if you have a stronger side, you may want to give more room on that side.

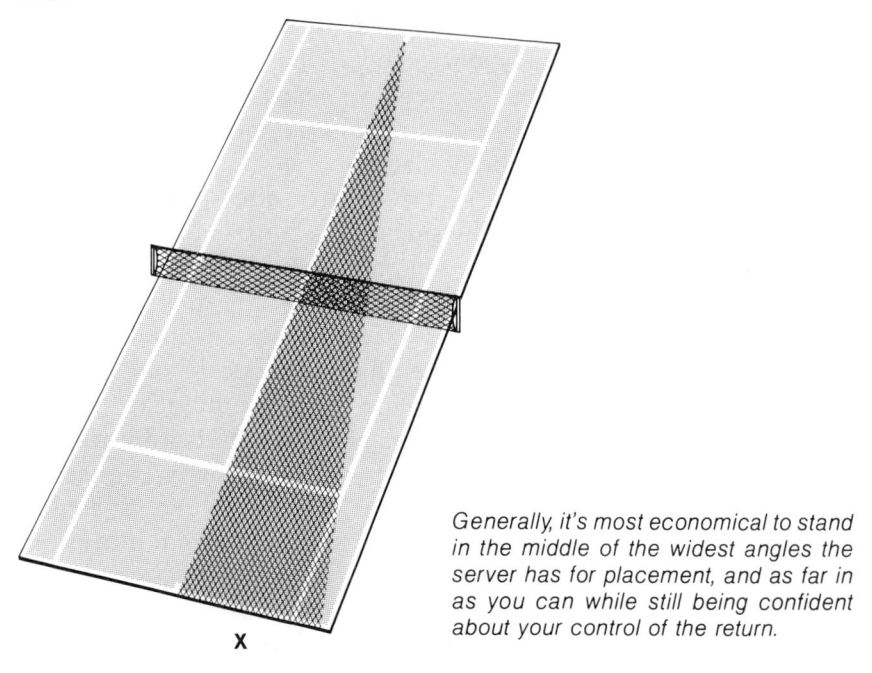

Generally, it's most economical to stand in the middle of the widest angles the server has for placement, and as far in as you can while still being confident about your control of the return.

How far **in** should you stand? It depends on the talents of both you and the server. Generally, the harder the serve, the further back you should stand. Staying back gives you more time to set your sights on the ball, but this also provides the server with more opportunity for hitting out of your reach to either side. Moreover, it gives the server who charges the net more time to get into effective volleying position.

Consequently, it's best to be in as far as you can and still feel confident in being able to hit under control, for three reasons: (1) any spin that the server gives to the ball will have less time and distance to work its effect; (2) since you'll be intercepting the ball earlier, you will not be drawn as far off the court by wide serves; and (3) there will be less time for the server to approach the net.

Getting Ready

As the server prepares to hit, remind yourself of a few things, partly to check that you're doing them, and partly to get your mind actively thinking **positive** things.

1. Hold the racket **loosely.**
2. Hold it in **front,** pointed at the server so that it can be quickly drawn to either side. Hold elbows comfortably in front of hips.
3. Have your weight **forward,** on the front of your feet. Pretend that a wedge has been pushed under your heels. Keep a flexed body.
4. Focus on the ball **early.** Zero in on it like adjusting a pair of binoculars. First see the total scene — server, racket, ball — then narrow in on the ball as it reaches the peak of the toss.

When waiting for the serve, be alive, alert, responsive. Keep the racket forward, held loosely, elbows in front of hips, and eyes riveted on the toss of the ball.

When the Ball is on the Way . . .

In the ready position, you should be primed to move **forward.** Go get the ball! **Pounce** on it! Meet it **early!**

Taking the ball as early as you can will keep you from being pulled off the court by a wide serve. It gives you less court to

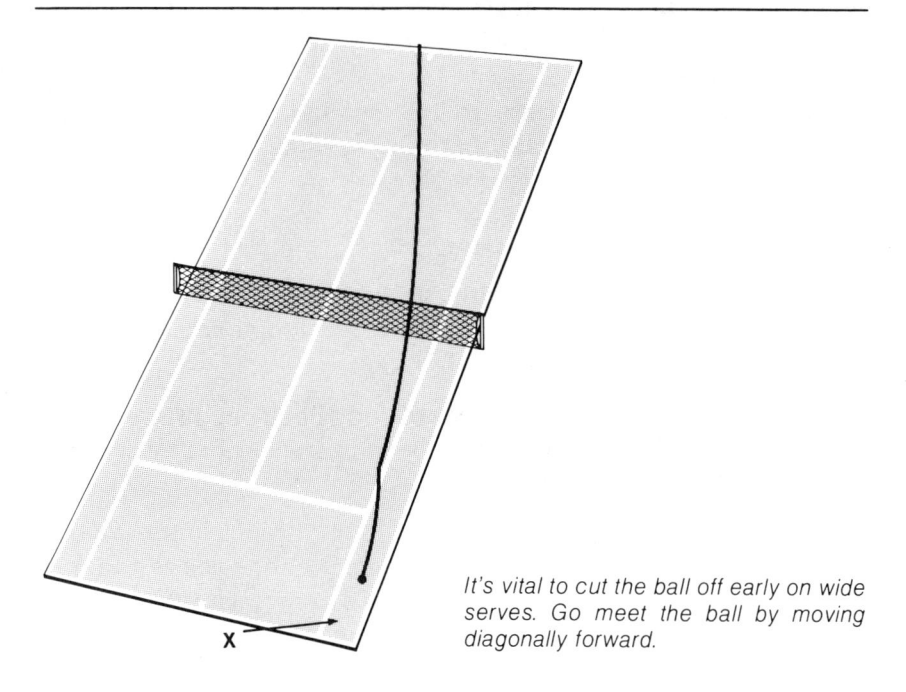

It's vital to cut the ball off early on wide serves. Go meet the ball by moving diagonally forward.

cover — less distance to go to intercept its flight. And by moving **at** the ball, you'll be able to put more weight into the return.

So don't step sideways. Turn your shoulders quickly, get the racket back, and make your first step **diagonally forward, toward the ball.**

Focus on the ball a second time. You honed your attention on it during the toss, now refocus again as it comes off the bounce.

Here comes a wide serve, and the receiver has turned to chase the ball . . .

. . . by running parallel with the baseline . . .

... thus being compelled into a strictly defensive return ...

... and being pulled too far off the court.

Here's another wide serve, but this time the receiver responds by going ninety degrees to the flight of the ball ...

... thus moving diagonally FORWARD ...

... to intercept the ball earlier in its flight ...

... and avoid being pulled as far off the court.

When the Ball Arrives ...

There's little time: take an **abbreviated** backswing, **tighten** the grip, and **thrust** the racket into the ball like you were hitting a volley stroke.

There is nothing tricky or fancy about returning a big serve. Use the power that is already on the ball. Keep a firm wrist, and shorten everything about your swing. Make it compact, but solid.

Some Refinements

The slower the serve, the more you can hit just as you would for a regular groundstroke. But the harder the serve, the more you must adjust the mechanics of your swing to the speed of the oncoming ball. On really hard serves there may not be time to get the racket further back than the shoulders, but always try to pivot the upper body to give solidity to the stroke. The key is how quickly you can get the racket into hitting position; thus, the importance of using the non-hitting hand (which should be cradled on the racket in the ready position) to either push the racket back for a forehand or pull it back for a backhand return.

What about a ball hit directly at you? Let self-preservation take over — get out of the way of the ball. Do this by pushing off one foot; quickly turn your upper body, opening your shoulders and pulling them **away** from the ball. Get the racket in front of the ball any way you can, and brace your grip for the impact.

Need more strength on those hard serves to your backhand? Try beveling the racket back a bit and bringing it into the ball slightly downward. In this motion you will use the stronger muscles on the back of your arm, and this, coupled with a hammerlock grip, will steady the racket head. Additionally, the downward motion of the racket will give it a little extra thrust to take the pace off the ball and turn it around. Be careful not to make this a "chopping" motion. Rather, imagine yourself sliding the racket across the top of a table. Hit with a swing that's similar

When receiving a forceful serve, get your shoulders turned as quickly as possible . . .

. . . using your non-dominant hand to help bring the racket into a shortened backswing . . .

. . . then return the ball with a firm downward and forward sweep of the racket head, keeping the wrist solid throughout . . .

. . . and finishing higher than the contact point.

to when you add backspin to a driving groundstroke: start just above the point of contact, bring the racket slightly downward, and finish higher than the contact point.

Still need more strength on the backhand return? Now is the time to try two hands.

Where to Send the Ball

The server's advantage disappears quickly if you can return the ball with a purpose. Don't think of trying to launch a missile, but keep some placement objectives in mind.

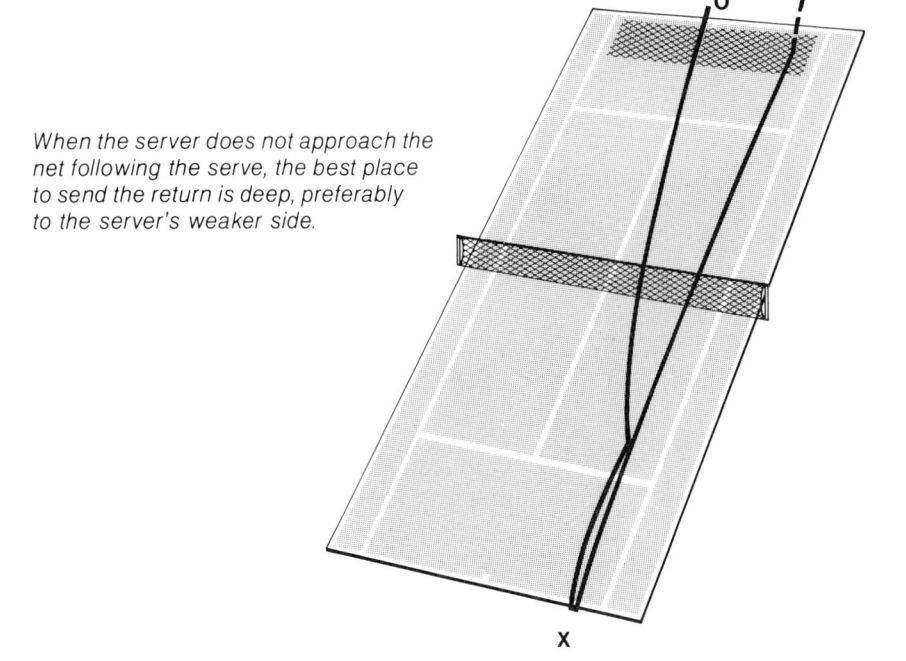

When the server does not approach the net following the serve, the best place to send the return is deep, preferably to the server's weaker side.

If the server does not rush the net, the return should be hit deep, preferably to the weaker side so there's less chance of being hurt by a strong follow-up shot. Be cautious about trying to chip the return just over the net, because (1) it's a difficult shot to transact if the serve has good pace, and (2) most players finish off their serve by "falling" into the court; therefore, they'll be in front of the baseline and in better position to retrieve your shallow placement. Furthermore, since they **are** in front of the baseline, a deep return will coerce them into backing up to take the ball after the bounce (very few players will attempt to hit the ball on the fly from that deep in their own court); thus, you will have taken all the momentum away from the server and compelled the play into an exchange of groundstrokes.

If the server comes up to the net, your placement must be more precise. If you try the same deep return that you used against the player who stays back, the ball will be too high and the net rusher may be able to put it away with a solid volley.

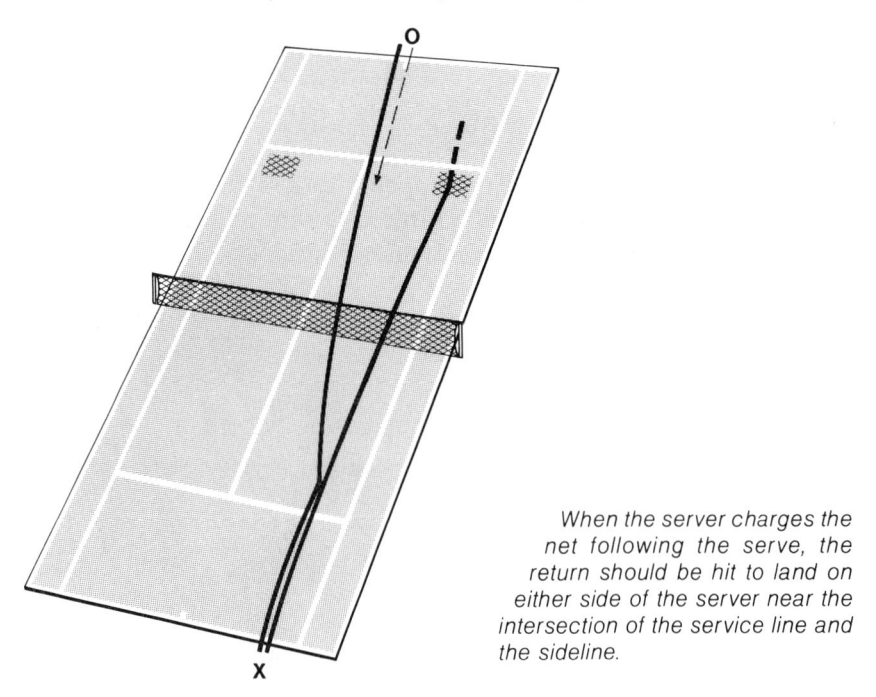

When the server charges the net following the serve, the return should be hit to land on either side of the server near the intersection of the service line and the sideline.

Instead, you must keep the ball low, bouncing it somewhere near the intersection of the sideline and the service line. That way the server will need to bend low and lift the ball up to clear the net, and therefore the ball will be hit more defensively.

It's commonly stated that the best place to return the ball against a net rusher is at their feet. While there is some logic to this (the server will be forced to hit the ball defensively, and it's a mechanically difficult shot), such a placement still keeps the ball within easy reach. You'll find that it's infinitely more effective to lay the ball off to the side of the net rusher. Make the server lunge for your return. Often, you'll be able to win the point right there.

Reminders

1. Think positive things as you wait. Keep your mind actively engaged on what you will do.
2. Keep everything simple.
3. Be ready to move **forward**.
4. Be ready to move **early**.
5. The harder the serve, the more the swing must be compact. But don't restrict the follow-through.
6. Move **at** the ball. Put life in your legs.
7. Keep a solid, firm wrist.
8. Have a "scrambling" attitude. Do anything to get the ball back.

Problem Solving

Problem	Probable Cause	Solution
Ball overpowers racket	Grip too loose	Hit the ball with a vice-tight grip
Hitting late	Slow racket preparation	Rotate upper body as soon as ball is sighted
	Too big of a backswing	Abbreviate the length of the backswing
No pace on returned ball	Moving parallel with or diagonally away from baseline	Go to meet the ball; move diagonally forward
Poor ball placement	Not following ball into strings	Rivet attention on the ball; see it twice, once at the top of the toss; refocus and see it again after bounce
	Not meeting ball early	

On the Court

Professional players, when waiting for the serve to be hit, go through a curious little dance. They will hop, jump, skip, bounce, or otherwise keep their feet moving before the ball is sent on its way. Then, as the ball is about to be struck, they will do a balanced hop forward which is timed to get their weight ready to spring at the ball. You'll see baseball infielders doing the same thing as the ball approaches the batter. It generates a better sense of energy buildup and keeps the weight from settling flatfooted on the heels. Give it a try in practice sessions. Make it a hopscotch kind of maneuver — a split-step that energizes your legs and keeps your feet from being lazy. Coordinate the hop so that you land just as the ball is hit. It'll give you an energized sequence of: ready-hop-**move**.

A bouncing split-step as the ball is about to be hit will give life to your whole body and responsiveness to your return.

One of the best ways to practice the return of serve is to have your partner stand inside the baseline (as far in as the service line, if you're brave) and bash serve after serve at you. Your reflexes will get a real test in this exercise. Or you could play practice games where the receiver automatically scores a point by landing the return inbounds, or perhaps between the service line and baseline. And of course the most direct practice can occur when you receive for your partner who wants to hit a bucketful of practice serves.

CHAPTER 6

Playing The Forecourt

The liveliest tennis occurs at the net. The pace is faster and the points are quicker. It's an adventurous game up there.

A player who stays forever in the backcourt is destined to spend their tennis time in too much of a defensive position. The forecourt is the life of the game. It's vitalizing, invigorating, daring, sometimes even reckless. But always it's the most arousing part of tennis.

Go to the net often, at every opportunity, for three basic reasons: (1) under the right conditions it presents a tactical advantage, (2) your presence alone can coerce mistakes from your opponents, and (3) it adds dimension to the game, making tennis more versatile, challenging, and enthralling.

Apprehensive about the forecourt? In actuality, playing the net is basic tennis. The techniques of play are straightforward and uncomplicated. Best of all, the strokes are exhilarating to hit.

When to Go

Sometimes a player's discouragement from experiences at the net comes from careless approaches to the forecourt in the first place. Everyone should carry a note taped to their racket that says: **caution — approach the net only under the following circumstances:**

1. **On a short ball.** As a general guide, when you hit from behind your own baseline, you should remain in the backcourt. But if your opponent offers a shallow ball, that's an invitation to the net. The further in front of the baseline you can move to hit, the more your response should be to automatically follow your shot into the forecourt.

The baseline is a guide; when hitting from behind it, stay back, but the further in front of the baseline you can move to hit, the more inviting the net becomes.

GREEN LIGHT — ALWAYS GO
YELLOW LIGHT — GO IF APPROACH SHOT IS WELL PLACED
RED LIGHT — STAY BACK DON'T GO TO NET

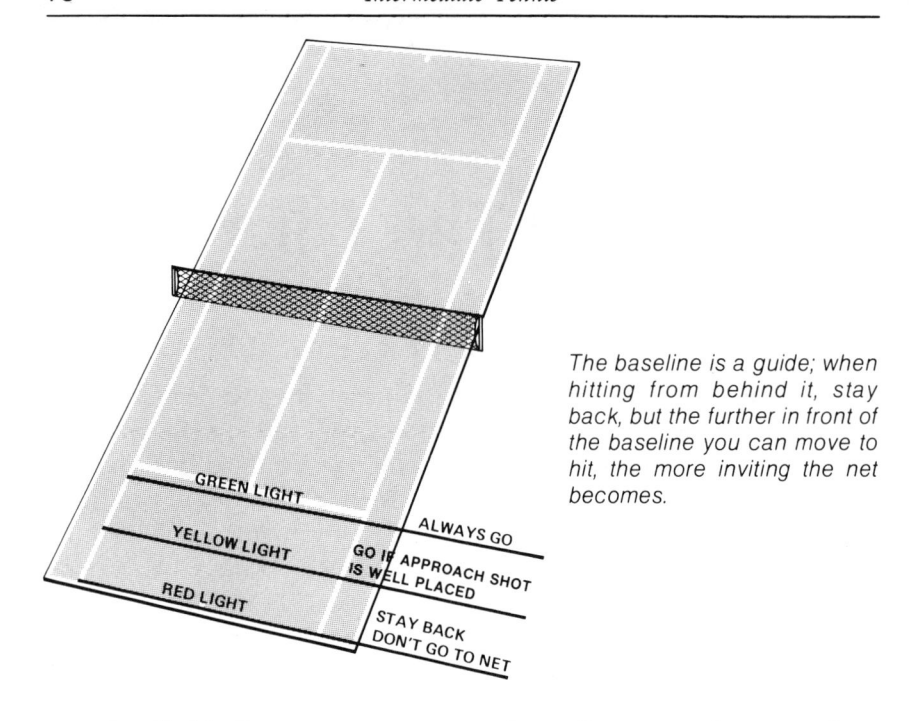

2. **Behind your own strong shot.** Go up to the net when you hit a ball that you believe will force your opponent to reply with a weak return. Usually this will be when you have your rival on the run or otherwise off-balance, or when you've rifled a shot to the weaker side. There are other times when you simply "sense" that your shot will be overpowering enough to extract a feeble return. The serve is such an example (which is the only time an approach to the net should be made from behind the baseline).

How to Get There

When you decide to go to the net, commit your mind firmly to that intent, but make sure that you execute the complete stroke first. Then let the following guidelines govern your trip:

1. **Hit the approach shot deep.** A cardinal sin of tennis is to approach the net behind a ball hit too shallow in your opponent's court. It makes you vulnerable, giving too many options to your rival. The objective of the approach shot is to put your opponent on the defensive, so send the ball deep, preferably to the weaker corner.

Playing The Forecourt

2. **Sacrifice pace for placement.** Try for a winner only if you have a wide open court, but never overhit the approach shot. Take a shorter backswing, stroke through the ball, and hit for depth rather than speed.
3. **Hit the ball at the top of its bounce.** Move in to catch the ball high, where you'll have more margin of safety for net clearance. You'll also be closer to the net, and your opponent will have a little less time to respond.
4. **Follow the path of the ball.** Wherever you hit the ball, go directly behind it, on-line with its flight path. This will keep you in the middle of the widest area of possible return from your opponent.

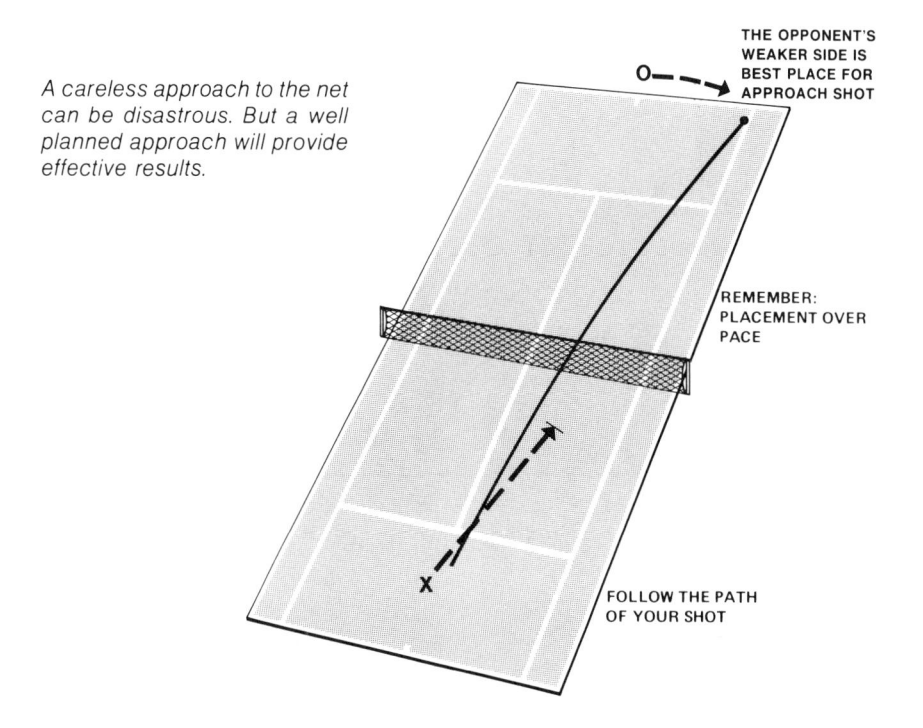

A careless approach to the net can be disastrous. But a well planned approach will provide effective results.

THE OPPONENT'S WEAKER SIDE IS BEST PLACE FOR APPROACH SHOT

REMEMBER: PLACEMENT OVER PACE

FOLLOW THE PATH OF YOUR SHOT

5. **Pause as your opponent is about to hit.** No matter where you are on the court, just as your rival is about to hit the ball, pull up to a controlled pause in your approach. Do a split-step to check your forward momentum. Hopscotch yourself into being ready to move any direction, including back to the baseline if your opponent replies with a lob.
6. **Keep your racket ready.** As you pull up into your jump-stop, keep the racket head in front of you, shoulder-high, where it's prepared for any kind of a return.

When you've hit an approach shot and you're on the way to the net . . .

. . . as your opponent prepares to return the ball, collect your momentum, and . . .

. . . do a hopscotch split-step . . .

. . . into a ready position, racket held high and in front, so you're prepared to respond in any direction.

7. **Be selective about going in behind serves.** Be cautious about following serves hit to the receiver's forehand, especially in the deuce court where the receiver will have better angle possibilities for returning the ball past you. The best time is on a serve hit into the far corner of the advantage court, where it will pull the receiver off the court and also compel a weaker return (assuming the receiver is right-handed).

At the Net: The Volley

You've heard it before, and you've been there before:

1. The volley is a short stroke. It's a compact and firm block of the ball — a punch rather than a swing.
2. The ball should be played in front, with a tight grip, and knees bent.

There's nothing elaborate about a volley.

Just take a short backswing, keep the grip firm . . .

. . . hit the ball in front . . .

. . . and punch it into your rival's court.

The mechanical story of the volley is short, because the basic stroke itself is short.

But as you gain in confidence, add more dimension to the shot. Hit a **drive** volley. Lengthen the swing, take the racket back a bit further, and give the stroke extra forward impulse. Instead of merely **blocking** the ball, **hit** it! Make the ball do something more than just using your strings as a trampoline.

When you have enough time, and the pace of the oncoming ball is not overpowering . . .

. . . step up to hit a drive volley. take a longer backswing, and . . .

. . . drill the racket into the ball . . .   *. . . for an affirmative, point-winning shot.*

You've come up to the net to finish off the point quickly. Win it as soon as you can. Drive the ball out of your opponent's reach. Hit it with an attitude of: "**there** — take **that!**"

Try hitting down on the ball, just like when you're giving backspin to a driving groundstroke. Thrust the racket into and down the back of the ball — not with a big karate chop as when you hit a drop shot, but with some definite downward quality to the swing. The main thrust, however, should be **through** the ball, not down. This will give the same benefit as a high-to-low swing on the return of serve — it will add strength to the racket and pace to the resulting shot.

To give stability to a volley stroke and pace to the shot, tilt the racket head back and . . .   *. . . come through the ball with a downward thrust of the swing.*

Another advanced habit is to actually **attack** the ball on a volley. Close in on the ball whenever possible — go **meet** it. It'll put you nearer the net for better angle possibilities, and it'll make the net less of an obstacle. Good volley players will try to avoid letting the ball dip below the level of the net before they intercept it.

Be aggressive at the net. Attack the ball instead of waiting for it to come to you. Defend the net like a goalie defending against a score.

How close to the net should you be? It depends on both you and your opponent. Feel quick today? Be on top of the net. Are you playing against someone who lobs a lot? Be more cautious. Does your opponent have strong groundstrokes? Stay back at least a couple of yards. But never find yourself caught near the service line. You'll lose the advantage of being able to hit angled shots, and the ball will often come to you below the level of the net, forcing you to lift it up and over.

Remember that if you have pushed your opponent off to one side of the court, you should follow by drifting to that side. The further off the court your rival is, the more you can forget about protecting against a shot that will come behind you, since you'll face few players who can pick up a wide ball and angle it crosscourt behind you to slip it inbounds along the sideline. An opponent's common tendency, when pulled off to the side, is to hit down the line.

Dazzle Everyone With Footwork

Then here comes a ball at the speed of sound, right at your sternum. And your life flashes in front of you.

But there's a way to save the moment. Take a quick step diagonally to the side and **forward,** and pull your upper body away from the path of the ball. Trigger an abbreviated shoulder turn, and hit with as much of a volley stroke as you can manage.

WHEN OPPONENT IS PULLED OFF COURT, DRIFT TO THAT SIDE

FORGET ABOUT COVERING THIS AREA

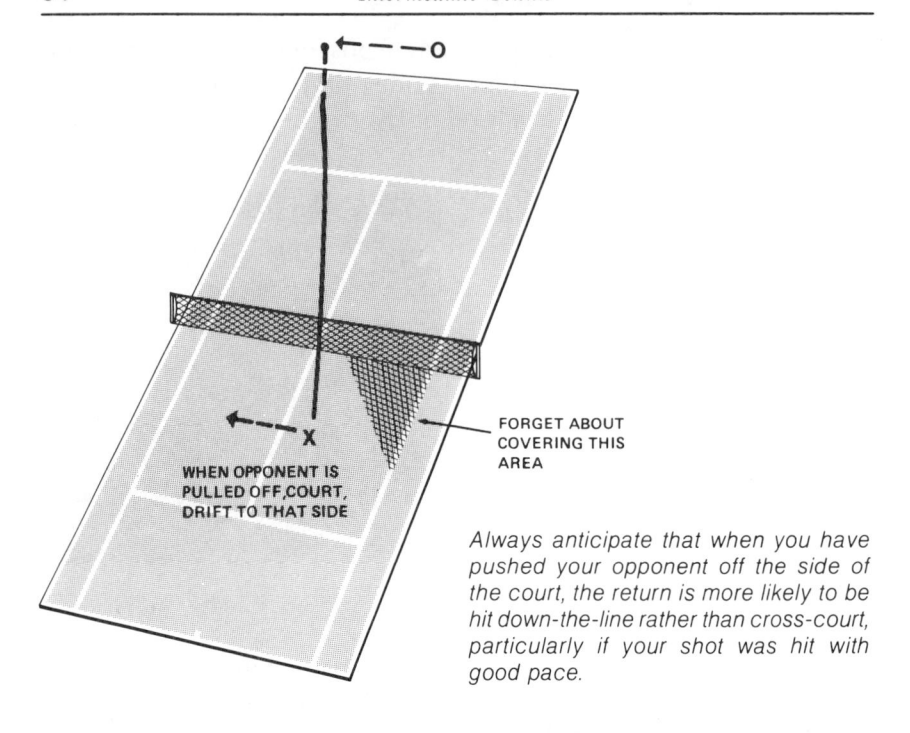

Always anticipate that when you have pushed your opponent off the side of the court, the return is more likely to be hit down-the-line rather than cross-court, particularly if your shot was hit with good pace.

When you're well stationed at the net, but your opponent sends a bullet right at you . . .

. . . take a quick step to the side and forward to facilitate a brief shoulder turn and get your upper body away from the ball. Keep a vice-tight grip, and block the ball back as best you can.

Not enough time to do even that? Then push your elbow out to the side and take the ball with a backhand. Brace your arm solid from the impact, and thrust the racket slightly downward if you can, but do **anything** to get the strings in front of the ball.

When you must lunge for a ball hit to the side, take a lesson from baseball. Picture a runner poised off first base wanting to steal second. As the pitcher delivers the ball, the runner first takes a short "jab" step with the right foot, then a cross-over step with the left. For close-range balls, a quick jab-step toward the ball should suffice. For a wider ball, a jab-step followed by a cross-over with the trail foot will be the fastest way to get to the ball. This two-step volley will be all you'll ever need to reach hard-hit, wide-ranging shots.

When you must lunge for a wide ball, take a short "jab" step with your lead foot...

... and follow with a cross-over step with your trail foot ...

... for a two-step maneuver which should get you in range to return the ball.

Reminders

1. Go up to the net only when you can hit from in front of the baseline (the serve is an exception).
2. Hit the approach shot deep.
3. Come to a split-step pause as your opponent is about to hit.
4. Keep your racket ready, in front of you.

5. Answer a hard shot with a firm punch, but hit a drive volley if there's time.
6. Defend the net like an ice hockey goalie. Attack the ball! Be aggressive!

Problem Solving

Problem	Probable Cause	Solution
Getting passed on way to net	Approach shot too shallow	Hit approach shot deep to backhand
	Not pausing on approach	Split-step and pause as return is about to be hit
Late contact	Arms held too tight to body in ready position	Hold elbows away from body; keep racket head up
	Too big of a swing	Reach out for ball, with minimal backswing
No strength to stroke	Racket head getting ahead of hand	Keep forearm behind racket on forehand, parallel to racket on backhand
	Grip not firm	Squeeze racket tight just before contact
Trouble controlling low volley	Dropping racket head down and scooping ball	Get down low, bend knees, lower head, and get racket arm parallel with court

Overheads

When you're at the net and you see your opponent

- Leaning back
- Taking a short backswing
- Tilting the racket face back

you can expect a lob. Start backpedaling in anticipation.

Now the fun begins. If your rival lofts up a too-short lob, you can let fly with an overhead. It's a sporting shot, hit for an attempted winner every time. There's an air of finality about the stroke that leaves the striker with a sense of vibrance which permeates the rest of the game.

The overhead is often likened to a serve — with added choreography. But there are two major differences:

1. The darned ball isn't where you want it. You must get under and **in back** of the ball. Skip-step into position. Keep your legs alive, with knees bent, for last-minute adjustments.
2. The windup is more compact. If you think of the overhead as similar to a serve, you might plug in your serve program, with its gyration of down-up-around-over, etc. By the time you go through all this, the ball may have clunked you on the forehead. Forget the fancy windup. Just get the racket up and over your shoulder, like you were an archer reaching back to pull an arrow out of the quiver.

Turn sideways as you arrive at your hitting place, and lift your free hand up to point at the ball — this will keep it in front of you. But the main reason why you point is to remind yourself to **rivet your eyes on the ball.** Bring your weight to your back

To hit an overhead, get into position behind the ball. Lift your free hand up and point at the ball to track its flight and focus your aim.

Get the racket back as for a serve, only with less windup. Keep the backswing simple.

Make contact more in front than for a serve. Hit the ball with as much power as you can control.

foot as you prepare the racket. And watch the ball. Keep your knees unlocked to make the final corrections in position. And oh yes — watch the ball!!

Now go for it! The overhead isn't a push or a punch or a shove. It's a **smash!**

That's its older name. It's a more descriptive term, for it tells you what to do with the ball. Crack off a winner — **smash it!**

Reminders

1. Get into position early. It's better to be too far behind the ball than too far under it.
2. Keep life in your legs for final adjustments.
3. Bring the racket straight back; nothing fancy.
4. Use your free hand to point at the ball.
5. Watch the ball intently.
6. Get sideways to the net.
7. Do what the word says — smash the ball.

Problem Solving

Problem	Probable Cause	Solution
Ball hit into net	Trying to hit too hard	Swing only as hard as you can control
	Pulling head down just prior to contact	Keep chin up until after contact
	Throwing hips back in jackknife during hit	Hit with forward-shifting weight, as in serve
	Letting ball drop too low	Hit at full extension of arm
Ball hit too long	Ball hit too far back	Set up behind the ball
	Elbow leading swing, racket trailing at contact	Use serve-like fling of racket, arm extending
	Punching at ball	Use fluid motion, not a push
	Sidearm swing	Get elbow up; bring racket up and over

On the Court

It's part mind-game, playing at the net. You wonder sometimes why any reasonable person would ever self-inflict that aspect of the game.

If you have those feelings, erase them. Take practice at the net as often as you can. Never let a rehearsal session go by without spending a good portion of it at the net. Ask your practice partner to give you a real test. If you have two friends, ask them to alternately hit ball after ball at you. It'll double your exhilaration and reduce the time by half to feel confident in the forecourt.

Should you switch grips, forehand and backhand, for the volley? If you normally do, and don't get tangled up in the process, then all is well. But when you feel experimental, try a Continental grip for **both** sides. One advantage is obvious: this no-switch is a time saver. But that's **not** the major benefit. The biggest bonus is that it naturally tilts the racket face back on both sides, and this works in favor of a swing pathway that is down and through the ball. Thus, a Continental grip is conducive to adding power to the volley stroke. It also keeps the racket in ideal hitting position for low balls, but it's devastating for high ones. In the final analysis, the major deciding factor about any grip is how well it gets the racket face into effective hitting position.

Here's an excellent volley drill that will help you evaluate your grip. You and your partner stand across the net from one

There is often a moment — when a ball comes high to your forehand — that forces a quick decision: should you smash it or hit a volley stroke?

The answer is direct; if you can't get your arm up and fully extended for a free-wheeling overhead, then volley the ball. Make sure you keep your arm firm for this high volley. Push the racket forward with a solid wrist.

another, each in the forecourt. Keep a ball alive, hitting firmly but within each other's reach. Play volley against volley, trying to hit as many consecutive shots as the two of you can manage. It'll remind you of how important it is to keep your racket in readiness and your feet alive when playing at the net.

Should you try to spin the ball on your overheads? Professional players seem to, and it's often suggested that it's essential for better levels of play. But in truth it's not necessary, at least not when hitting from near the net. Besides, spinning the ball slows it down and gives your opponent an extra chance to catch up to it. Devote your attention instead to hitting the smash cleanly, without adding anything exotic.

It's generally agreed that the smash should be aimed deep in the opponent's court. But don't be excessively concerned with placement. As long as the ball is well hit, and is inbounds, it should be a winner.

Here's a vibrant skill to learn during practice. Go up to the net, and have your practice partner hit some offensive lobs for you. Do a quick retreat of a few shuffle steps, then...

. . . lunge into a jump overhead. Spring off your feet for the smash. Give the swing plenty of whip from your arm and wrist.

Finish off the stroke. It's common to be conservative on a jump overhead. Instead, hit the ball with an attitude of flair in your swing.

Ask your practice partner to lift up some really high lobs. Know where your threshold is — at what point is the ball too high to be effectively smashed from flight, and when should it be allowed to bounce first?

Hit some of your practice overheads flat-out, with no holding back. Learn how hard you can swing and still control the destiny of the ball. And feel the raw exhilaration of being able to hit with full conviction. Then dare your next opponent to hit you a lob.

CHAPTER 7

Tactics For The Lob

The poor lob. It's the orphan of tennis — often ignored, much unused. It seldom gets the recognition it deserves. Usually it's devalued as a shot hit only in defense. Sometimes it's seen as a sign of weakness.

It's unfair. The lob can be used for an outright winner, and it is one of the truly finesse shots in tennis. It also provides one of the game's most satisfying moments — when you loft a ball just over an aggressive net player's reach and watch that player's hopeless effort in trying to chase it down. To hit such a shot is a sign of a finished player.

There are other uses for the lob. It can drag down a strong hitter with its change of pace or discourage an offensive forecourt player from coming to the net. And it can buy time when you need to recover your court position.

Two Kinds of Lobs

The lob has two variations, each with its own purpose. An **offensive lob** is hit against a player who is at the net. It is lifted just over the player's reach and aimed into the backcourt, where it should outrun the retreating player's attempt at retrieval. Thus, an offensive lob is hit as a concluding shot, with the anticipation of it being a point winner.

On the other hand, a **defensive lob** is hit as self-preservation by keeping the ball in play to salvage a later opportunity for a winner. Its most common use is when an opponent has driven you off the side of the court, and you need time to get back. It can also be hit whenever your rival has coerced you into an awkward off-balance predicament that keeps you from hitting a strong return. Thus, a defensive lob is hit higher, its virtue being to allow you to recollect yourself for the next shot.

Hit Offensive Lobs for Winners

An offensive lob is the right shot for the right time. Hit it when your rival has taken up a station at the net. Lift the ball so that the highest point of its travel is just above your opponent, a couple of feet higher than their reach.

Let the racket do most of the work. There's no need to change the grip, for the lob is essentially a groundstroke hit high. Make your swing more compact, shortening the backswing and using less shoulder rotation. Tilt the racket face back to align it for the upward hit.

Come into the ball from below the point of contact, low to high, and let the racket head follow-through **into the direction in which you want the ball to go.** In this way the racket head will literally tell the ball how high its path should be. Have the strings, at the moment of contact, exactly ninety degrees to the intended trajectory.

Relax your hitting elbow as you bring the racket forward, but keep your wrist steady to avoid the tendency of giving an extra flick of the wrist in a subconscious effort to lift the ball.

An offensive lob is a compact ground-stroke . . .

. . . where the racket is brought into the ball from below the point of contact, with wrist held steady . . .

. . . and the racket head finishing by following the trajectory of the ball.

Bend your knees more than for a groundstroke as you prepare for the lob, then unbend them with your swing to help add direction to the racket.

For most players, the lob is more difficult to hit on the backhand side. If you have trouble with this side, emphasize the upward follow-through of the racket head, and give yourself extra room for error by lifting the ball higher than on a forehand lob.

On the backhand side, bring the racket up into the ball from below . . .

. . . and emphasize the height of the follow-through to give more lift to the ball and thus provide a greater margin for error.

Give Defensive Lobs Height

You desperately need a defensive lob when your opponent has dragged you off the side of the court and has come up to the net ready to pounce on an errant return. The more you're pressed into hitting on the run, the less likely it is that you'll be able to get off a fully controlled shot. To attempt an offensive return in this quandary might result in a ball hit too low, into the waiting racket of your appreciative opponent, who now has your entire vacated court to hit into. So drop the racket head down extra low; tilt the face way back; let fly with a limber-arm upward swing; do whatever you can to send the ball back **high.** Use the shot to push your rival away from the net, and to give yourself time to recover your normal court position.

94   Intermediate Tennis

When your opponent has pushed you off the side of the court and has an established net position . . .

. . . it's usually best to respond with a defensive lob . . .

. . . whereby you need to drop the racket head extra low . . .

. . . and come up under the ball . . .

. . . to give the lob plenty of height . . .

. . . so you have lots of time to apply the brakes . . .

. . . and recover your court position.

Don't be bashful with defensive lobs. Lift them into the stratosphere. Give yourself enough time to retie your shoelaces and still get back to the court.

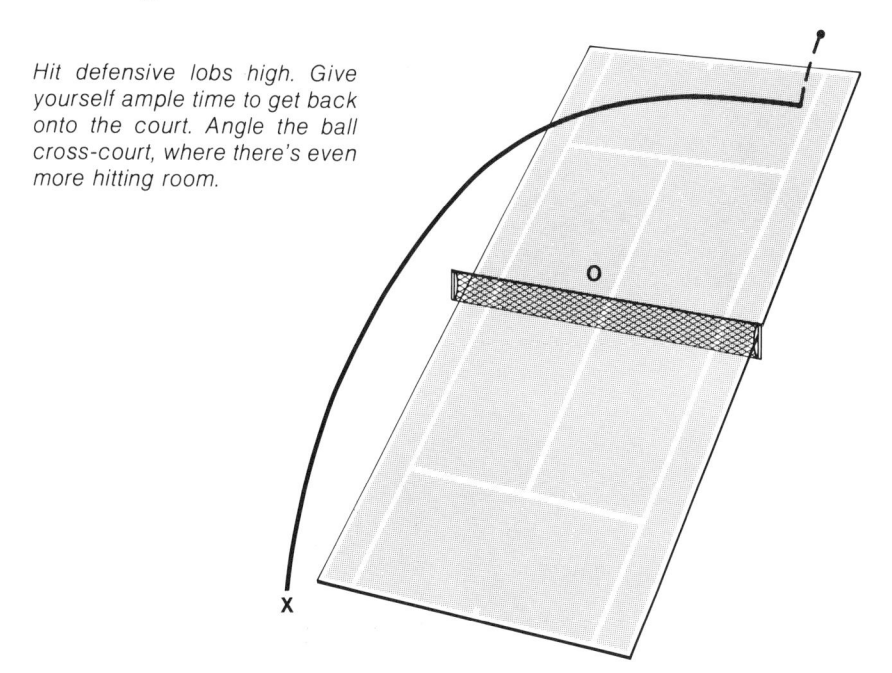

Hit defensive lobs high. Give yourself ample time to get back onto the court. Angle the ball cross-court, where there's even more hitting room.

Spin on the Lobs

The topspin lob — it's one of the joyful sights of tennis. The ball arches just over a flabbergasted net player, then bends into the court and kicks toward the fence, far out of reach. When you hit a successful topspin lob, it's difficult to keep from laughing out loud as you watch the flight of the ball and the bewilderment of your opponent.

But — it's also a very difficult shot to hit. It's a risky maneuver with a high chance for error. And it's not really necessary to hit spin on the lob for it to be a winner. Consequently, the topspin lob is a shot to be mastered only at the top of the tennis echelon. Notwithstanding all this, it's still worth a try.

To give topspin to the lob, you must get the racket head especially low to start. Let your elbow relax and lay your wrist back, then let fly with the most vigorous upward flail of your arm that you are able to generate without losing control. Finish high above your opposite shoulder. Fling the racket like you were going to throw it at an airplane passing overhead. Use lots of wrist.

The topspin lob is a flamboyant shot that . . .

. . . is hit by sweeping the racket up into the ball from several feet below the point of contact . . .

. . . with a dynamic upward fling of the arm and wrist . . .

. . . that finishes on the opposite side of the body.

Tactics For The Lob

The shot cannot be hit from a contact point below the waist, and it's difficult to control when the oncoming ball has good pace, or when you're on the run. Furthermore, it's almost impossible to hit at all from the backhand side.

By contrast, giving backspin to a lob is sometimes a handy asset, with less fickle results. It's generally a defensive response, used most commonly when your opponent has given you a strong offensive shot, such as a smash, or even a crushing serve. It's also effective when caught on the run, for it will keep the ball in the air longer and give you more time for recovery.

The swing for a backspin lob is short, with a distinctly firm wrist. The racket face must be tilted back and lifted above the anticipated point of contact, but make the swing essentially parallel with the court. Let the tilt of the racket provide the spin. Be generous with the height of the shot. Give yourself enough time to catch a deep breath and be in good position to watch your opponent stagger when trying to figure out how the ball is going to bounce.

To give backspin to a lob . . .

. . . the racket should come into the ball on an essentially level plane . . .

. . . with the strings tilted way back . . .

. . . to provide the spin and plenty of loft.

Using the Lob in Match Play

A lob can be hit anytime. Don't keep it in reserve just for when your opponent is at the net. Use it whenever you are pinned into a defensive position and you need time to recollect yourself, or as a change of pace against a strong hitter, or simply to break up the rhythm of a prolonged rally.

If the sun is a hazard on one side of the court, use it often when it'll force your opponent to look up into it. But don't lift a lob into a wind that is behind you, for you might watch it get carried like a kite beyond the court.

Hit every lob with enough height to accomplish its objective. If you make a mistake, let it be in hitting too **high** instead of too low.

Go cross-court with the lob when the opportunity is available. The logic is the same as for a cross-court groundstroke: there's more room for placement when angling the ball to the far corner. Otherwise, hit the ball over the backhand side of a net player. Few players can effectively hit a high backhand, so even if you fail to give the ball enough height, it's unlikely that you'll get burned by a strong return from that side.

Anytime you hit an offensive lob over a net player, your first impulse should be to follow it to the net. Even if your opponent

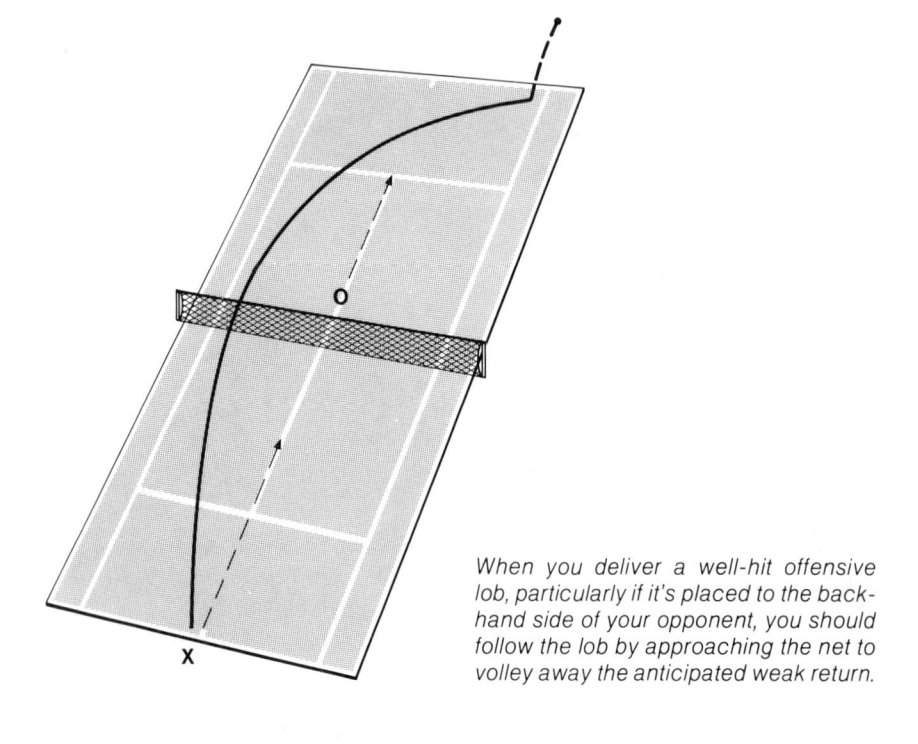

When you deliver a well-hit offensive lob, particularly if it's placed to the backhand side of your opponent, you should follow the lob by approaching the net to volley away the anticipated weak return.

manages to chase the ball down, it'll be on the run away from you, and the return will have only diluted strength. In many cases, your rival will toss up another lob in desperation. Either way, it will be opportune for you to be in the forecourt to volley away the weakened reply.

It's often suggested that you should try to conceal the lob by coming into the ball as if for a groundstroke, then lift up a lob at the last instant. In truth, very few players, even at an advanced level, will react by quickly retreating from the net when you openly show that you are about to lob. So don't camouflage your plan at the expense of hitting the ball well.

In every match, hit a few lobs early, even if your opponent is not at the net. There is a tendency to hit the first few lobs of a match too short, probably because the muscles are still a bit tight. By lofting some high shots early in the match, you'll get your bearings set for the first time you need to go up over your opponent's head.

Reminders

1. Hit the lob as an offensive shot whenever you can. Try to win the point with it.
2. Hit defensive lobs only when necessary. Give them plenty of height.
3. Always provide enough clearance — hit too high rather than too low.
4. Swing your racket directly up in the same plane as the height you want to give to the ball. Try to hold the ball on the strings as long as possible, and follow-through into the path of the ball.
5. Keep a firm wrist for the stroke.
6. When under pressure, do anything to get the ball up.

Problem Solving

Problem	Probable Cause	Solution
Erratic control	Stopping racket too soon	Hit through the ball

(Continued)

Problem Solving — continued

Problem	Probable Cause	Solution
Hitting too short	Racket head not dropped below contact point	Get racket down; come up under ball
	Wrist too flaccid	Keep firm wrist throughout swing
Hitting too long	Flicking at ball with wrist	Keep a steady wrist and forearm
	Too big of a swing	Keep backswing short, but still follow through

On the Court

When hitting lobs in match play, there is often an irresistible urge to keep a wary eye on your opponent — and this causes your arm to tighten up. Practice the lob by trying a camera trick: focus on the ball and make the background fuzzy. You're still **aware** of the background (where your opponent is), but it's out of focus, while the ball is a clear image.

The best practice is to have a willing partner or two. Ask your friend to stand at the net and feed you a bucket of balls, one after the other, then try to groove your swing so that at the end of the supply you can land every ball within five feet of the baseline. If you have two friends, have one feed you from the baseline, while the other stands at the net to crash away every ball you hit too low. Ask the feeder to start pushing you from side to side, in rapid succession. In a match, as fatigue begins to have an effect, there will be an increasing tendency to hit lobs too low. But in this tiring practice you will learn how much more you'll need to lift the ball to have it accomplish its task.

Occasionally, hit some lobs really high. See how far into the clouds you can send the ball while still keeping it in bounds. Then your regular-height defensive lobs will seem like a cinch.

It's the offensive lob, however, which often gets ignored in practice sessions. Hit dozens of them. Learn to desensitize yourself from the net player by pretending that a ten-foot-high fence is at the net. Think of the **fence,** not your opponent. Then lift shot after shot adroitly over the fence-net.

CHAPTER EIGHT

Making Extraordinary Shots Ordinary

The game would be so much easier if it could be played against a ball machine. You could take your time, set up properly, prime your swing, and hit perfect strokes as each ball floated lazily into your racket.

Opponents don't happen to see it that way. They mostly try to hit the ball everyplace except where you want it. So you spend a lot of time in a match hitting running forehands, lunging overheads, half-volleys, double-jointed backhands, and other shots that you never think of practicing yet are part of every set you play. Because tennis is a sport of constant motion, your success depends a great deal on your ability to adapt and hit from unconventional positions. Here are some suggestions to help you handle such situations.

Hitting on the Run

The most frequent occurrence is having to chase down a wide shot and make the return while on the run. To get off an effective shot in such cases, try the following:

1. *Cut the ball off early.* Just as with the return of serve, try to intercept the ball before it has moved too far off the court. Make a quick pivot, and go on a direct path ninety degrees to the flight of the ball. This means that you'll be running diagonally **in,** relative to the baseline, to reach the ball. If you run parallel with or diagonally away from the baseline, you'll have a longer distance to travel to catch up to the ball. Cut it off early, before it gets out of your reach. By this habit you'll also give yourself a better chance to get some weight behind the shot.

2. *Delay your backswing.* Never mind trying to get your racket back early. Pivot and run, using both arms in a pumping action to help your acceleration. Your first objective is to get to where you need to be; the second is to execute the swing. Start your backswing as the ball is about to bounce. Abbreviate its length to conserve time. But add a little loop to help the timing and to make the movement continuous instead of having to interrupt the momentum of the racket head with a straight back-straight forward swing.

3. *Let your arm propel the racket.* When you take the ball on the run, you won't be able to get your shoulders rotated in normal fashion. So you must rely on your arm to do most of the work. Keep your arm loose. Give it a whip that feels like the motion came from your shoulder socket, and add some flick of the wrist. Don't try to muscle the ball over the net, for this will only reduce the flinging action of the racket head and rob the swing of impulse.

4. *Provide an extra margin of safety.* Don't try for a net skimmer. Lift the ball higher over the net than usual to allow for any loss of control. Add a bit of topspin if you can to give even more room for error. Usually the safest retort is to aim down the line, even though the net is higher there. Often your opponent will be coming up to the net when you are on the run, and an errant attempt at a cross-court return could drift the ball right into your opponent's hands. Make sure that you provide the same margin of safety as you did for the net clearance: aim a couple of yards inside the lines. But if you're caught on a full sprint and can't get prepared for a decent swing, then toss up a defensive lob.

5. *Recover quickly.* As soon as you can after your hit, reverse your direction to recover your court position. Get to the spot from which you'll hit as fast as possible, trying to give yourself time to collect your momentum at the end, maybe even making your last step toward the net. Then pivot and get back to the court. If you're pressured into having to hit on a flat-out run, as soon as you can slam on the brakes. Don't loop your run to come back to the court in a circular path. Get your feet out in front of you to stop dead in your tracks, then turn and get back.

6. *Hit on the run only if you have no other choice.* Sometimes there's nothing to do except scamper after a ball and get it back any way you can. Form becomes nonexistent. Only results count. But never hit on the run unless you must. Try to accelerate as quickly as you can, then slow down as you

If you're forced to hit from the side of the court, while on the move, give some extra whip to your arm for the shot . . .

. . . then slam on the brakes . . .

. . . and quickly recover your court position.

near the ball. This is especially true for approach shots. As you come in to retrieve a shallow ball, try to time your run so that you'll be able to pull up for a near-normal swing. Hitting while on the run toward the net does not add any strength to the shot and may in fact increase the chances of hitting out.

The Half-Volley

Any player who goes to the net often will get caught in situations where the ball arrives low, at the feet. Taking a ball from flight as it's descending is a menace. The drop of the ball makes it feel like it has extra weight, and it'll respond like a rock on your strings. You need a tight grip and firm arm to play such a ball. Hit with a volley-like stroke. Don't be anything other than defensive with this return. Push it back deep.

Whenever you can, play a much safer stroke — the **half-volley.** This is where you catch the ball on a short bounce the way a baseball infielder scoops a ground ball from a short hop. It's a useful and not too difficult shot that, when hit from the forecourt, can be an effective defensive response. But when hit from the backcourt, it takes on many of the qualities of a groundstroke and can therefore be used as an attacking weapon.

When hitting a half-volley from in front of the service line, just put the strings behind the ball. Turn quickly to the side and point the head of the racket toward the sideline — there's no time for any backswing. Meet the ball just an instant after the bounce, with a stable wrist. Tilt the head of the racket back to let the ball rebound up and over the net. Bend your knees — lower your seat. Get your head down and try to keep the racket handle parallel to the court. If you can give the ball direction, sweep it down the line where you'll have a better chance to cover the possible return. Make sure that you clear the net with plenty of spare room.

When caught in the middle of the court, the ball often arrives low, where it's difficult to return aggressively.

If you take the ball from flight, before its bounce, use a short backswing and brace your wrist for the "heavy" impact.

Punch the ball back, defensively, sending it deep into the opponent's court.

From this middle-of-the-court position, a half-volley is usually a more reliable shot.

To hit a half-volley, bend your knees to get down low. Keep your racket parallel to the court. Let the ball take its bounce and make contact just an instant thereafter.

Give more forward impetus to your swing than when you hit a descending ball. Make the swing more characteristic of a groundstroke than a volley.

From deep in your own court the half-volley is essentially a groundstroke hit from a short hop. The main ingredient is timing. There's no need to bend as low, but don't just drop the racket head and try to shovel the ball either. Make your swing resemble a normal groundstroke, only with less backswing preparation. Once you get the feel of this stroke, you'll use it as an approach shot. Give it a try! You'll quickly discover how easy to hit and useful it is.

Handling a High Backhand

Here comes a ball high to your backhand side — and suddenly it's panic time! What to do with it? Try to flick the racket for a badminton-like stroke? Roll the wrist up and over? Simply slap at the ball?

Two things will help. First, lift your whole arm, not your shoulder; keep the racket at the same angle to your forearm as for an ordinary backhand. Second, keep your arm straight. You can swing much more comfortably at a high ball when your arm stays extended. This means that you must adjust your position so that your contact point is further away from your body than on a normal backhand.

Don't try to hit down on the ball, particularly when you're deep in your own court. Push the racket out and straight through the ball. Accept your predicament: you've been caught in a defensive position, so hit defensively. Play the ball back high and deep.

To hit a high backhand, lift your whole arm, keep it straight, and . . .

. . . punch through the ball. Play it safe; push the ball back high and deep.

But if you're at the net, and you feel adventuresome, you may want to let fly with a backhand smash. Make sure that the ball is high enough to allow your arm to extend for the hit. Then get your shoulders turned well around, sideways to the net. Lift your hitting elbow, bend your arm, and cock your wrist to bring the racket back and down, forearm now parallel to the court. Hit by unbending your arm, wrist coming up and over your elbow, and add "whip" to your forearm and wrist for extra pace in the racket head. It's a fairly difficult shot, but if you don't overdo your exuberance when hitting, it will discourage opponents from thinking they can win an easy point by lobbing over your backhand shoulder.

When hitting a backhand smash, get your shoulders turned well around, as much as for a backhand groundstroke...

... then lift your arm and drop your racket head down...

... and snap the racket into the ball with a vigorous whip of your arm and wrist.

Returning Deep Lobs

Suppose you're at the net and an unobliging opponent gets off a good lob. But you've retreated quickly, and you'll catch up to the ball, albeit on a run toward the fence.

With your back to the net you'll not be able to use much upper body rotation to give strength to your swing, and with your momentum carrying you away from the net, an offensive return is out of the question. So reply with a lob of your own. Return the lob with a lob. Take whatever backswing you can, then lay your racket open and lift your arm upward, coming under the ball to spank it back high. Give your arm a loose-limbed fling, and add some wrist snap to help get the racket moving.

There'll be a tendency to hit too short on this lob, so give the ball plenty of lift and height. No trials at offensive lobs here. Think of getting the ball back to the middle of your rival's court — to the "T" where the service line and center line join. That'll give you maximum margin for error in all directions.

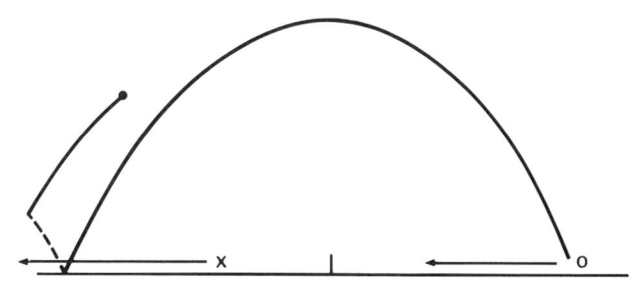

Suppose you (X) are pushed away from the net by a well-hit offensive lob. Your opponent (O) may follow the shot by taking over the net as you retreat. The safest return is to hit a lob of your own, giving the ball plenty of height and aiming to land it in the middle of your opponent's court.

Get into position for the shot by running back parallel to the flight of the ball, but a bit off to the side so that you can swing around your shoulder. Watch the ball out of the corner of your eye as you run. Never mind trying to see whether your opponent has come up to the net. Just fix your mind on three things: hit the ball back high, hit it to the middle of the court, and don't whack yourself on the head with your follow-through.

On a full-out retreat to chase down a lob . . .

. . . lay your racket strings toward the sky, take as much backswing as you can, and . . .

. . . give your arm a whip-like fling to get the ball back the best you can.

In other instances your rival will chase you away from the net with a lob that is so high you'll have plenty of time to retreat and get into hitting position. First do what experienced baseball outfielders do when a ball is hit over their head: take a quick sighting on the ball, then turn and run flat-out without bothering to watch its flight. Go well behind the spot where you think the ball will land, then turn and resight the ball again. Make sure that you've gone far enough so that the adjustments you'll need to make allow you to move forward into the ball instead of watching it bounce over your head. Then hit with a serving-like stroke. Keep your side to the ball. Lift your free arm up toward the ball to guarantee staying sideward and to set your sights on the descending ball. Make the point of contact further back than for a serve, and use a **topspin** motion. If you hit flat on this ball you'll simply have to punch it, but if you give it topspin you can hit with the same freedom you do for a serve, while enjoying the whole court as your target.

If you can catch up to a lob and get into position for hitting an overhead . . .

. . . go around behind the ball, lift your free arm up to track its path, and . . .

. . . keeping your shoulders turned side-on to the net, get your racket back as for a topspin serve . . .

. . . then rip into the ball with a topspin motion, contacting it further back than for a serve.

The "Anything-Goes" Shot

When you're on a full sprint toward the fence, trying to run down a deftly hit lob, about all you can do is to fling your racket at the ball, send the ball into the ozone, and hope. Or if you're at the net and your adversary rips a bullet right at you, anything you do to get the ball back is acceptable.

The better you get at tennis, and the more aggressively you play, the more you'll find yourself in emergency situations. In these instances there is no style. When you're pressed into awkward shots, use lots of wrist, or hit off the wrong foot, or slap at the ball — anything to get it back. But do not try for an all-or-nothing shot. Just stay in the point. Give the ball lots of height to provide yourself with recovery time. Send it to the middle of the court, or if you can, deep.

Using Touch

Moments arise in a match when a soft shot is opportune. The ball is hit with little pace, away from an opponent, sometimes with spin. They are the so-called "touch" shots of tennis, the name suggesting the finesse that is necessary to make them successful. Essentially, they are the following:

1. *Drop shots.* This shot, hit after the ball has bounced, is intended to fall short of a deep opponent. Use your normal grip, bring the racket back above hitting height, relax your forearm, and push the racket down the back of the ball. Finish low.

Play the shot less frequently the farther back you are in your own court. In fact, a drop shot should be played from behind your own baseline only when your rival has fallen down behind their court near the fence. It's a risky shot if it isn't precisely placed, because if it's pushed too far, it becomes a setup for your opponent.

2. *Drop volley.* It's generally safer to try to drop a shallow ball from a volley, but only when you're right on top of the net and your opponent is behind the baseline. The objective is to take the momentum out of the ball. There are two ways: either by relaxing your grip almost to the point of letting the racket fall out of your hand and merely letting the ball sink into the strings, or by sliding the strings down the

110   Intermediate Tennis

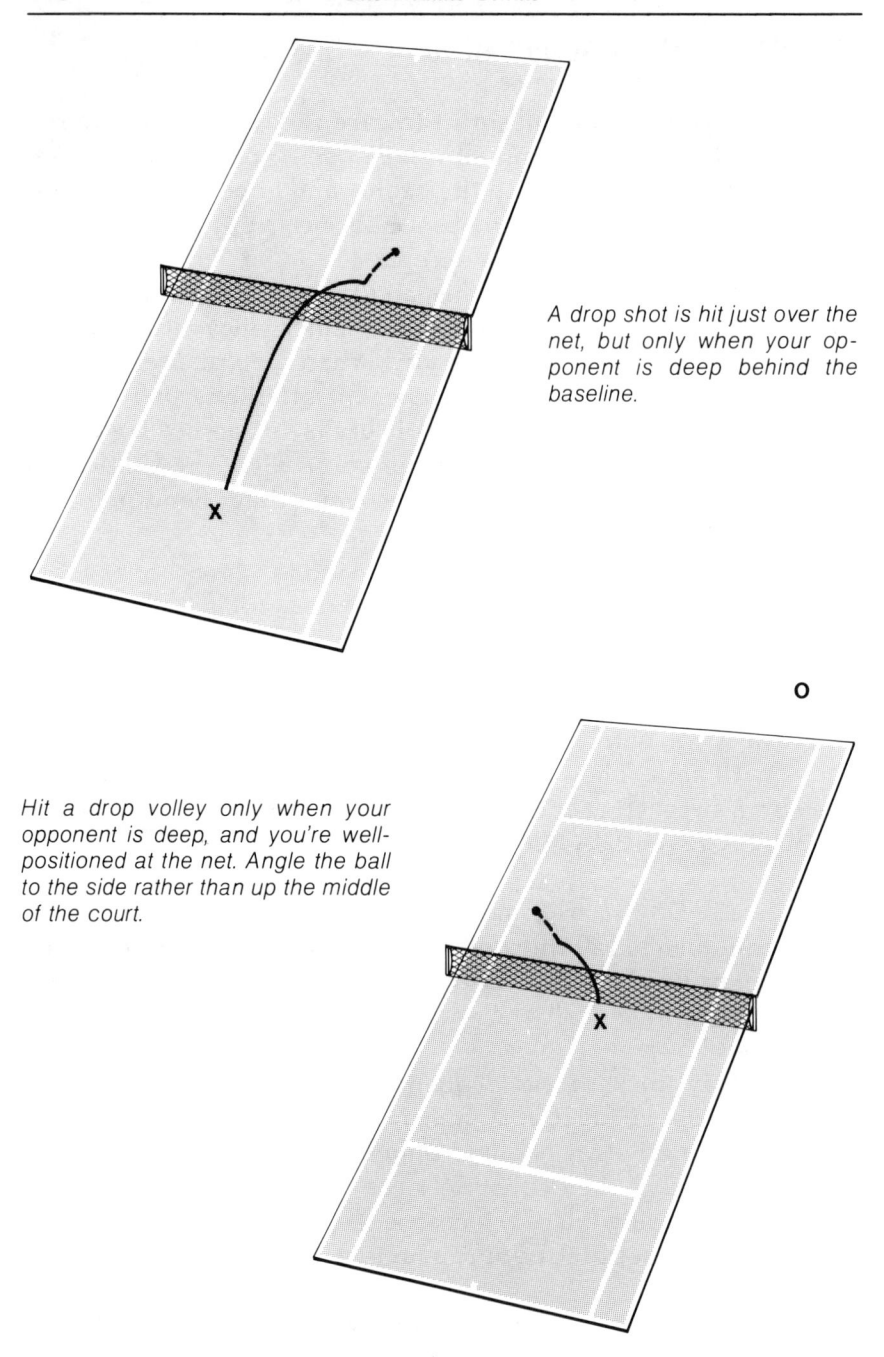

A drop shot is hit just over the net, but only when your opponent is deep behind the baseline.

Hit a drop volley only when your opponent is deep, and you're well-positioned at the net. Angle the ball to the side rather than up the middle of the court.

back of the ball at contact. Try a combination, and be sure to tilt the racket face back. Don't let the ball kick too high off your strings where it'll give an opponent time to chase it down. Keep it low over the net.

On both a drop shot and a drop volley, relax your grip and tilt the racket face back.

Slide the strings down the back of the ball to take away its momentum and to impart some backspin.

3. *Dinks.* Anything that's left over after all the other shots have been made is seemingly called a "dink." But in fact it usually refers to a soft, shallow, cross-court shot that is hit from inside your own baseline against an opponent who is at the net. Thus, it is hit behind an opponent, anticipating that it will catch your rival moving the wrong direction as they come over to cover the side of the court you are on. When you can hit this shot reliably, you'll be ready for the tour.

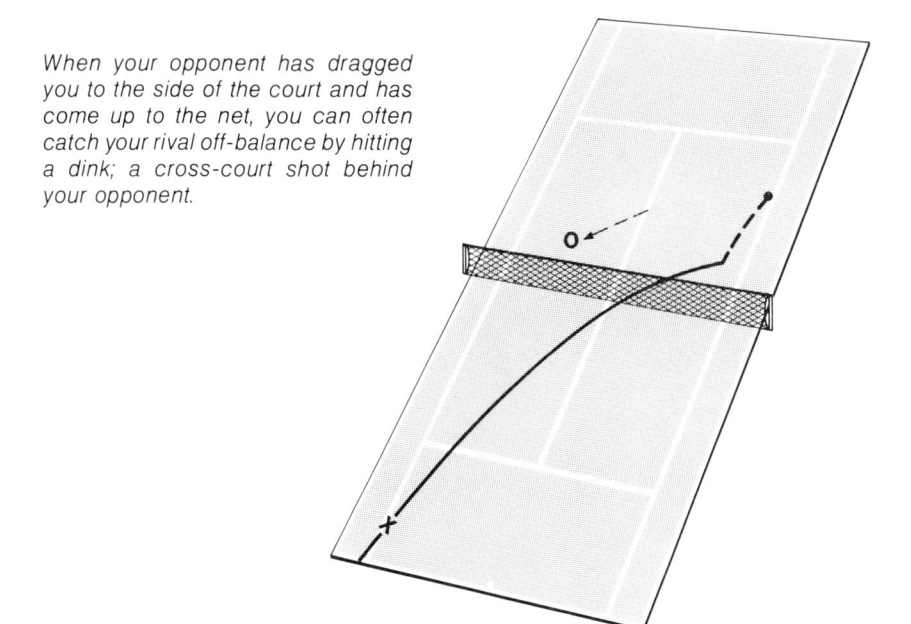

When your opponent has dragged you to the side of the court and has come up to the net, you can often catch your rival off-balance by hitting a dink; a cross-court shot behind your opponent.

Touch shots can be overused. They are only for select situations. But learning them is important for developing an all-around game. When you can intentionally shift gears, you can keep an opponent guessing just as a baseball pitcher keeps a batter off-balance with changes of pace. And touch shots make your power shots more domineering. You'll control the rhythm of a game and you'll be better able to handle a wider variety of opponents.

Be Creative

Develop versatility for **all** your strokes. Be creative; experiment with different spins and trajectories. Learn to hit a wide assortment of shots with the same stroke. For example, make your forehand a reliable weapon for hitting a regular flat drive, or a topspin looper, or with heavy backspin, maybe some slice, and so on. Develop a variety of modifications for each stroke. The more options you have with your strokes, the easier it will be to come up with an answer to any awkward situation in a match. In the bargain, your practice sessions will be more fun, and during matches, you'll hear more gasps of amazement from your opponents when you pull yourself out of desperate predicaments.

CHAPTER NINE

Strategy For Singles

It is in the blood of some people to want to hit a tennis ball for its own sake. They can find carefree pleasure in the non-competing spirit of prolonged exchanges with another of like interest, where the principle objective is to keep the ball alive as long as possible. It's infinity tennis, and in an unadulterated sense is a pure way to enjoy an art form of sporting endeavor.

But "the game's the thing," as an old English proverb goes. It means that until you can prove your acquired skills in a competitive performance, those skills cannot be considered complete. No matter how satisfying the unopposed act of simply whacking the ball around may be, the more decisive ambition should be to put your craft to the test of match play. Tennis is, after all, designed to be a contest.

Competition is an Attitude

In actuality, tennis is composed of only about half a dozen strokes. But in application they multiply into hundreds of variations. Add the compatible playing size of the court, and the game affords the room to be generously varied in strokes and strategy. Thus, tennis appeals to a mathematical mind, where shot selection and ball placement are based on the laws of probability. And it also appeals to a creative mind, where situations of play require second-by-second inventions of strategy.

Sometimes, however, there are night and day differences between one's performance in practice and in games. In the unchallenged free hitting of a practice session, the body may work in smart coordination. But start keeping score, and the muscles might take a vacation. Notwithstanding this, from one viewpoint competition could be seen as the ultimate practice, because it coerces you into hitting each ball not with detached commitment, but with forethoughtful intent as to direction, spin, and pace. Furthermore, through games the results of your playing techniques become more apparant, since feedback is liberally supplied about what is working well, or what may need some refinement. Games make practice more meaningful, and practice in turn provides more diversity to games.

Simplify the Plan

Conceivably, a fretful reason why some players are apprehensive about their ability to do well in competition is their feeling of unpreparedness about tactics of play. In part this may come from an unfortunate belief that the strategy of the game is highly complicated — far more involved than can be judged from watching a typical Sunday afternoon televised pro match. But in truth the strategy of tennis has been sinfully overestimated. The best laid plans are unabashedly straightforward. There is nothing complex about sound, logical strategy.

Everything originates out of the direct objective of trying to hit the ball so hard or place it so well that it cannot be returned; or if returned, is hit so defensively that it provides a chance for a point-winner on the next shot. From this all other tactics follow — where to stand, where to go, when to go, where to hit, what kind of shot to hit, and so on. Most situations in the game have automatic answers, or at least, sensible responses. And this makes for a comforting state of affairs, knowing that the effective strategy is remarkably uncomplicated, even for top-level play. It is a great relief for the mind to not need an excessively analytical game plan that would only clutter, rather than clarify, the tactical side of tennis.

The First Law: Keep the Ball in Play

The obvious primary intent of tennis is to hit the ball over the net, land it inbounds, and do this one more time than an opponent on each point. It is, pure and simple, the first law of strategy. But this law is often broken. Not so much because of a lack of ability, but more because of a lack of **sense**-ability.

The worst mistake anyone can make is to hit the ball into the net. It's a dead loss, never giving an opponent a chance to commit an error. Usually it happens from trying to hit the ball too hard, thus having to skim the net to keep the ball in the court. If you are a frequent victim of this, ease up on your stroke, loft the ball more (to clear the net by several feet), and thus you'll keep it in play. Even if a shot of yours is sailing errantly too long, there is always the chance an impatient opponent will swat at the ball anyhow before its bounce to attempt a return.

A related mistake is to hit the ball too wide. This is generally indicative of trying to rifle an angled shot too near the sideline. Always aim several feet inside the lines, where there's an allowance of room for some inaccuracy.

The Second Law: Keep the Ball Deep

An associated tactic, equally direct and equally effective, is to habitually place the ball deep. This will compel an opponent into staying back, and hitting incessantly from behind the baseline, with little chance to come up to the net and with reduced opportunities for hitting angled, cross-court returns. You'll also provide yourself with more time for moving into ideal hitting position on each ball, thus allowing full concentration on a rhythmical, forward-flowing swing.

During practice, monitor your rally to see if you can consistently land the ball at least behind the opposing service line, and preferably within a yard or two of the baseline. Such deep placement will be effective against any opponent, and on any court surface.

Know When to Use Angles

Keep the ball alive, and play it deep. They are the first two requisites for consistent tennis. But when your opponent offers a shallow ball, one that you can play from inside the baseline, then think of taking advantage of cross-court angles.

The more favorable opportunity is when you get a return that is not only shallow, but also off to one side. Suddenly your rival's court has added width, for now you can either fling a cross-court winner in front of your opponent, or plunk the ball into the near corner behind your surprised adversary. Of the two choices, the cross-court is generally the safer.

When your opponent forces you to hit from behind your own baseline, you are usually left with only the retort of returning the ball deep. However, when your rival hits an inviting short ball:

1. the further inside the court you can move to retrieve the ball, the greater the potential for successfully angling a shot toward either sideline. But,

2. the more you are pulled off to one **side** of your own court, the more favorable the situation becomes for a **cross-court** return.

Even if your adversary has pushed you far behind the baseline — but still off to the side — a cross-court shot is a more logical choice than a down-the-line attempt because:

1. the distance to the opposite diagonal corner is greater than the distance to the near corner, thus providing more room for the placement;
2. the ball will cross the net near the middle, where the net is six inches lower than at the sides;
3. the ball will be moving away from your opponent, whereas a down-the-line shot will swing the ball back toward your rival; and
4. you are in better position following the shot to cover the potential area of return from your opponent.

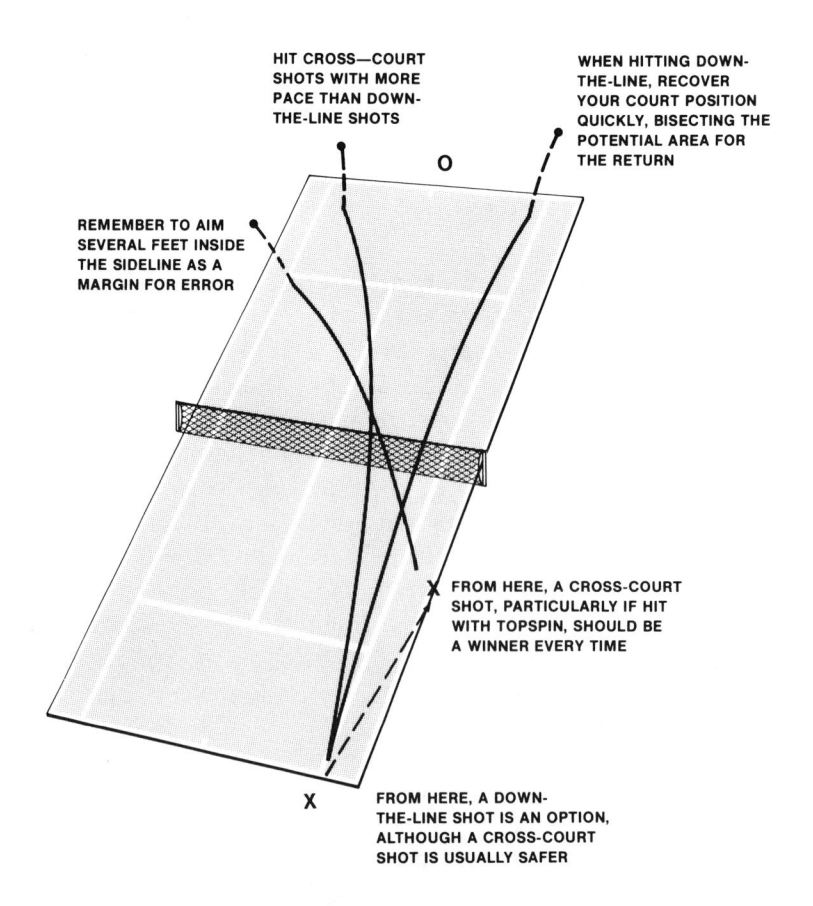

How to Beat a Strong Groundstroke Player

Add one more ingredient to the (1.) keep-the-ball-alive and (2.) play-it-deep components of successful tennis. It's (3.) keep the ball in the **middle** of the court, and now you have the prime tactic to use against a player who has solid groundstrokes.

This might sound contradictory to what you've always heard. Tradition has it that you should run good groundstroke players from side to side, presumably to tire them out or to force them into hitting off-balance shots. This **does** hold some logic, but only if you can consistently produce sufficient pace on the ball to keep your rival from getting into position to hit strong returns. Otherwise, the **last** thing you want to do is provide a good groundstroke player with opportunities for hitting angled shots, for that opponent would then have the same advantages of a wider placement potential as previously discussed.

It is especially vital to keep the ball deep and in the middle of the court if your adversary can hit topspin. Against such a player, an unforgiving mistake is to hit a ball shallow and to the side, where it is an open invitation for a cross-court winner.

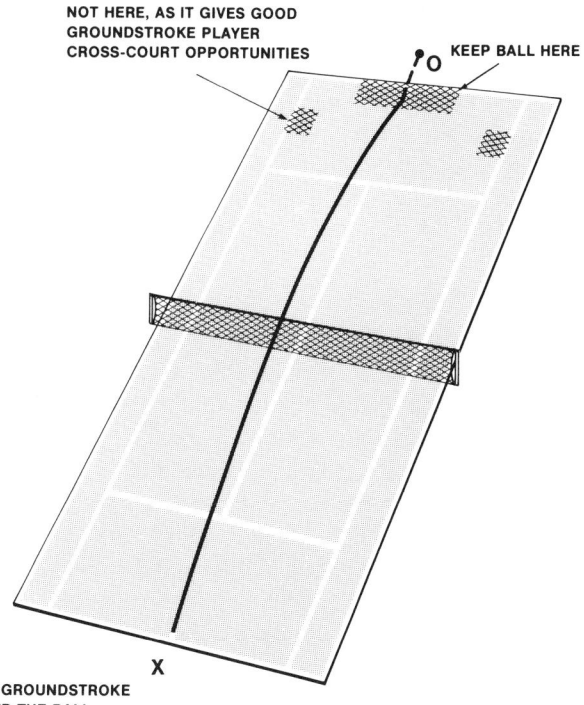

AGAINST A STRONG GROUNDSTROKE PLAYER, TRY TO KEEP THE BALL DEEP UP THE MIDDLE, PARTICULARLY WHEN YOU HIT FROM BEHIND YOUR OWN BASELINE

If Your Opponent Is A Slugger

The keep-the-ball-alive philosophy is particularly valuable against a rival who likes to hit hard. Usually, such a player will determine the outcome of virtually all points, either by winning them outright with put-away shots, or by losing them on errors. But sluggers are often impatient. If they haven't won a point after a few exchanges, they may become anxious and try for an overly aggressive shot that has a higher probability of failure. So the objective is to keep feeding the ball to this player, allowing plenty of chances for that player to create their own mistakes.

Additionally, it's difficult to generate pace off a ball that does not itself come with much speed. A big hitter will prefer the ball to arrive with some pace, so instead offer this player a "nothing" ball. Float the ball back with good net clearance, and land it deep. Hit occasional semi-lobs, and frequently use backspin to slow the ball both in flight and after its bounce. Remember that by beveling the racket back and swinging slightly down on the ball, you not only create backspin, but the racket is also stabilized to more effectively take the impulse out of strong returns.

Try another tactic: bring the big hitter up to the net. Sluggers often prefer to stay back and bash away at the ball from the baseline, whereas they may feel uncomfortable at the net, where touch and finesse are necessary. Find out by dropping the ball just over the net. It's imperative to backspin these shots, for if you mistakenly hit the ball a bit too far into the court, the halting action of its bounce will still make it more difficult for a power player to get their full weight into a shot.

If Your Opponent is a Human Backboard

Suppose you're up against a player who is the opposite of a power hitter — one who scrambles to return every ball, although usually with little pace. Now the direct ploy of keeping the ball alive will have less effect in compelling your foe into making mistakes, so it's up to you to make something else happen.

It's difficult to beat consistent groundstroke players in a baseline rally. They have confidence in their own ability to keep the ball alive and will not likely become impatient during a prolonged exchange. But they're also less apt to try for put-away shots. So moving these players from side to side will not invite the cross-court winners that it does from the big hitters.

Add a little extra pace to your shots, without being coaxed into the same impulsive attempts (with consequent loss of accuracy) that you were trying to extract from a power player.

Since a consistent baseline player often hits defensively, your extra pace will increase the chances of getting a shallow return that allows you to step up into the court and take advantage of the angles. You'll also have more opportunities to approach the net, and the typically slower ball that defensive players hit will give you added time to make the trip. Be wary that your backboard-like opponent may have good command of the lob. But if you do your preliminary work of sending your approach shot deep, your rival's potential for tossing up an offensive lob is reduced, and it's highly unlikely that you'll get passed by a strong drive hit out of your reach to one side.

Use the Forecourt Often

One mark of a confident, aggressive player is an instinct for coming up to the net at every opportunity. Against some opponents, when you show an intent to make frequent use of the forecourt, you inflict a plaguing mental diversion that constantly interferes with their concentration. They'll keep an apprehensive eye on you and hit more cautiously, trying to keep you in the backcourt. And, when you do come to the net, your very presence alone may be enough to press a jittery opponent into committing unforced errors.

Recall from chapter six that the approach to the net has the following qualifications:

1. Come in only when you can hit an approach shot from inside the baseline; or, behind your serve, if it's strong.
2. Hit the ball, for an approach shot, at the top of its bounce.
3. Send the ball deep, preferably with backspin, to your opponent's weak-side corner.
4. Sacrifice pace for placement.
5. Follow the path of the ball on your trip into the forecourt.
6. Just as your opponent is about to hit a return, come to a split-step pause in your advance.
7. Finish off the point as quickly as you can.

When stroking the approach shot, the higher the ball bounces, the easier it is to attack, and the more placement choice you have. If the ball is low, forcing you to hit more up and over the net, it is wiser to play it to your rival's weaker side in anticipation of a subdued return.

If you play an approach shot from near the sideline, it's marginally safer to hit cross-court, but this also opens up an inviting area of your court for your opponent to hit a passing shot into. Consequently, the better choice may be to hit down the line. This will make it easier to cover the widest possible angles that your opponent will have for a return. If you do prefer a cross-court approach shot, use it more often when you can leave the open court on your strong side, which usually means (assuming both you and your foe are right-handed) that you'll hit a backhand cross-court to your opponent's backhand side, thus forcing a weaker return and leaving the open space on your stronger, forehand side.

Go to the net as often as you can, even if you're still uncertain about your ability. Each trip will add to your confidence. Generate an attitude of **always** looking for a chance to move forward. Productive groundstroke play is essentially a matter of keeping the ball alive until your adversary offers a shallow return. Then, take the invitation and step up to the net.

Hit It Where Your Opponent Isn't

Once at the net, the intent is never to prolong a rally, waiting for a mistake from your rival. Instead, win the point as soon as possible.

Where to hit the ball? Anyplace it's not likely to be returned. There's an old baseball adage about how to be a successful batter: "Hit the ball where the fielders ain't." The principle is the same for net play in tennis. Fling the volley someplace your opponent isn't, out of their reach.

It's the same for an overhead, but for this shot don't be too precise with your placement. Let the **force** of your shot command much of the influence.

Against a Net Rusher

Nobody's perfect. Occasionally you'll inadvertently drop a ball too shallow, and your assailant will take the net. Keep a cool head, and let your rival's approach shot tell you what to do.

If it's deep, forcing you to hit from behind the baseline, the logical retort is to lift a lob over your opponent's backhand shoulder. If you can, make it an offensive lob. Some players will rush the net flat out, and thus you can float the ball just over their reach and possibly win the point right there. Otherwise, if the approach shot is short, the further in you can move to play the ball, the more the percentage turns in favor of a passing shot. If you are pressed toward the sideline, hit the ball down the line, because it'll get to the net-rusher quicker. If you're in the middle of the court, hit the passing shot to either side, aiming to land it near the intersection of the service line and sideline. This will force your onrushing rival to lunge for the ball and drop the racket head down low to reply with a defensive shot that must be lifted up to cross the net. Suddenly, it's you and not your opponent who will have the offensive. Or, your passing shot may do just that — pass your opponent to resolve the point in an instant.

SEND THE LOB TO THE BACKHAND SIDE PARTICULARLY WHEN OPPONENT IS STILL ON THE WAY UP TO THE NET

KEEP PASSING SHOTS LOW, LANDING THEM NEAR THE SERVICE LINE

FROM HERE, HIT PASSING SHOT AGAINST AN OPPONENT WHO IS AT THE NET

FROM HERE, HIT A LOB

Hit Shots in Sequence

If tennis is like chess, to which it is often likened, then one of the similarities is the sequential pattern of the play. Both require patience and a plot for openings. One move leads to another in a logical, planned order.

The first lesson in playing chess-like tennis is simply to maneuver your opposition from side to side. Although deep and down the middle is the foundation of steady backcourt play (besides reducing the potential for cross-court returns), sometimes an alternating series of shots to the flanks will produce weakened returns from a scampering opponent. It also sets up a chance for you to fling the ball **behind** your rival, into the area of the court that they just vacated. This will "wrong-foot" your surprised adversary, and you can expect to either win the point directly, or to get a feeble return that lets you pounce on the ball to hit a put-away.

Another frequently suggested sequence of shots is the "up-back" philosophy: drive your opponent deep behind the baseline, then lay a drop shot just over the net to catch your rival stranded too far back to retrieve the shallow, low-bouncing ball. Or, even if your opponent does manage to get to the ball, you'll probably be presented with a placid return that allows you to hit an easy lob to finish off the point.

The weak link in this cycle is the drop shot, for unless it's deftly hit, it could become a sitter for an angled, point-winning shot from your foe. Another variation, usually safer, is to start the sequence by hitting deep into your opponent's forehand corner, then follow with a short placement along the opposite sideline. This makes for a longer run, and if your rival still chases the ball down, it will probably be from a sprint that produces only a weak return and leaves your opponent off the side of the court. Then you'll have plenty of time to send the next ball back into the now empty, forehand corner.

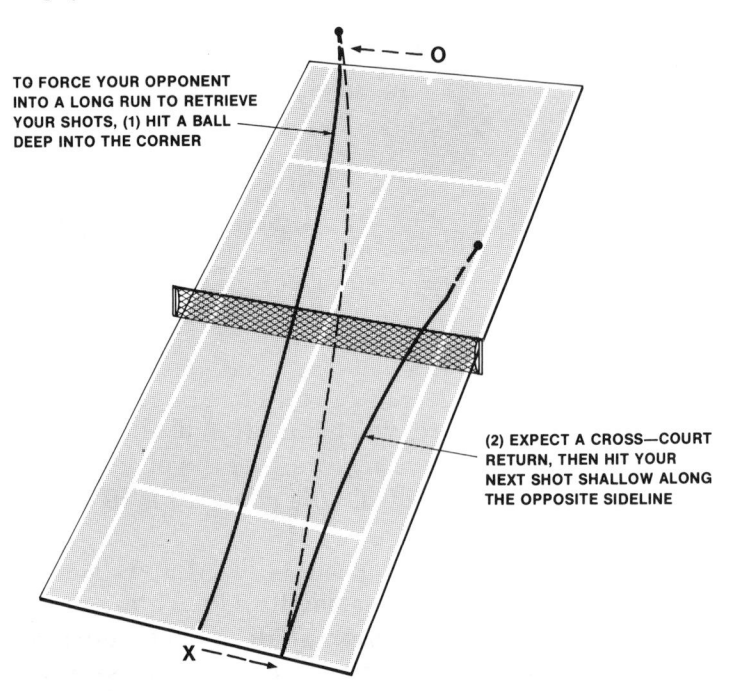

TO FORCE YOUR OPPONENT INTO A LONG RUN TO RETRIEVE YOUR SHOTS, (1) HIT A BALL DEEP INTO THE CORNER

(2) EXPECT A CROSS—COURT RETURN, THEN HIT YOUR NEXT SHOT SHALLOW ALONG THE OPPOSITE SIDELINE

If you initiate this sequence of (1) deep to one corner, then (2) shallow to the opposite sideline by first hitting into the backhand corner, you can expect a subdued reply that could be a candidate for a rousing topspin forehand winner. In fact, **any** ball that you hit deep into your rival's backhand corner should heighten your readiness for moving in to catch the return early and pull off an angled put-away.

Make Things Happen

The overall objective to playing a series of chess-like shots is to create some activity. It is to **cause** events rather than waiting for things to happen. Thus, by variable ball placement you can take the offensive, compelling an opposing player into hitting off-balance returns and increasing the chances of extracting an error.

You can do much the same by varying the pace and spin of the ball, or by adding extra velocity to your shots to induce defensive returns. Always, the intent is to do something that will make an opponent respond to **your** actions rather than the other way around. It will create openings and allow you to be more opportunistic. And you'll have more influence over the outcome of points.

Don't be overzealous, however. If you get pressured into a defensive predicament, accept your fate and respond with a defensive return. But even when you're hitting defensively, you can still be working for the advantage. Sometimes it's enough just to stay in a point by scrambling to get the ball back any way you can. Or if the momentum of an exchange of shots has put you on your heels, try lifting the next ball higher over the net than usual, even as a semi-lob. At some instant the momentum may change, even from a purely defensive return, and you'll gain the offensive again.

Play Within Your Ability

It is sometimes tempting, when the opportunity arises, to try to pull off a dazzling point winner with an unusual miracle shot. But probably you've never practiced such shots. Therefore, it's better to hit shots that you know you own. Keep your technique within your ability. This is especially vital in two circumstances: when you have an easy put-away, and when you are playing crucial points. The first instance draws on emotion rather than skill. When your opponent offers a "sitting" ball, it's tempting to hit with more-than-necessary force, as if to make some kind of declaration of dominance. But missing an easy shot leaves you with an agonizing feeling of disbelief, while the opponent can be rejuvenated by the reprieve. So do only what is necessary to win these easy points.

Relatedly, do not try unusual shots on big points. A drop shot is an example — it needs a fine touch, a small area of effective placement, and the right opportunity. If it is poorly hit, it's either netted or becomes an easy setup for the opponent. Therefore, do not try such surprise shots when you are playing a crucial point (for instance, when you could lose the game off that point). Save them for the middle of a game, when you still have time to recover if they fail.

Get the First Serve In

All too often players assume that they should bash away at the first serve and, upon failure, push the second. Instead, it would be well to slow down the first serve and increase the pace of the second.

First serves should be made successful on at least half the attempts, mainly to keep your opponent hitting from behind the baseline. In addition, a first serve that can be consistently hit in bounds is a great psychological boost that adds spirit and confidence to your entire game. Moreover, the most opportune time for coming to the net will be behind the first rather than the second serve.

Analyze your second serve not so much by whether it's being made good, but rather by how often it wins points. For instance, if you are successful on nearly all your second serves but find that you are losing more than half the points, it could be that your second attempts are too slow, allowing opponents to step up and hit winners. Therefore, you need to risk a lower percentage of success by hitting the second serves harder, thus forcing your opponents to be more defensive, and in the process boosting your point-winning percentage off these serves.

In reality, you never need to hit any serve harder than necessary to win points. If you find that your opponent cannot handle even your second serves, then slow down your first serves to make them successful even more often, thereby further reducing any risk of double faults.

Where to Hit the Serve

There are basically three areas for placement of the serve: (1) the far corners, (2) the near corners, and (3) directly at the receiver.

1. Serves hit to the **far corner** of either court will pull the receiver wide and open up a roomy area for a volley of the return. When hit to the far corner of the ad court, the serve not only drags the receiver wide, it also attacks the weaker side (of a right-handed player) and thus presents the best opportunity to follow the serve into the forecourt (to volley away the soft return).

A topspin or slice serve is particularly effective in the far corner of the deuce court (opposite for left-handed servers), since it moves away from the receiver during its flight. If you can generate a good deal of spin on the ball, occasionally try to place it shallow along the sideline. You'll need to slow down the pace of this ball, but give it your best topspin or slice. Even with the slower pace, it's often an outright winner.

2. Serves hit **down the middle** have the benefit of reducing the receiver's potential to hit cross-court returns. And, since these placements bring the receiver to the middle of the court, a charge to the net following the serve will not have as much risk of being hurt by an opponent's angled return.

3. When the serve is hit **directly at the receiver,** it may force that player to waste a fatal fraction of time deciding to take the ball with a forehand or backhand. Besides, a ball coming directly at someone is more difficult to judge for flight characteristics than one that can be seen at an angle. When using topspin, direct the ball just off-center a bit toward the receiver's backhand side. The curving arc of the ball will bring it into any receiver's most vulnerable spot: tight on the forehand side, thus forcing an awkward response and a virtually assured weak return (usually a short ball) and favoring a net charge.

There is a basic law in serving: second serves should be hit to the receiver's weaker side. Almost without exception. But never be so predictable that the receiver can be primed for your placement. Throw an occasional second ball right into the receiver's strength, just to keep your opponent in a constant tentative state, not knowing where the ball will arrive.

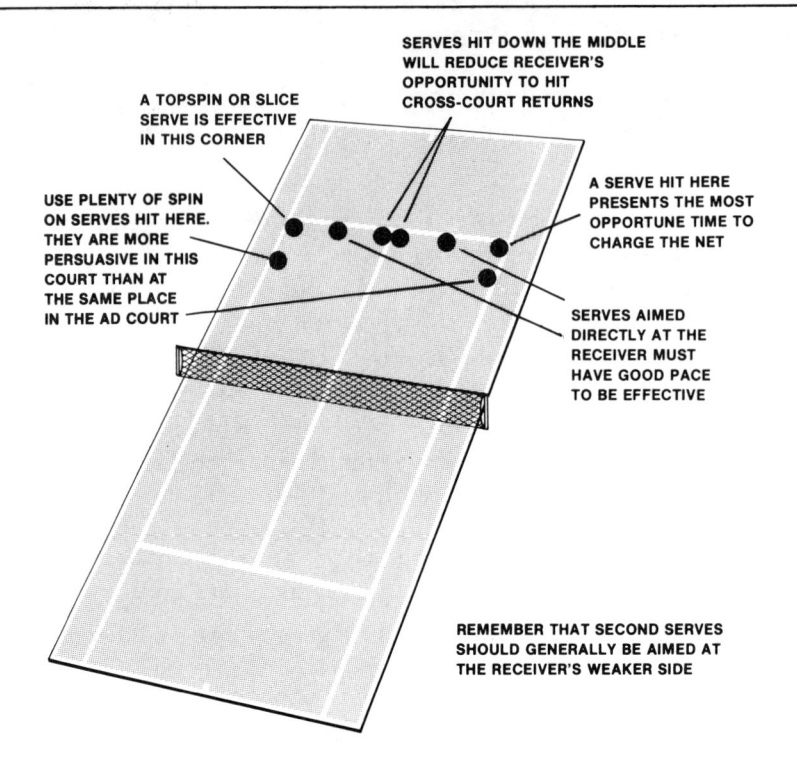

A TOPSPIN OR SLICE SERVE IS EFFECTIVE IN THIS CORNER

SERVES HIT DOWN THE MIDDLE WILL REDUCE RECEIVER'S OPPORTUNITY TO HIT CROSS-COURT RETURNS

USE PLENTY OF SPIN ON SERVES HIT HERE. THEY ARE MORE PERSUASIVE IN THIS COURT THAN AT THE SAME PLACE IN THE AD COURT

A SERVE HIT HERE PRESENTS THE MOST OPPORTUNE TIME TO CHARGE THE NET

SERVES AIMED DIRECTLY AT THE RECEIVER MUST HAVE GOOD PACE TO BE EFFECTIVE

REMEMBER THAT SECOND SERVES SHOULD GENERALLY BE AIMED AT THE RECEIVER'S WEAKER SIDE

Adapting to the Court Surface

Somewhere in time there will be a perfect court surface, inexpensive to build, suitable for all weather conditions, and having no maintenance requirements. Until then, we'll play on clay, cement, grass, asphalt, synthetics, pulverized brick, and other surfaces.

No court surface will make an elite player out of a mediocre one, or vice-versa. Nor should any player discard their own personal playing strengths on any court surface. For example, a player who likes to attack and volley should use that style even on a slow court, in spite of what is commonly believed about the illogic of such a ploy. The court surface should never **dictate** your game, but merely temper the tactics. Here are some suggestions:

Slow-Court Strategy.

The soft, granular surface of "slow" courts will grab the ball on the bounce, slowing it down and making it bounce higher. Consequently, the biggest adjustment is to anticipate longer rallies. Therefore:

1. Play more patiently, keeping the ball alive, trying less frequently for put-aways, and being more selective about going to the net.

2. Spin is more effective on slow surfaces. Use topspin often, particularly on serves. But wide serves will not slide off the side of the court as much as on a fast surface, so slice serves will not be as influential.
3. Slow down the first serves to get them in more often, since aces are less likely and power is less compelling. Furthermore, you do not want a receiver coming in to attack your court-slowed second serve.
4. Keep groundstrokes deep, with topspin, to discourage opponents from coming to the net.
5. Since footing is less sure, make your opponents change directions often. Use angled shots and touch shots, and hit behind your rival more often. Use more changes in pace to keep opponents from maintaining rhythm.

Fast-Court Strategy.

On hard-surface courts, the play is faster because of the tendency of the ball to skid and stay low after the bounce. Accordingly, it's more important to make things happen rather than just trying to wear down an opponent.

1. Footing is more sure, so come around behind the ball to get into ideal hitting position and to put more weight into each shot. Be aggressive with the groundstrokes. Go for the open court more often.
2. Because the ball does not slow down as much from the bounce, prepare your racket earlier and shorten the backswing, especially when returning serves.
3. Attack the net more often to put added pressure on your opponent. Go in behind your serve and, if possible, on your opponent's second serve.
4. Hit strong serves. Use a flat serve more often, and slice the ball to the far corner of the deuce court where it will pull an opponent especially wide.
5. Use backspin more frequently on driving groundstrokes, since it will make the ball skid and will pave your way up to the net.

Play Percentage Tennis

In the final analysis, logical strategy is a matter of percentages. Shot selection should be based on the probability of success at any given moment, or at least doing what will keep you in the point. It means doing what makes sense, and the guiding principles are:

- What do you do best?
- What does your opponent do worst?

In its simplest form, strategy is a process of linking the two together. Does your opponent have a weak backhand? Play to it often. Do **you** have a weak backhand? Run around it often, and make no apologies for doing so. "Go with your best!" is an old athletic saying. If you are confident with flat serves, hit flat serves. Use your strengths. That way you'll **win** instead of having avoided losing.

CHAPTER TEN

Strategy For Doubles

There's nothing formidable about doubles play. It merely requires lightning-fast reflexes, winged feet, quicker-than-the-eye hands, uncanny finesse, unfailing accuracy, extrasensory anticipation, infinite patience, and unshakable nerves.

Played poorly, doubles can be a drag. But played well it's a supremely exhilarating challenge and fiery game of dexterity. It's much more than simply playing singles with a copilot. The strokes are the same, but their employment is different. Here are some characteristics of doubles:

1. It's a net game. The basic and overriding objective is to gain control of the net, from where most of the points are won.
2. Points tend to be longer. The doubles court is only nine feet wider than the singles court, but with twice as many players protecting it, the points are not likely to end after only one or two shots.
3. There's a premium on accuracy. Singles is a game of speed; doubles is a game of placement.
4. It's a team endeavor, with the same requirements for cooperation and compatibility among partners as for any other team game.

Choosing a Partner

You've signed up for the intramural or club doubles tournament. Who should be your partner?

Theoretically, the best doubles teams feature a tactician — one player who sets up points with steady placements — and a finisher who hits put-aways. The extremes of both types can be frustrating. If your partner is someone who hits every ball with magnum force, then you won't have much activity. And if your partner is a feeble hitter, you'll spend a lot of time ducking away from your opponents' smashes. But in the final analysis, the major criteria is psychological: find someone with whom you enjoy hitting.

Starting Positions

At the start of each set, the stronger server of the two partners should serve first, without exception. Even in a short set, it's assured that player will serve twice. If by contrast you start with your weaker server and the other team starts with its stronger server, and the better servers on each team hold their serves while the weaker servers lose theirs, your team will drop the set 6-4.

When receiving, the steadier and/or stronger player normally takes the ad court, since that's where the most crucial points are played. Additionally, the ad-court player usually hits more shots in a match because of having the right-of-way to return balls arriving up the middle (since that player will be able to hit with a forehand).

If one player is left-handed and the other right-handed, the lefty should usually take the ad court so that both players can return wide angled shots with forehands. Remember that the rules allow you to switch your arrangement to start the second or any subsequent set.

Take the Net

At all levels of play, the doubles team that can effectively control the net will win. You get more **opportunity** to win points at the net. A team of two, firmly entrenched at the net, presents a nearly impassable wall, being vulnerable only to a lob, and then only to well-hit offensive lobs.

The two of you do not even need to be particularly strong net players to win from the forecourt. But if you stay back and the other team takes up a station at the net, then you **must** have talent to either lob cunningly over their heads or hit needle-threading shots between them. It's maddening being trapped behind the baseline trying to hit over or through two omnipresent net players.

So get up to the net at every opportunity. Take command of the point. Go in behind your serve and on your opponent's second serve if you can. Use every shallow ball from your opponent as a chance to charge the net. Get into the forecourt sometimes even when you wouldn't in a singles match. The net is where doubles points are **won**.

Serving Strategy

Decrease the strength of your first serves to get them in more often, mainly because you do not want the receiver pouncing on your second serve and drilling the ball through your net-playing partner. Hit to the receiver's backhand side more often than in singles, for the following reasons:

1. The return will generally be slower, giving your partner more time to reach the ball and volley it away for a winner.
2. The receiver will be more likely to return the ball with backspin than topspin, further slowing its pace and making it an easier ball to volley.
3. Since it's unlikely that the ball will come back with topspin, an approach to the net following the serve will not be vulnerable to a sinking return hit at the feet of the server.

You might throw in an occasional serve to a right-hander's forehand in the ad court, but almost never in the deuce court where it invites a cross-court return.

Hit your best controlled serves. If you have command of topspin, use it almost exclusively. Hit a slice or flat serve only to surprise the receiver, and then only if you have unfaltering control of those serves.

Remember that you are responsible, following the serve, for playing your half of the court (divided down the middle). So serve from a position farther away from the center mark than for singles. Then approach the net by going straight forward instead of following on-line directly behind the path of the served ball as in singles.

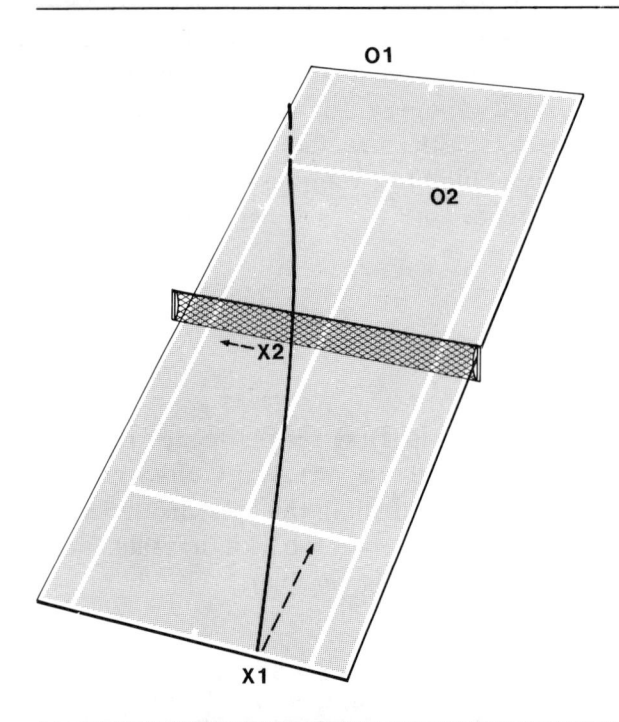

The diagram above shows the server's starting position in doubles (which should be closer to the sideline than in singles) and the proper straight-ahead line of approach to the net following the serve. When the serve is hit into the far corner, as this illustration shows, the net player should take a quick step toward the sideline to protect the alley. In the photo the straight-ahead approach of the server shows that it maintains optimal court coverage, while the receiver in this case has performed the appropriate tactic of hitting the return away from the net player, back toward the server.

The Job of the Server's Partner: Take Everything

The partner of the server should stand in the **middle** of the service court. Forget any neurotic compulsion to protect the alley. Few receivers will be talented enough to send the ball back along the doubles sideline. Get out into the court where the return is more likely to be hit. You'll be a more menacing figure there, and even if you do tempt a receiver to hit behind you, that player will have been coerced into aiming for a much smaller target than if they threw the ball back into the wide area in front of the server.

Try this little trick: stand with your feet together before the serve is made, and bend low to get your head out of the firing line. Then watch to see where the serve lands. If it's hit right to the middle of the service court, do a quick on-site split-step to get ready for the return. If the serve is hit to the outside, take a long step with your outside foot toward the sideline to get into a ready position. And if it's hit up the middle, take a step toward the middle of the court.

Then have the attitude of an aggressive soccer goalie. Good, confident soccer goalies will go after the ball at every reasonable opportunity. They **want** the ball, for it's the only way they can control the game. Do the same at the net. Go after every ball — you have first rights to every shot that comes back. Take advantage of your position to punch away every low ball and smash every lob.

Poaching

Any dictionary says that poaching is trespassing on private property, usually for hunting. In tennis, it's when the net player trespasses over into the not-so-private empty area on the other side of the court to hunt and kill a cross-court return of serve.

There are two ways to do it. One is to wait until the receiver is committed — when they can no longer change their mind about where the ball is going to be hit. Then **go!** Quickly! Take the ball early. Shove it right down at the feet of the receiver's partner (if that unsuspecting player is up at the net), or volley it out of reach if both are back at the baseline.

The other technique, often called a **drift,** is where you openly reveal to the receiver that you intend to cross over. You **want** the receiver to notice you, and thereupon the receiver might take their eyes off the ball and possibly change their mind in midswing about where the ball should be hit, or your move might force an

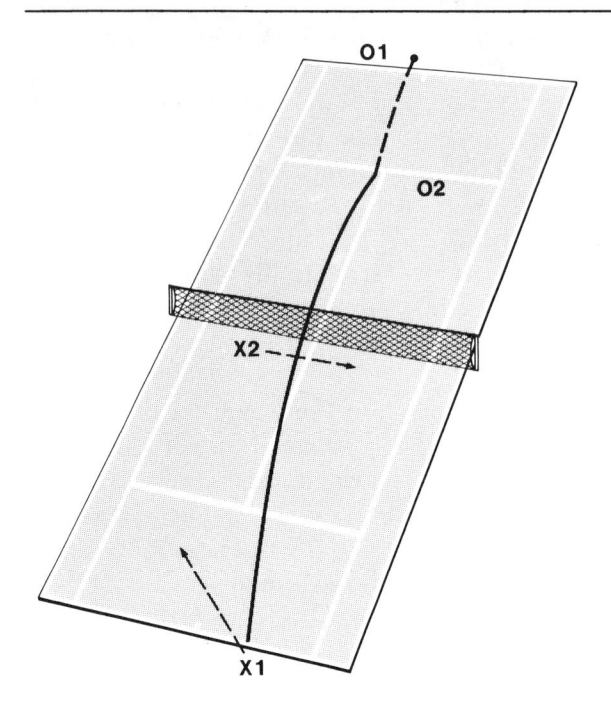

Here's the poach in motion. The server's partner has started to cross the court, while the server moves over to cover the net player's side of the court. The diagram illustrates this switching maneuver, which often produces its best results when the serve is hit down-the-middle in the deuce court, where it attacks the receiver's backhand and eliminates any possibility of a sharply angled return.

outright error. So you start this move earlier, while the serve is still on its way. This also opens the door for a **fake,** whereby you indicate that you will poach; and then having persuaded the receiver to hit the ball toward your just-vacated area, you suddenly turn and go back to your original net position and, **plunk!** — there's an easy volley awaiting you.

Remember your own partner, the server, who must know when you will poach. As you cross over, the server is obliged to follow by coming into your emptied side of the court. It's a scissors act, net player poaching and server crossing over to cover behind the net player's original position.

Commonly, the net player will show the plan to the server by a hand signal, held behind the back to conceal it from the opponents. A closed fist, for example, could mean that the net player will stay put, and an open hand would mean that there will be a poach.

Poaching is the caper of tennis. It gives the two of you more of a sense of being a team — of having planned moves. And it's also intimidating to opponents. After you do it a few times early in a match, you'll find the receivers being hesitant with their returns. The best time to pull it off is when the serve is hit down the middle in the deuce court, to the receiver's backhand. But try it often, and eventually you will have literal control over where the receiver will aim the return. Even when you don't poach, the threat of it will force the receiver to keep a wary eye on you, thus having one less to focus on the ball. And the shell-shocked partner of the receiver will no longer take up an offensive position at the net during the serve.

Returning the Serve

There are two objectives for returning the serve in doubles:

1. Get the ball past the net player.
2. Keep the ball low enough so that the server can't ram it back for a winner.

Generally, this means hitting a cross-court return, with backspin if possible, and driven right at the shoestrings of a net-charging server, or aimed at the singles sideline if the server stays back. But if the serve is difficult to handle, swallow your pride and lift up a lob, preferably over the net player.

In general, it's best to return the serve, whenever possible, toward the intersection of the singles sideline and the service line, where it will either be low and away from an onrushing server, or it might be an outright winner by passing out-of-reach of a server who does not charge the net.

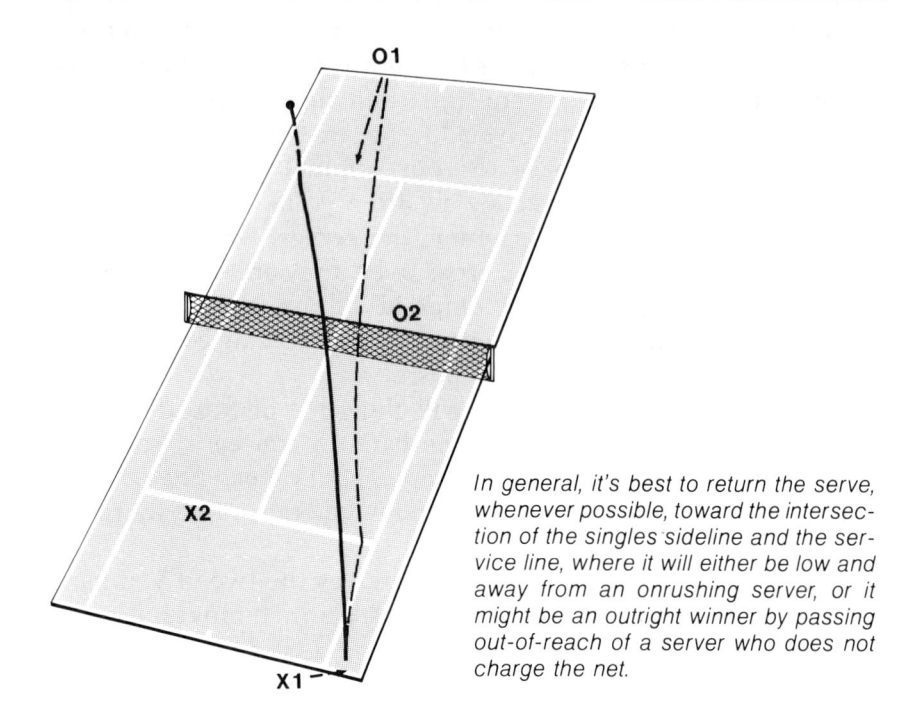

The Receiver's Partner

It seems that at the start of every point there's nothing for the partner of the receiver to do for awhile, since the ball must cross the net at least three times before this player can get involved. But the receiver's partner often provides the point-finishing shot; i.e., the serve is made, an effective return is hit which forces the server to reply with a floater, and **wham!!** — the receiver's partner is there to smack it away for a winner.

To play this role means being up at the net, just as the server's partner is, at the start of the point. From there, sometimes you'll go dizzy watching the ball being incessantly hit between the server and your partner, but you will also have cut off half the court as a target area for your opponents.

Be aggressive from this net position, just like you are when playing up while your partner is serving. Take everything that you can effectively reach. Crunch every ball you can get your racket on.

But . . .

If your partner has trouble handling the serve, you may need to have your baseball catcher's equipment on. Stay up at the net only if your partner can hit pacing, low returns. Otherwise, it's healthier to stay in the backcourt.

The Influence of Lobs

When both opponents are at the net, and your team is at the baseline, take the high road with your shots. Lob often. Push your opponents away from the net and take it yourselves.

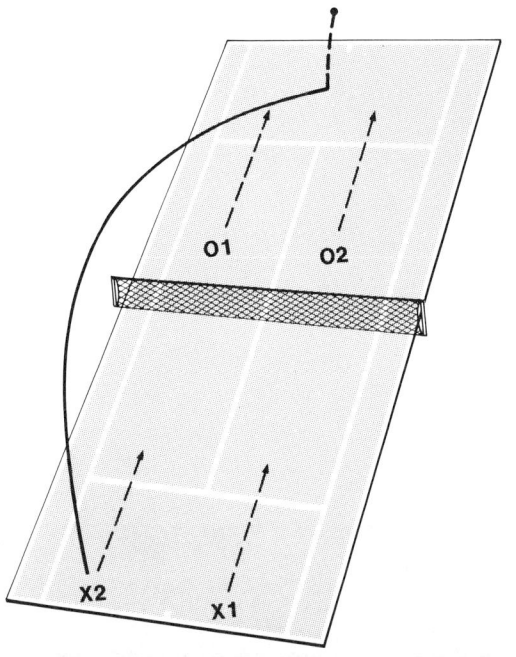

Doubles teams should usually try to maintain a side-by-side relationship, thus when both partners are at the baseline and the opponents are at the net, a lob hit over the net players should be followed by both partners advancing to the net, as the illustration shows. The photo shows this in action — the far team has hit an offensive lob and now begins to approach the net, while both partners of the near team retreat toward the baseline.

138   *Intermediate Tennis*

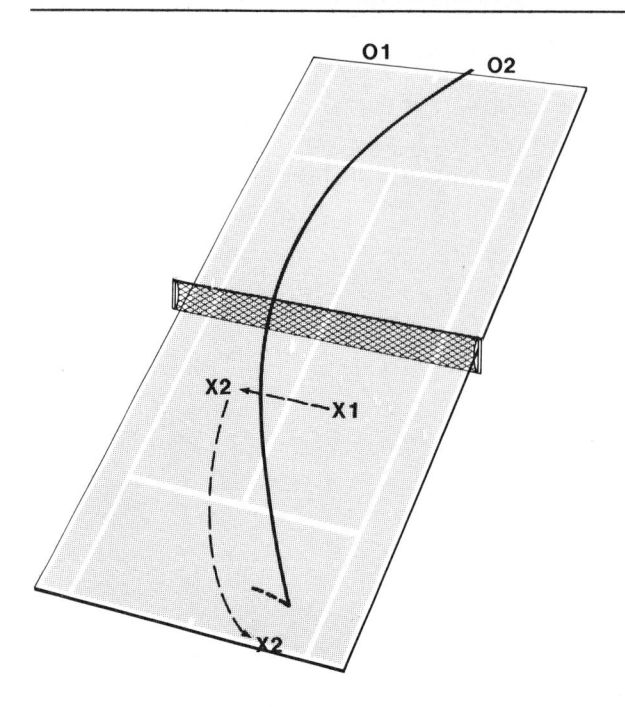

Here's an exception to the side-by-side rule. The illustration shows a lob hit over the head of player X1, but high enough to allow player X2 to retreat and hit a forehand smash, thus player X1 maintains the offensive net position by crossing over to cover the area vacated by X2. The photo shows the start of this "scissors" maneuver, while the far team, realizing their fate, does not charge the net. A smash return would be far less likely if the lob were hit over player X2.

Lob early in a match to show aggressive, net-swarming opponents that you intend to keep them on the defensive. Hit the ball over the player on your right so that if that player's partner comes around to collect the ball, it will need to be hit with a backhand.

If both of you are at the net and a lob is hit over your heads, both of you should go back together. Whichever player feels that they have the best play on the ball should call for it. Usually this is the partner who can return the ball with a forehand. If it's a well-hit offensive lob you're chasing down, answer with a lob of your own. Don't bother to look where your opponents are. They probably will have come up to the net, but even if they haven't, send back a helium ball that's high enough to give the two of you time to recover and get up to the net again. Play the "fifty-foot rope" game. Pretend that a fifty-foot rope is tied between your team and your opponents. When they're up at the net, you stay fifty feet away from them, but when you lob over their heads, let the imaginary rope pull your team up to the net as they retreat. Always keep in mind the basic law of team play in doubles: **both players go up together, or stay back together.**

Exploit the Middle

Doubles teams will often be overprotective of the alleys. As a result, they play too far apart and are vulnerable up the middle. Hit the ball there often, for three reasons: (1) the net is lower; (2) the opponents will have less chance to send back an angled cross-court return; and (3) the two of them may hesitate a fatal moment deciding who will take the ball. You don't even need to hit the ball hard, just land it low between your two opponents.

Conversely, who should take a ball that comes back between you and your partner? There are two rules: (1) whoever is closer to the net has priority, otherwise (2) it should be the player who has the strongest stroke. If you're both at the baseline the strongest stroke will probably come from the player who can hit with a forehand but when both of you are at the net, this may not necessarily be the case. One player might have a stronger backhand volley than the other partner does on the forehand side.

Make these decisions before the start of a match. Otherwise it could be: Mine! Yours! Crash!

Cover the Empty Space

Use another imaginary rope, this one tied between you and your partner. If your partner is forced off the side of the court, let the rope pull you over to cover the now-wider area of potential return space that is presented for your opponents. Always try to stay in the middle of the court space that's left over when your teammate is pushed out of position.

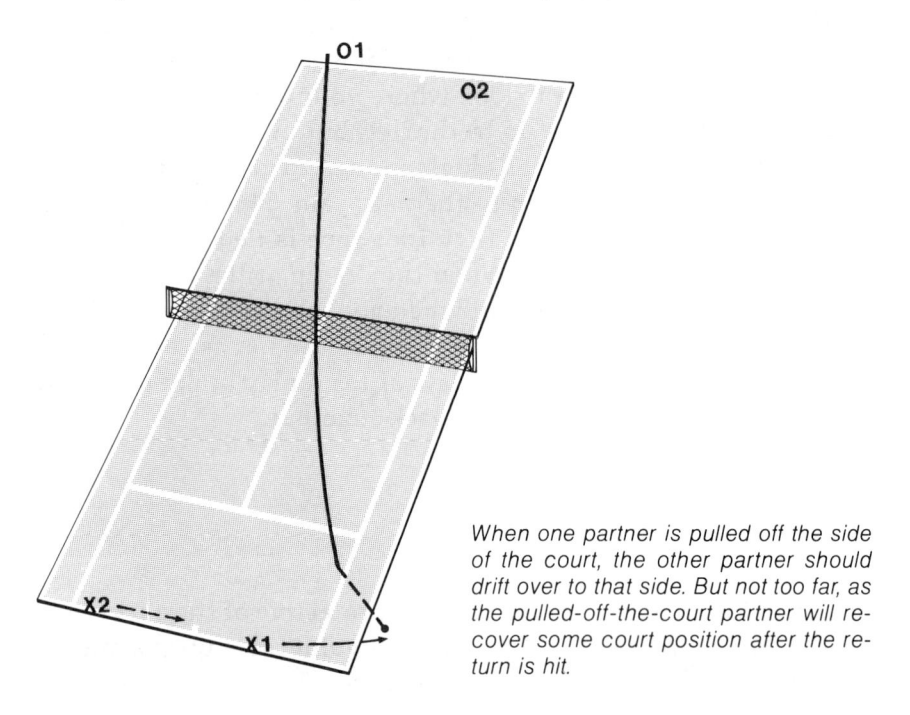

When one partner is pulled off the side of the court, the other partner should drift over to that side. But not too far, as the pulled-off-the-court partner will recover some court position after the return is hit.

Try an Australian Serving Formation

There is no rule which says that the server's partner must take up a net position diagonally on the opposite half of the court from the server. So give variety to your serving by sometimes (often?) using an **Australian formation.** This is where the partner of the server takes a station in the same half of the court as the server, thus being directly in front of the server.

Why try such an act? As a surprise for the opponents, for one reason. And just as a novelty, for another. But it also presents some intriguing poaching possibilities, and it clamps a lid on the receiver's cross-court potentials. Further, it can be used to protect both of your backhands when serving into the ad court.

Strategy For Doubles

Here's the start of the Australian serving formation, with both the server and the server's partner on the same half of the court. Note that the server stands near the center mark, as is typical for singles.

Here the server has done the proper job, from the Australian formation, of serving the ball into the far corner, then charging the net on a diagonal path rather than straight forward. In this setup, the serving team has virtually assured themselves that their next shot will be a forehand.

It's especially effective when the server hits to the far corner of the ad court, then takes a few steps over into the empty side, for now the two of you have perfect court coverage, and it's a virtual guarantee that your next shot will be a forehand (off a presumably weak return as a bonus).

Mixed Doubles

Add this to the long list of credits for tennis: it's one of the few sports where men and women compete as teammates, against other mixed teams, including at the professional level.

Mixed doubles is what you make it. It can be a friendly socializing, or an enjoyable diversion, or darned good tennis. Above all, it's like any other doubles: four people enjoying tennis instead of two.

Certain traditions became established over the years regarding mixed doubles play. For example, it was customary for the male partner to be the first server in the rotation, and for the female partner to receive in the forehand court. Those days are gone. Today the criteria are the same as for any other doubles match: the **most capable** partner serves first, and the **most dependable** partner receives in the ad court. No favors asked, and no reservations granted. There are no special rules, and no special provisions. Nor **should** there be. And that's a factor which makes this a truly beautiful game; the old timeworn statement of "Tennis, anyone?" could easily be paraphrased to "Tennis is for everyone." It's for both sexes, and all ages, at the same time, and anyplace.

CHAPTER 11

The Mental Game

It's predictable. When you're playing well you feel great! Everything is in sync; mind and body together. The ball looks big as a grapefruit and seems to be coming in slow motion. Your swing has infinite harmony, and every shot finds its mark.

Yet at other times, you can be in total disillusion with your play. You get caught frozen between points, your shots have no life, and the ball is erratic. It's maddening!

When you play well, you're exhilarated. But play poorly, and you feel terrible. Naturally.

But the fact is, it's usually the other way around. You play poorly **because** you feel terrible. And you play well as a **result** of feeling good. Court performances are commonly a **product** of states of mind rather than a **cause** of them. You play how you **feel,** not vice-versa.

The Body Has A Brain

Mind and body are not separate. Mental and physical phenomena are interrelated, each dependent on the other and each influencing the other. How you feel on the inside will be reflected by how you respond on the outside. The proper emotional states will help you to mobilize the energy sources that are crucial for optimal performance; or by contrast, negative states of mind could be devastating to your game. You can feel alive, energetic, confident — and your shots will have vivid resolution. Or you can be nervous, frustrated, angry — and your play will be sloppy.

Champions of tennis have excellent mental composure. It may not seem that way when watching the volatile behavior of a pro who is disputing a line call. But when the next point starts, the best among them will have put away all their grievance and will instantaneously gain full command of their emotional resources.

Overall, the professional players have high levels of success-oriented determination, coupled with a strong belief in their own ability to play well. They are ultra-confident and are extraordinarily capable of focusing their mental attention on the task at hand. Their competitive intensity is high, yet they are generally able to play in states of calm, with no overwhelming sense of pressure, even though they may be involved in a tense match. They are, in a true regard, fine examples of idealized mind/body unity.

But many a weekend player, when faced with a tough match, will react with emotional states that interfere with their play. Nervousness, mental anguish, indecisiveness, and so on, will dictate their performance. Their backswing on groundstrokes typically becomes shorter than usual, there is less acceleration in the swing, and the ball often lands shallow. The toss for their serve is too low, and shots hit from the net are tentative. Footwork may become careless and off-balance hits common. Even their body language changes: slumped shoulders, lowered head, nervous fiddling with the racket strings. And they may utter verbal expletives such as, "Here we go again — another bad day," or "I never get any breaks!" or, "I just can't get it together."

What can be done about all this? How can you create the right mental climate for optimal performance?

Start by generating positive mental attitudes that will transfer into positive play. Forge an upbeat emotional tone that will stimulate rather than restrict your game. Be enthused! Feel inspired! Talk yourself into an optimistic frame of reference. Convince yourself that all is well.

Handling Stress Before a Match

Before a match even starts, it's common to feel a generalized state of anxiety. If you're about to play someone you've never competed against before, there is a natural apprehension about the unknown. Or if it's an opponent who you've previously played and lost to, you might fear a repeat performance. Perhaps there will be friends or club members watching, and you do not want to play poorly in their presence. Or maybe it's a doubles match and you do not want to let your partner down. Stress might even come from feeling that you are not dressed well enough or do not have the latest in racket styles.

Whatever the source, pre-match tension is universal. If it's anything more than a friendly Saturday morning hit-around,

everyone has anxiety before the start. The pros do. The club player does. The serious weekender does. In fact, some pre-match anxiety is healthy, for it assures you that your mind is in more than just a casual state of attention for the competition.

The problem, however, is not usually in trying to get psychologically "up" for the match, but rather in the need to come "down" from a too-high level of tension. If you are often too keyed up before competition, the following may help.

1. *Think constructively.* If your mind starts to build a series of potential reasons why you might not play well, you will invariably hurt your own cause. You may find wandering thoughts that could convince you there's too much wind, or the sun will be in your eyes, or your elbow hurts, or you didn't get enough sleep, or you don't have your lucky wristband along. Rid your mind of such mental ramblings. Think instead of the things you will be able to do in the match — focus on the skills that you know you have. Visually picture them. See yourself doing well. There's only a given amount of room in your brain, and if you fill it with constructive thoughts, they will crowd out the negative ones. You might even let your mind hover on the very **fact** of the ensuing match — considering how enlivening it is to have the opportunity to use your talents in a competitive atmosphere.
2. *Be honest with yourself.* Admit that there is, after all, only so much you can do in the match. There's no way to make last-minute changes in your ability. You are what you are — nothing more, but certainly nothing less.
3. *Bring enough equipment.* Two rackets are a must, as insurance for a broken string. The spare racket should be one you've played with before. Also, bring new tennis balls, a towel, water, and extra shoestrings.
4. *Be on time.* But not too early. If you must wait a long time before the match, tension might multiply by the moment. Some players will stay away from the court until exactly match time. If you're on time, and your match is unavoidably delayed, you may want to ignore any other ongoing games, since watching them might heighten your anxiety.
5. *Find a place to relax.* For some players, this means being alone. Others may want to socialize to keep their mind off the match. In either case, keep the activity low-key. At some point, sit or lie down to take your weight off

your feet. And stay out of the fatigue-inducing rays of the sun.

On the other hand, if you're **really** uptight, and can't relax passively, then do something active instead. Walk around, do a few calisthenics, even jog a bit. But only use your **extra** energy, not the reserves you'll need for the match.

6. *Be physically ready.* Not only in sound physical shape, but also prepared on game day. Avoid any unnecessary drains of your strength on that day. And get your stomach ready, having consumed some high-carbohydrate calories the night before and taken your last full meal at least four hours before the match.
7. *Treat it as a game.* In the final analysis, match play should add **enjoyment** to your life, not frustration. It's a game, the purpose of which is to **reduce** stress, not create it. You're an amateur, without being financially dependent on winning for a living. No matter how well or poorly you play, after the match is over everything will still be intact. You'll still have your job, your college credits, your wallet, your stamp collection, everything. Best of all, since it's a game, you'll still have your psyche.

What to Do During the Warm-up

The warm-up prior to the start of a match is more than just a ritual. It's actually a fairly critical event, for it can generate intensity levels and fashion appropriate psychological preparation. Use it to alert all your resources — organize both mind and muscles. Create the right state of mental and physical readiness.

1. *Actually WARM-UP.* Get your body temperature elevated. Do little hops between your practice shots. And stretch your limbs out, giving flexibility to your muscles. Be **physically ready** to go all out on the first point of the first game. Often a trend is set early in a match — one player hitting aggressively, the other sinking into a defensive attitude. Be ready to assume the offensive at the very start.
2. *Prepare all your strokes.* Practice every one of your strokes, not only forehands and backhands, but also volleys, overheads, even lobs (there's a tendency to hit too low and shallow on the first few lobs of a match). In particular, make sure that you have hit plenty of serves,

not only to prepare your arm but also to prevent muscle pulls.

Hit all your strokes easily at first, then with increasing pace. Try especially to sense the rhythm of your swing. Remind your muscles of how it feels to hit with the fluid freedom that comes so easily during a practice session.

3. *Create positive energy.* Of **course** you're nervous! So is your **opponent!** And if you weren't wired, you wouldn't have much chance of being ready. All you need to do now is channel your supercharged state into positive form.

    As soon as you walk onto the court, start working immediately to collect positive energy. Feel alive. Be optimistic. Sense the very thrill of being able to play. Take the nervous energy you had before the warm-up and use it to create electricity in your muscles.

    Listen to what your inner voice is saying. If there are negative feelings, stop them right away. Replace the negative inner talk with constructive conversation. Talk yourself **out** of any negative attitudes and **into** positive feelings. They're **your** emotions. You'll be amazed at how easy it is to influence them with self-talk. Grab hold of your psyche and mesmerize yourself with positive inner conversation.

4. *Nothing fancy.* Make up your mind that you are going to play with the talent you have, not trying anything you haven't yet acquired in your hitting repertoire. If you've practiced topspin lobs, for example, but do not yet feel prepared to hit them with self-assurance, then discard any thought about using them for the match.

5. *Evaluate your opponent.* Take an inventory of your rival. Notice if there is a weaker groundstroke side. Offer varieties of pace to see the response. Get your rival up to the net to observe talent and aggressiveness. But don't overdo this analysis. How someone hits during the warm-up may not be how they will hit in the match.

6. *Center on yourself.* It's possible to become psyched-out before the match begins by things that have no relationship to the contest. If your opponent is wearing sophisticated attire and has expensive equipment, this could be intimidating. Or your rival's court behavior might be irksome. Perhaps it seems like your adversary isn't taking you seriously enough. You might even fret about getting the ball to where your opponent can easily hit it.

The more your emotions get tied to your opponent, the more they are pulled away from yourself. But the major objective of the warm-up is to get **yourself** ready, not to become obsessed with the characteristics of your rival. This is **your** time. Use this fleeting moment to focus attention on the rhythm and timing of your own strokes. Alert your muscles to the job you have for them. Become self-centered.

When the Match Begins

One factor that consistently emerges as a common trait among top-level athletes — in any sport — is an ability to focus attention on what is relevant to their performance. They are able to block out extraneous stimuli and concentrate on their task. They use **selective attention** — being alert to what is meaningful and ignoring the rest. The finalists in any pro tennis tournament are focusing on the execution of their strokes, not on the crowd, the wind, the sun, the television cameras, the prize money, or anything else.

It's similar to when you want to study and there are distractions around; conversation going on, a stereo being played too loud, traffic outside your window. You must ignore all this and selectively attend to your work.

Everyone does this automatically in a lot of ways. It isn't meaningful, for example, to attend to how your socks feel on your feet. Nor is it meaningful, during a tennis match, to waste attention on your overdue rent, or the unfinished term paper, or the distractions on the neighboring court. The only stimuli that are meaningful are those which are directly related to the performance of your strokes. Extraneous stimuli must get ruled out — tennis in. It is the first requirement for effective game performance: selective attention to information that is meaningful to the task.

Each Point Is An Entity

It's vital to selectively attend not only to the match as a whole, but also to isolate on each point — in fact, on each **ball**.

Bill Tilden, who dominated tennis in the 1920s and who is often credited as the greatest player ever, once said that he never considered his skills extraordinary, but thought instead that his success came mostly from an ability to hone his attention on every shot. Spectators thought that Tilden played in a trance, so complete was his concentration. Tilden's own description was that he saw each ball as an event, independent of the previous ball.

Accomplished players can tunnel their attention to the present moment, not being affected by the past. Thus, their performance in a previous game, or a previous point, or even the last ball of an ongoing exchange, does not influence their ability to give full and positive concentration to the next shot.

If you hit a poor shot, do not discredit yourself, since this will potentially make you tighter and more cautious for the next point. Put it out of your mind and self-talk confidence back into your attitude. Loosen your muscles, take the racket out of your hitting hand, and bounce a few times on your toes. You'll recover your alertness and positive frame of mind more quickly by relaxing than by fighting yourself after an errant shot. Be ready to hit rhythmically, again, on the next ball. Forget the past. Selectively attend to the present.

Try this technique: play every point as if it were the deciding one in the game. That way you'll focus on one point at a time, and collectively it will add up to a higher level of concentration for the whole match. Remember — you have to fight each battle to win the war.

Make sure that you're ready for the start of every point. If you're serving, bounce the ball a few times, gather your emotions, fix in your mind where you want the ball to go, then **sense** the spin and pace you will give to the ball — all of this **before** you start the windup. If you're receiving, try to build your focus in coordination with your rival's serve. First think rhythm, engendering your muscles with a feeling of fluid readiness, perhaps doing a few hops to help the feeling. As your opponent bounces the ball, begin to collect your alertness. See the server as a whole, but when the toss is made, zero in on the ball, like a zoom lens, to where you have a heightened visual clarity just as the ball is served.

Believe in Yourself

Top-level players have an encompassing belief in their own ability to play well, particularly under pressure. They are intensely self-assured. It's the only way they **can** feel. They could not get to the top if they didn't believe strongly in their ability to get there.

Your ambition isn't likely aimed at becoming the best in the world. But you still want to play well, maybe to win the intramural or club championship, or to beat everyone in class, or at least to play the best you can play.

It's been stated earlier, but it can't be overemphasized: positive states of mind are a great help. If you start a match thinking that you're going to lose, it's difficult to get into the proper frame of mind to be competitive. Or if you're about to play a crucial point and you find yourself wishing that you were somewhere else, it will be difficult to play that point with determination. Remember that your body responds to your mental attitudes. So give it a chance. Tell it positive things. Believe that you are capable. Then hit your backhands freely. Belt your serves with conviction. Hit your volleys with confidence. Tell yourself how good you feel, and your nerve-muscle machinery will respond.

Play Positive Tennis

When you are optimistic, believing in your own ability, then you can play **positive tennis.** It means trying to **win** points rather than trying to avoid **losing** them.

There's a difference in style. The player who tries mostly to avoid making mistakes will hit cautiously, conservatively, without spontaneity. The player who wants to **win** the point will hit with affirmative, free-swinging strokes. Both will make mistakes. The player who hits to avoid errors will make **negative** mistakes: dumping the ball into the net, hitting too shallow on approach shots, pushing the second serve. But the player who hits to win will make **positive** mistakes: the ball will be hit too **long** rather than too short. Still, it's a sign of energetic, optimistic play, and in the end this style will win out.

If you play with a feeling of impending doom, you'll hit defensively when it's not called for, and in the end you'll actually take yourself out of points instead of keeping yourself in them. Accept the inevitable: you **will** make mistakes, no matter how skilled you are. But **positive** mistakes are a sign that you are trying to make things happen. They indicate that you are playing with freedom in your style, and probably even that you are enjoying the game more.

Believe That Your Serve Will Go In

Arnold Palmer, golfer extraordinaire, once said that when he hit a perfect shot he was never surprised, since that's what he

wanted to do. He was only surprised, he said, when the ball did **not** go where he wanted.

Serving is no different. If you anticipate failure, you'll never be surprised when you double fault. And getting the first serve in is cause for astonishment.

It's another example of negative tennis. Instead, believe that **every** serve will go in. To facilitate such a mindset, walk slowly to your serving station, then take only one ball in your hand for the first serve — stick the second one in your pocket. Collect yourself both mentally and physically before starting the motion. Have all your decisions made: where to hit the ball, with how much pace, how much spin, and what you will do after the serve. Physically "feel" your swing and mentally "see" the ball go in, even before you make the toss. Then just let your body act out the mental image that you have created for it. Be positive. Think success. Don't start your motion until you've **felt** and **seen** a good serve. In this preparation, you'll hit more serves in, and not one of them will be a surprise.

Act Like A Winner

Relatedly, no matter how you may be playing at the moment, act like a winner, even if it's an **act.** The way you behave **physically** will transfer to how you **feel.**

It's long been known that it works the other way around — how you feel is reflected by how you act. Studies in body language have demonstrated that external physical behaviors are indicative of internal attitudinal states. But what is also true, though less considered, is that physical conduct can influence mental states.

Watch a champion. There is confidence in every manner — the way they approach the line to serve, the way they flaunt playing talents, even defiant amazement at losing a point. You can tell a winner just by the way they walk onto the court. A winner is energetic, animated, and lively. By contrast, an unsure player will walk around the court two inches shorter than he/she actually is. The whole body droops, and confidence stays down with it.

So be **tall.** Put confidence in your style. If you're nervous, shake out your shoulders and walk **calm.** Slow down and be **deliberate.** Have a controlled, affirmative air to your behavior. Use your physical self to persuade your mental self that you are capable and ready to play well.

Close Out Your Opponent

Altruism has its place. But not in tennis matches. The basic law of all sports is that someone wins.

Some players actually feel guilty about winning. Symptoms are: easing up on the serve if the opponent can't handle it, not hitting to the weaker side, turning conservative and "courteous" after building a big lead, hitting an easy shot to keep a rally alive, giving breaks on line calls, and not coming up to the net.

In actual fact, such behavior is seen by experienced players as discourteous. Not performing at your best can be an insult to an opponent and a discredit to the spirit of competition. No one should ever feel apologetic for playing well.

This does not suggest that you must always play with a vindictive "killer instinct," or that you should try to humiliate an opponent. There will be times when you are so superior to your opponent that a subtle "easing off" will go unnoticed and will provide you with a chance to concentrate more on the rhythm of your strokes instead of trying to drive the ball with power. Such cases provide an opportunity for you to use your second serve to start a point, or to attend to your footwork, or to practice the useful art of hitting the ball deep up the middle. But when you have an opponent on the ropes, and victory is imminent, then finish your work.

Sometimes, against an opponent who is skilled, if you build a lead then subconsciously slacken your competitive intensity, you may find it impossible to regain your edge later in the match if your opponent makes a comeback. There are certain times in a match when this is more likely to happen, in particular, right after having broken your opponent's serve. At this moment you might experience an inadvertent letdown, feeling that your accomplishment is an end in itself and now you can relax somewhat. And yet this is the very time to come with your best, for if you now lose your own serve, your rival will be rejuvenated and may forge into having the upper hand. Slam the door instead of opening it.

If You're Losing ...

...Get control of yourself. Maintain your cool. Use self-talk to stay relaxed. When you fall behind in a match, there is a tendency to tighten up, to abbreviate your strokes, and to play defensively. So exaggerate your relaxation routines. Consciously ease your grip. Take the racket out of your hitting hand between points. Take more deep breaths. Bounce more on your toes.

Take time between games to analyze both your game and that of your opponent. If you are beating yourself with errors, concentrate more on rhythm and on watching the ball. If your opponent is winning with power, change the pace of your shots. If you haven't been rushing the net, try that. But don't press yourself into making wholesale changes in your game. Only make the changes that you are capable of doing. No opponent can play perfect tennis for an entire match, so keep the basic fundamental of strategy in mind: know what you do best, figure out what your opponent does worst, and link the two together.

Superstitious? Go Right Ahead

In a time past, if a player was superstitious, a tennis psychiatrist would try to desensitize that player from such beliefs. "What's that you say? You can't play without your lucky socks on? Let's confront that and see how meaningless . . . etc." But today it's, "So you play better with your lucky socks on? Then make sure you have your lucky socks on."

It's a sugar pill. A doctor gives a powerless sugar pill, tells the person that they will feel better, they take it and do. It doesn't matter that there's no reason, physically, for it to work. What's important is that it **does.**

Maybe you play better if you have pizza the night before. Maybe you need to sleep on the floor — or go jogging before a big match. Or warm up by kicking a soccer ball around. Or bounce the ball exactly four times before serving. Or avoid stepping on any lines as you walk back to your starting position after each point.

Whatever it is, if you feel more secure in doing it, then do it. You are, quite simply, trying to recreate the conditions that in the past were related to your playing well. Don't feel silly about that. What you want is to feel **right** and to play your best.

How to Break Out of A Slump

Inevitably there will be times when nothing goes right. The north of your body does not communicate with the south, or the east with the west. No matter what you do, the court seems too short and the net too high. Frustration builds, adding to your decline in play. You're in a slump.

It happens to everyone. Weekend players. The pros. Baseball players. Salespeople. College presidents. Everyone.

What to do?

Try the following:

1. *Don't make panic changes.* If you play poorly several times in succession, you may think that your game needs a major overhaul. So you change your grip, toss the ball lower on the serve, avoid going to the net, and so on. But slumps usually have **psychological** rather than mechanical causes. Realize that the higher you go on the skill ladder, the more likely it is you'll experience variability in your performance. It might even be that what you think is a slump is actually a plateau in your progress. Therefore, don't let a few "off" days pressure you into making sudden alterations in your style.

2. *Get a second opinion.* If your poor play **does** persist, despite your patience, there could in fact be some mechanical reason. Maybe your elbow is coming up on your backhand. Or your serving stance is too open. Or you had a sore ankle that forced you into a habit of hitting off a stiff forward leg. Whatever the origin, another person may be able to discover a flaw that is going unnoticed to you. Ask your instructor to watch the part of your game with which you're having the most trouble. Often, an outside pair of eyes is better than inside feelings.

3. *Do something new.* Sometimes, the **routine** of playing can get you down. Too much sameness. So find new opponents. Go play on a different court. Use different balls. Buy some new equipment. Get a new tennis outfit. Have your racket restrung. Take some lessons. Even read a tennis book.

4. *Use mental practice.* Refer to the next section of this chapter.

5. *Stop playing for awhile.* A slump can come from fatigue. And it can build faster if you're playing often. If you can't seem to break out of it, take a break from playing for a week or two. Get your term paper done instead. Go backpacking. Increase (or start?) your fitness program. When you come back to the court, you'll be rejuvenated, refreshed, and eager. Then watch the ball jump off your strings with renewed life.

How to Mentally Practice This Game

The most widely used mental tool in sports today incorporates the human mind's lucid capacity for imagination. Through a technique of visual dramatization called **mental practice,** an athlete will, while in a state of quietude, create a mental image of their own performance, trying in the process to generate all the sensations and environmental conditions of the skill, including the actual feel of the execution. It is a virtual dreamland of rehearsal, and it grows more powerful in effect as a person gains in experience.

Extensive research has shown that using mental practice in combination with overt physical practice can produce greater improvements in performance than either method used alone. The technique is quite simple but requires the important prerequisite of knowing **what** to visually rehearse as well as **how** to effectively perform the skill in the first place. Consequently, mental practice is far more effective for an experienced player than a novice who, because of minimal background, could conceivably visualize doing mechanically wrong things.

The best results occur when you are in a quiet, nondistracting environment and your mind is not oppressively cluttered with thoughts or feelings unrelated to tennis. There are two ways to use visualization. One is to see yourself performing as if you were an observer — a spectator watching your own game. The other is to stay inside yourself, seeing the events of a tennis match as you would with your own eyes when actually playing. Research suggests, though not conclusively, that the second of the two may be more beneficial for those who have either extensive playing experience, or who have made mental practice a regular habit.

Following is a general guideline for using mental practice:

1. Choose a time and place where you can be undisturbed.
2. Close your eyes, breathe deeply, and relax as completely as possible. Feel your muscles go limp.
3. Clear your mind. Imagine a blank white screen. Think of emptiness. Free your mind of all thoughts.
4. Select an aspect of tennis — serve, forehand, whatever. Visualize yourself performing the skill, including all parts of the execution. For example, if you are rehearsing the serve, see yourself stepping up to the line, bouncing the ball, setting your sights, and so on, right through the end result of the landing and rebound of the served ball.

5. Visualize your performance in as much detail as possible.
6. Visualize in color, making the colors as vivid as you can. For instance, emphasize the contrast between the color of the ball and the sky or the playing surface.
7. Try to **feel** the movements of the game. Create the very physical sensations of the performance.
8. Give some time to freewheeling imaginations, allowing spontaneous visualizations to arise of, for example, a rousing exchange of strong shots between you and your imaginary (or real) opponent.
9. Have spectators in your visual game, including both strangers and close friends.
10. End each session by seeing yourself hitting some emphatic, convincing, point-winning shots.

At the end of your mental practice, you should feel good, persuasively optimistic, and psychologically energized. It should leave you with a feel of being prepared, mentally, for your next match.

Here are some additional considerations for visualization sessions:

1. It is sometimes said that you should mentally practice only successful performances, yet research indicates that there may be some value to occasionally seeing yourself hitting a bad shot, but then recovering to hit a **good** shot on your next attempt.
2. Mentally practice with all your senses. Not only should you **see** and **feel** the skills of the game, you should also **hear** the sounds of tennis, such as the thwack of the ball on your racket, or distracting noises like passing traffic or loud chatter from a neighboring court. Imagine the heat of a midsummer day, or the crisp air of an autumn morning. Even try to smell such sensations as new-mown grass around the court, or the characteristic scents that radiate from clay courts.
3. Mentally practice all aspects of the game, including the more difficult skills, such as a high backhand, as well as the standard strokes.
4. Rehearse the emotions of tennis, especially seeing yourself in full command of your psyche during stressful points of a match.
5. Sometimes visualize in slow motion, trying to be critically analytical of your skill during these slowed-down performances.

6. Don't prolong the sessions. Several brief sittings of five minutes or so are better than one long session.
7. Make mental practice a regular routine. Gradually try to incorporate it into your on-court playing so that you can give yourself quick visual reminders between points, or during an exchange of ends, or before a serve.

Mental practice is not a utopia. In no way does it substitute for on-court physical practice. But it is a remarkable compliment to it. The results can be dramatic. So use it often. Go see the movie that's in your head.

CHAPTER 12

Realistic Practice

Practice makes perfect, it's commonly said. There are also other myths about athletic skills.

Practice alone does **not** make perfect — it merely makes more **permanent** the things that are practiced. Thus, a problem arises: it's possible to practice the **wrong** things, thereby making **flaws** in performance more permanent. Every time a faulty movement is executed, the nervous system remembers, until it's a habit. And habit is practice long pursued until it's difficult, if not impossible, to do it any other way.

But if you're a member of a tennis class, you are fortunate, for the lessons are designed to help you neurologically forget any flaws and ingrain your nervous system with efficient movement. Otherwise, you might rarely practice at all, since it's typical to find practice dull compared to games. Or if you did practice on your own, without a discerning observer nearby, you would potentially run a higher risk of strengthening your flaws as well as your proficiencies.

Make Practice Like the Game

Any practice session should be realistic. That is, it should simulate the actual game, or small segments of the game, so that it's more "real-life" than merely hitting the ball incessantly back and forth without purpose. Creating game-like circumstances makes practice more interesting and gives reason to do well.

For example, if you're uncertain about your play at the net, instead of starting a practice point with a serve, start instead by dropping the ball down and hitting a groundstroke, and have your practice partner agree to feed you a half-speed shallow ball which allows you to come in to hit an approach shot. After that, play the point out as normal.

Or, say you have trouble returning serves. Have your practice partner hit off-speed serves to you, with no follow-up charge to the net, and agree that you will score a point each time you get the return back between the service line and baseline. But your partner can also score by winning the ensuing exchange, so after the return of serve, anything goes.

Having trouble handling pressure in a match? You can practice that as well by introducing some pressure into these game rehearsals. For instance, you could play "one serve" points where you get only one chance to make the serve good. Or you could reduce the court by agreeing with your partner that any ball which lands in front of the service line will be called out. Or you could play an entire set of tie-breaker games.

Pick out your weakest, or least confident aspects of the game, and create situations that will help you develop the necessary skills. Put aside your insecurities and openly admit that you have some parts of your game which need work. Don't try to hide them from your practice partner by, for example, running around your backhand to hit a more reliable forehand. In fact, if your backhand is a troublesome area, you might play some practice points where only backhands are allowed. Remember that the more advanced you become in this game, the more your weaker areas will be exploited by opponents. So devote most of your practice time to fixing any inadequate parts of your play.

Don't ignore your strengths, however. You also need to keep your already-mastered skills finely honed. Therefore, a well-rounded practice session will include attention to the total game, without overlooking such often-neglected apsects as second serves, half-volleys, and drop shots.

Creating Muscle Memory

The idea is to practice **something.** If there is no structure at all to practice save for getting the ball over the net to keep a rally going, it's too easy to slip into lethargic habits such as not bending the knees, or failing to transfer the weight properly, or letting the ball bounce more than once before returning it. Nonetheless, there **is** some advantage to unqualified free-lance hitting, for it allows concentration on the performance of the strokes, with full attention given to the style of their execution. This is, however, still a practice of **technique,** whereas tired and purposeless hitting of the ball is an invitation to making flaws habitual.

In effect, what happens each time a ball is hit is that a neural pathway is electrochemically set off in your brain. It reverberates around in your cranium and becomes more and more permanent each time the same pattern is used. Then, in the future, any similar situation (such as a real match) will kick into action the same neural pathway that had been used during practice. Consequently, it's important to develop a "muscle memory" during practice which is technically correct and easily transferable to match play.

Try especially to ingrain a muscle memory for a big put-away shot. For example, if you find that you have reasonable control of (and enjoy hitting) a cross-court topspin forehand off a ball that comes to you just above waist height, then devote plenty of time to hitting that shot. Have your practice partner set you up for repeated trials, and otherwise hit it every chance you get. Implant the pattern so deep into your nervous system that each time the opportunity to hit the shot in a match arises, all you need to do is pull the switch and: **click!** — another topspin cross-court winner!

Rehearse Both Offense and Defense

Many times in a practice session both partners will tune up only their offensive shots, such as when one player hits serves but the other does not take advantage of the opportunity to practice returns, or when partners take turns setting each other up for chance after chance at cracking off winners. While practice sessions **should** in fact be geared toward the offensive side of play, defensive shots should not be overlooked. For example, it's unlikely that during a practice time either player will devote any attention to retrieving a lob while on the run away from the net, or intentionally stand in the middle of the court to hit defensive half-volleys. Yet both these circumstances will occur in a typical match.

When playing an offensive shot, the intent is to hit the ball with enough pace and/or effective placement to either win the point outright or to force a weak return that allows a follow-up shot to be hit for a winner. Offensive tennis, therefore, is built around the following:

1. Hitting the ball into the corners.
2. Hitting overpowering serves.
3. Coming to the net behind a strong serve or a well-placed approach shot.
4. Hitting offensive lobs.
5. Hitting the ball out of the opponent's reach.

On defense, the objective is to stay alive in a point; to play the ball in a way that will keep the opponent from hitting the next shot for a winner, or at least giving the opponent another chance to make an error. Thus, in a match you would:

1. Hit a defensive lob.
2. Retrieve a ball while on the run.
3. Return strong serves.
4. Stretch for a wide volley at the net.
5. Play any defensive predicament with a return hit deep and up the middle.

Basically, in a tennis match you either (1) make things happen, or you must (2) respond to things that happen. Practice sessions tend to focus on the first of the two. Yet in many, or even most cases, the rehearsal of an offensive shot by one partner will also present an opportunity for the other partner to practice defensive returns of that shot. Moreover, when an offense-defense setup is staged, the player hitting the offensive shot gets the bonus of feedback which tells whether the shot is being effectively hit.

For example, one player might hit aggressive topspin groundstrokes, while the other player tries consciously to loft the ball back with an off-speed return. In this way one player has practice at crunching a slow-moving ball for a winner, while the other can rehearse change-of-pace shots that will be used against a big hitter.

A Typical Practice Session

There are no ultimate practice routines. The major objectives are quite simply to:

1. Have a partner who is willing to **practice** instead of just wanting to play games.
2. Rehearse the things that will **actually happen** in a match.
3. Make the sessions **enjoyable.**

Accordingly, a typical day of practice might go something like this:

1. **Warm up** properly, including stretching, before hitting a ball. Examples of stretching exercises are given in the next chapter.

2. **Hit easily** for the first few minutes, using only groundstrokes. Have no target area other than keeping the ball within easy reach of your partner. Concentrate on the form of the strokes and the rhythm of your swing.

3. Now give your shots more **dimension.** For instance, try to land every ball within a yard of the baseline. Or try hitting a "heavy" ball by emphasizing the acceleration of the racket head.

4. Next, try some **placement** hitting, where you aim your shots toward a specific area of the court. For example, hit only cross-court with your partner, corner to corner, and increase the intensity of this drill (further illustrations are in the next chapter).

5. Now play **rapid fire,** where both of you stand across the net from each other, just inside the service line, and hit volley after volley, trying to keep the ball in play as long as possible.

6. Then it's pure **setup** time, where your partner feeds you exactly the shot you want. Often this is best accomplished if your partner hits a bucket of balls to you, without attempting to return your shots. After the bucket is exhausted, then switch so that you can feed your partner.

7. Add **serve** and **receive** practice. Hit maybe half a bucket (to avoid going too arm-weary) while your partner hits returns. No playing points out — just concentrate on serves and returns. Then your partner serves while you return.

8. Now for some **match play** drills. Try to stage actual playing situations. Be inventive with these drills, but don't overcomplicate them. Make the situations as close to reality as possible.

9. Devote time to **specialty shots,** such as drop shots, dinks, or backhand overheads. And give attention to the shots you'll be forced to hit defensively in a match.

10. Finish off the day with **free hitting** again, focusing solely on rhythm and form. That'll get you in the right frame of mind to feel good about the day, about yourself, and in a positive reference for the next match.

Just for the Fun of It

There's always the potential of losing sight of the purpose of tennis. It's to enjoy playing — to have pure, unadulterated fun. This is, after all, a **game.**

Practice should be likewise. If it's drudgery, little benefit will emerge. There may even be some negative outcomes.

Make practice fun. Add variety to the sessions. Use the time to experiment with different spins, or new ways to hit the ball. Even be crazy sometimes by doing such things as hitting the ball with the racket in your non-preferred hand. Or play some points where the only rule is that the ball must cross over the net. Or agree that after every shot you must run up and touch the net with your racket. If you have enough players, try the tennis version of the party Ping Pong game where you start a rally off, then hand the paddle to another person who must keep the rally going, then hand the paddle to another player, and so on.

Let these whimsical little games be totally therapeutic. Use them to spark renewed interest in practice. In the bargain you'll have a blast and be reminded that tennis is a sporting endeavor, the end result of which should be, above all else, to add enjoyment to your life.

CHAPTER 13

Aerobic Conditioning For Tennis

An hour or so of tennis — it's not the most physically brutal thing you can do to yourself. But the game **is** physically challenging, and it can be a fairly stern test of your state of fitness. A couple of snappy sets may well determine not only who is the most talented, but also who has the best resource of stamina. Other things being equal, it will be the most physically fit player who will usually win out. This is increasingly true as you move up the skill ladder, where rallies become longer and points more intensively contested. Accordingly, to play consistently excellent tennis requires both a well-rehearsed stroke repertoire and a ready state of physical preparedness.

How Much Fitness?

One way to be in shape for playing tennis is to play tennis. But such a direct objective never provides you with any reserve. It would be like building an automobile engine with a top speed of 50 miles per hour, then running it at 50 every time out.

More logically, a fitness program should be based on the **overload principle.** That's where you train at a level that is **more** than is needed for playing. That way your engine will be capable of doing 120 miles per hour, so when you run it at 50, it'll be smoothly coasting along, with an available reserve for kicking into passing gear to chase down a wide ball.

To be complete, a conditioning program for tennis should provide you with reserves of:

- **strength,** to hit the ball hard and to get from here to there in a hurry.
- **endurance,** to go full-out from beginning to the end of a match.

- **flexibility,** to reach high and bend low and swing unrestricted through a full range of motion.

Tennis isn't weightlifting, nor a marathon, nor gymnastics. But it has elements of all three. Following are some suggestions for developing each area.

Strength

Tennis does not make uncompromising demands for brute strength. But being responsively strong will help you to get quickly from one side of the court to the other, or to more effectively block a crushing serve, or to put more drive into your groundstrokes. Furthermore, it will increase your chances of staying injury-free.

The strength that's compatible to tennis is not raw, weightlifting-type brawn, but rather **explosive power** — the ability to contract muscles quickly. Consequently, disciplined exercises should concentrate on weight **training** instead of weight **lifting.** Weight training is using lighter weights and more repetition of movement than weight lifting. The product is not "bulked-up" muscles, but muscles that are alert and responsive for the quick-trigger action of a tennis match.

Some areas of the body need more attention than others, in particular the muscles on the front of the thighs (the quadriceps) and the back of the thighs (hamstrings); the chest muscles (pectorals); the upper back and shoulder (trapezius and deltoids); and the back of the upper arm (triceps). Remember that any workout with weights should:

- be preceded by a warm-up including stretching,
- take the muscles through a full range of motion, and
- never be pushed to the point of strain.

Endurance

In the tie-breaker game of a third set, you need fuel reserves. You need endurance. To prepare yourself for long, intense matches, you need some off-court exercises that will elevate your heart rate to at least 120 beats a minute and keep it there for 20 or 30 minutes. Walking won't do that. Nor will a leisurely bike ride. But an eight-mile-an-hour jog will. So will anything else that has you perspiring freely after ten minutes. But fair warning! If you're not accustomed to vigorous exercise, take it easy in the beginning.

But there's more. The sustained exercise program is to help you maintain your peak performance as a match wears on. In the meantime, the game-by-game demands are stop-and-go; stop-and-go; stop-and-go; ad infinitum. So the training program should also include lots of sprint-type bursts of energy.

You can easily include these in a jogging regimen. Jog for a given distance, then sprint for ten full strides, then jog again, then sprint ten strides, and so on. Or come to a sudden stop and run backwards a short distance. Or sideways. Or run and bend down frequently as if hitting a half-volley. Or twist your upper body as you run like you were hitting a backhand. In these actions you'll be imitating the moves of a tennis match, besides adding variety and extra fun to your jogging.

Flexibility

When your muscles are supple and your joints flexible, you'll be better able to spring from the crouch of a ready position to a flat-out run for chasing down a drop shot. And you'll more easily crank the racket into the backscratching position for an emphatic topspin serve. And you'll be more responsive for reaching a wide ball then slamming on the brakes to scramble back into position.

Moreover, these moments of sudden exertion are prime times for muscle pulls. But you can avoid pulls by a conscientious program of stretching. It'll not only reduce the risk of injury — stretching before a match will actually elevate muscle temperatures, so it's a true form of "warming up." And stretching after a match, when your muscles are warm and limber and can be extended fully, will help eliminate soreness and stiffness.

Remember some general rules about stretching:

- Do only static stretching. No bouncing! Curiously, bouncing actually works **against** the development of flexibility, because a muscle that is quickly stretched will react by contracting, thus resisting the stretch and increasing the chances of being torn during the exercise. So stretch **slowly.** And hold the end position for awhile.
- Don't push to pain. If it hurts, stop. Pain is your body's way of telling you to go easy. Don't force the stretching, and what hurt today will be an easy position to achieve next week.

Before a match, stretch your muscles out, for three reasons: (1) it'll reduce the risk of a muscle pull, (2) it actually elevates the temperature of your muscles, and (3) it gets your muscles into a responsive state, more prepared to do the job you have for them.

Circuit Training

Circuit training involves a series of stations, each one having a specific exercise routine spread out over a course. At each station you perform the given exercise, then walk, jog, or run to the next station where another exercise is performed. The objective is to complete the circuit in as short a time as possible, and/or to increase the number of repetitions at each station whenever the course is run.

Circuit training is terrific conditioning for tennis. It fosters the kind of physical preparation that is needed for the game. And the circuit is individualized, because you set your own pace and number of repetitions. Best of all, you can easily design your own circuit, without any need of equipment. In final appraisal, a circuit offers a combination of strength, endurance, and flexibility exercises all in one plan, besides being an appealing way of achieving excellent overall fitness.

Bent-knee situps.

Here's a sample circuit course. Start by doing some stretching, then jog or run to each station, where you stop for a specific exercise.

Trunk twists.

Half-knee dips.

Pushups.

Knee raises.

Leg lifts.

Heel raises.   *Push up off ground, clap hands.*   *Jump and reach.*

An Aerobic Workout

The term **aerobic** is now household. It means, literally, "with oxygen." Aerobic exercises, therefore, are those that can be sustained over a period of time because they do not demand more oxygen than the blood can supply.

When you sprint to catch a bus, you can only go at top speed so far because your muscles run out of oxygen. That's an **anaerobic** activity. But if you swim laps at a leisurely pace you are doing aerobic work, for your muscles will receive a continuous supply of adequate oxygen.

Aerobic workouts are great for tennis, because they can use the game itself for the design. Practice sessions can be arranged to incorporate both a rehearsal of skills and aerobic conditioning. In this way your body will become accustomed to hitting skilled shots while being pressed into a high level of energy output. It's also a fun way of adding variety and dimension to practice.

You can readily design your own aerobic workout, focusing in particular on the parts of the game that you want to practice the most. The seven drills illustrated on the following pages are offered as an example.

Injuries

Unfortunately, evolution hasn't completely prepared us, anatomically, for tennis. Elbows were not designed for serving, nor shoulders for backhands, nor ankles for the constant starts

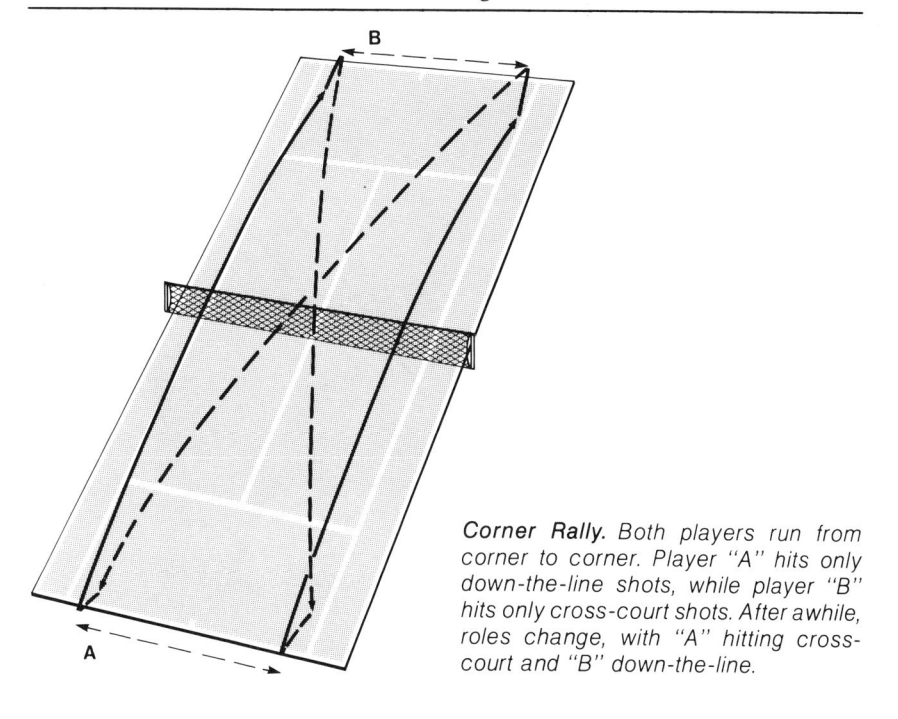

Aerobic Conditioning For Tennis

Corner Rally. Both players run from corner to corner. Player "A" hits only down-the-line shots, while player "B" hits only cross-court shots. After awhile, roles change, with "A" hitting cross-court and "B" down-the-line.

Hit-and-Advance. Both players start from behind the baseline, each carrying two or three balls ready for play. A ground stroke starts a rally, each player advancing a few steps toward the net after every shot. If a ball is misplayed, another is immediately put into play. Eventually, both players are across the net from each other, playing rapid-fire volleys.

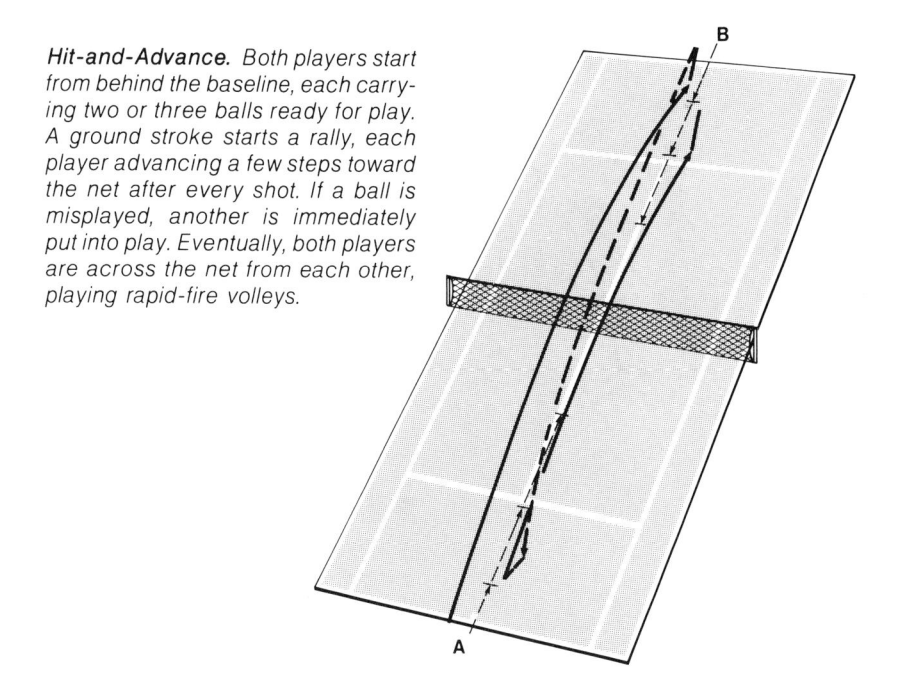

Serve-and-Volley. "B" serves and advances toward the net. "A" does not attempt to return the serve, but hits a ready ball to "B", who plays a volley, and the point is then played to its finish. As a variation, "A" could have another ball ready to provide a lob after "B" has hit the volley. After the point, roles switch.

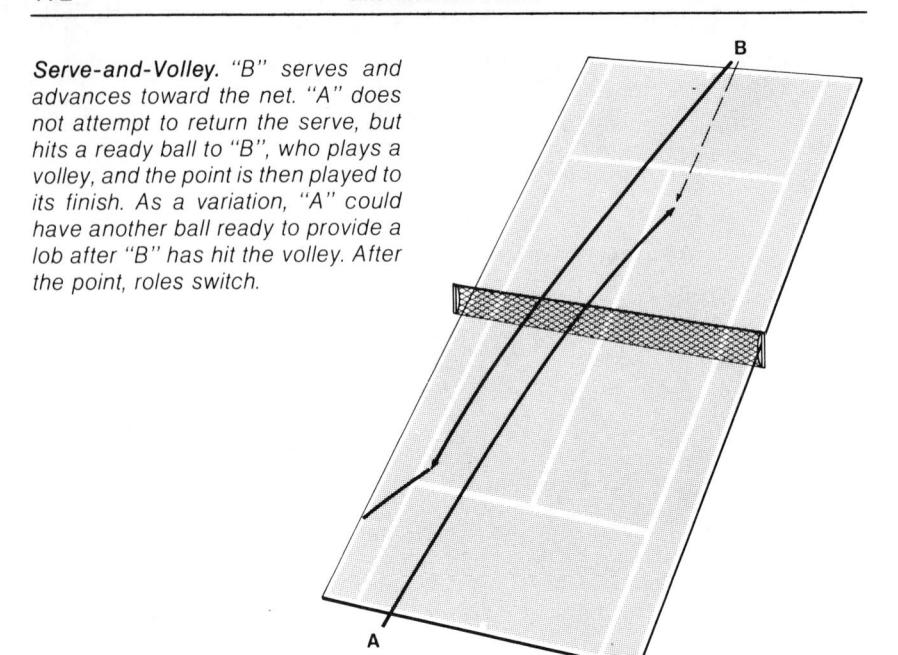

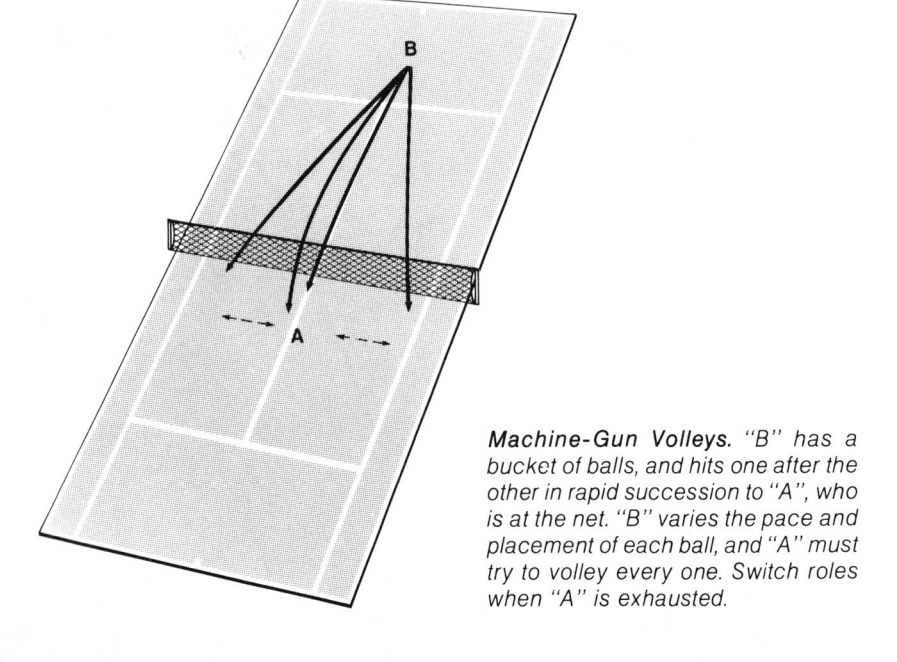

Machine-Gun Volleys. "B" has a bucket of balls, and hits one after the other in rapid succession to "A", who is at the net. "B" varies the pace and placement of each ball, and "A" must try to volley every one. Switch roles when "A" is exhausted.

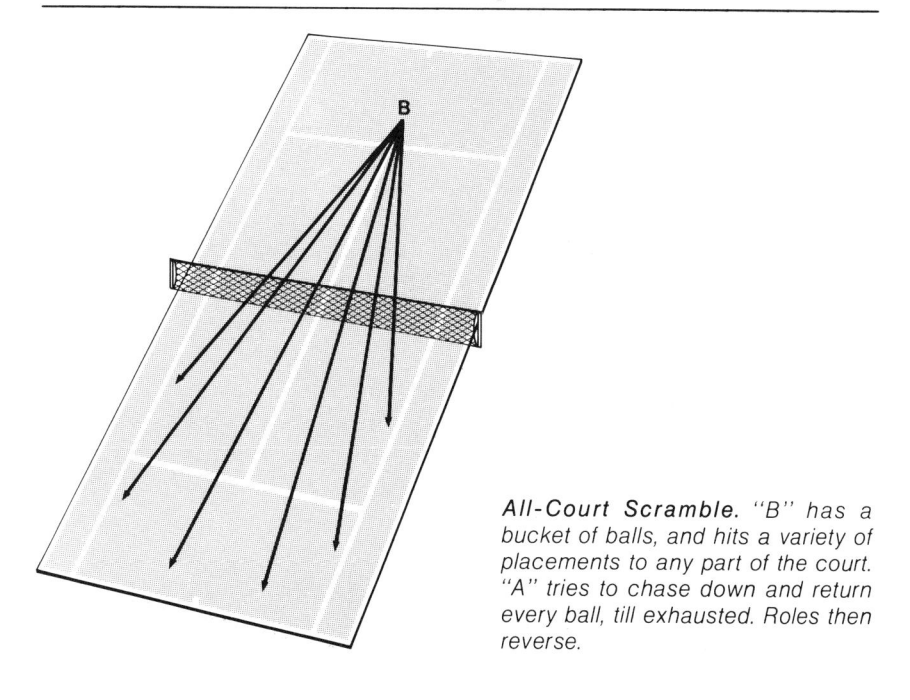

Aerobic Conditioning For Tennis

All-Court Scramble. "B" has a bucket of balls, and hits a variety of placements to any part of the court. "A" tries to chase down and return every ball, till exhausted. Roles then reverse.

Up-and-Back. "A" stands between baseline and service line, with a bucket of balls, and first hits a short ball that "B" must run down. Then "A" follows with a lob which "B" retreats to hit, and "A" provides another shallow ball. "A" does not try to return any ball, but alternates hitting shallow and deep setups.

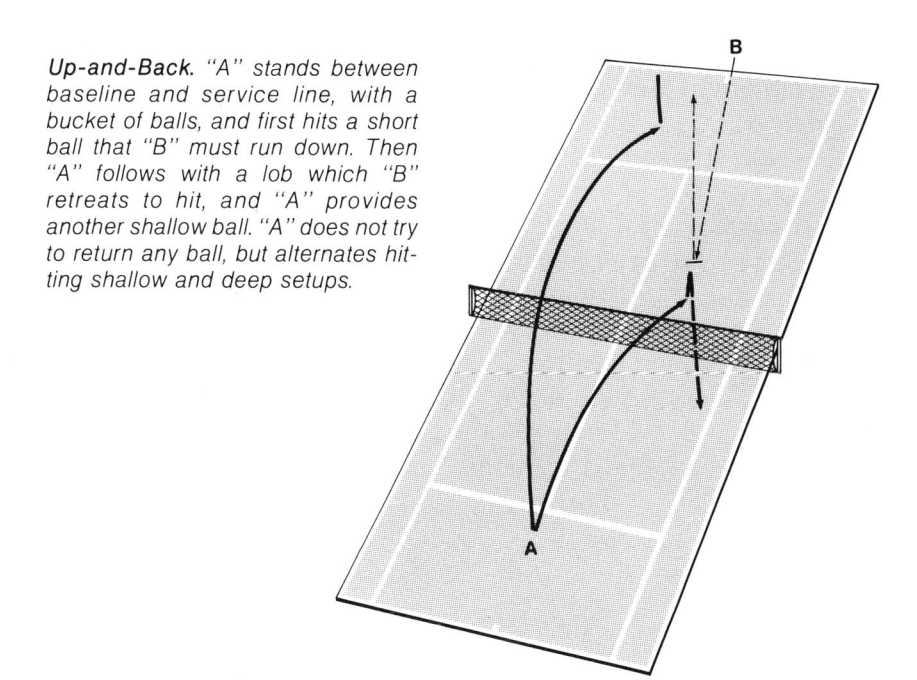

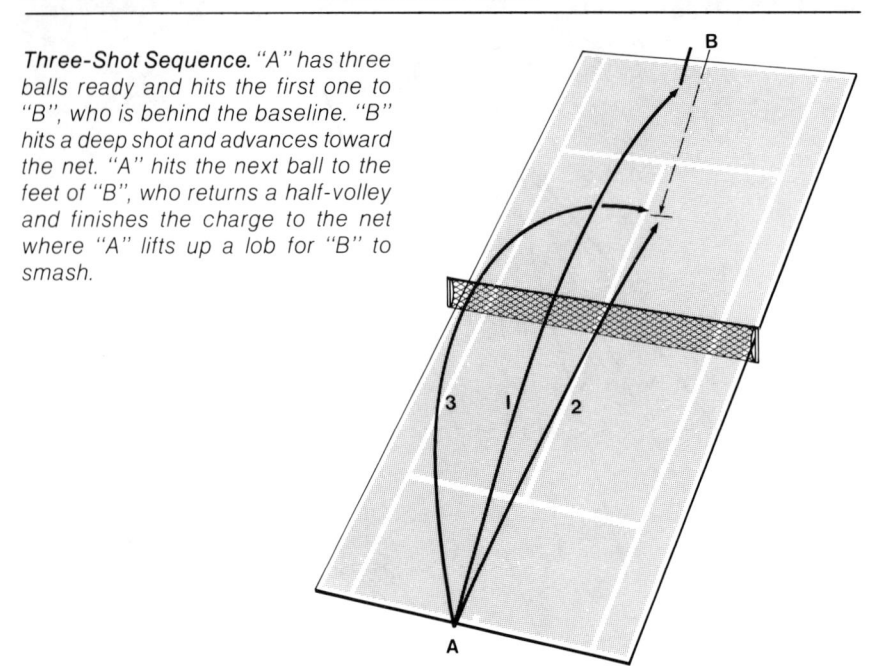

Three-Shot Sequence. "A" has three balls ready and hits the first one to "B", who is behind the baseline. "B" hits a deep shot and advances toward the net. "A" hits the next ball to the feet of "B", who returns a half-volley and finishes the charge to the net where "A" lifts up a lob for "B" to smash.

Four-Ball Rally. (Not Illustrated) *Each player gets two balls ready. One player starts a point by hitting a second serve, just to get the point underway. As soon as a winner is hit or an error is made, the second player hits a new ball into play, within the other player's reach, and the point continues until all four balls have been played.*

and stops of the game. So the body sometimes rebels. Being killed by an opponent is bad enough, but if your body is killing you, it's self-defeating.

TENNIS ELBOW. The poor elbow. It's notoriously susceptible to injury. Statistics show that about half the people who play regularly will, at some time in their playing life, have an elbow problem.

The infamous "tennis elbow" is usually a tissue tear or in some cases a calcium deposit. Most commonly it comes from the stress of serving, but it can also occur from a faulty "leading-elbow" swing in the backhand, or off-center hits, or even poor weight transfer into the shot. When you have tennis elbow, there will be local tenderness, sometimes outright pain, and difficulty in moving your arm through a full range of motion. Your elbow has told you to quit for awhile.

That's the easiest treatment — no playing for at least a week, or until your elbow stops complaining. In the meantime, do muscle strengthening exercises. Especially helpful are elbow-extending exercises such as pushups. Also do wrist curls with weights, and carry a tennis ball around with you to squeeze during idle moments. Add full-range-of-motion exercises to increase joint flexibility.

When you decide to play again, take some aspirin before going to the courts (to keep inflammation down), do **plenty** of calisthenics to warm up, and then play the way your sensitive elbow is reminding you the game should be played in the first place: keep a limber arm, use your whole body for each shot (not just your arm), have good weight transfer, and hit the ball early (late hits put more trauma on your elbow).

There's one more suggestion, but it's an expensive one: buy a new racket. Read Chapter 14 of this book, then get the racket that has the best vibration damping and largest sweet spot you can find. It'll take some of the shock off your elbow by better absorbing the concussion of the ball.

FOOT PROBLEMS. By incidence, the feet are the second most commonly injured area of the body. Sooner or later, it seems that everyone will incur a bruised heel, resulting from a hard landing or sudden stop. While it hurts at the moment, in a few days it will be ready for play again, without any treatment. But a heel spur, where calcium deposits can form, will not disappear in a few days, and if you have a persistent pain, it may be notice for an X-ray.

A stubbed toe, while uncomfortable, will also disappear in a few days. But a stress fracture will not and needs X-ray analysis.

Sometimes ankles will roll too far during a sudden change of direction. When they do, ice is needed and aspirin as an anti-inflammatory medication. Later, an elastic support will ease the discomfort and help the recovery.

Exercise is the best preventative. Strengthen your ankles by standing with your toes on the edge of steps and do heel raises. Add flexibility by rolling your ankles through a full range of motion. And running figure eights or other shuttle types of stop-and-go activity should be a regular part of your training program. Finally, though it may seem trite, make sure that your shoes fit properly.

THE LOWER LEG. The runner's scourge, shin splints, is not really common to tennis players. It's also a non-specific term, for it refers to any lower leg pain. Should you ever have enough pain in your lower leg to prevent your continuation of playing, a specific medical diagnosis is necessary. Otherwise, if a decrease in playing time and/or a change of shoes lessens the discomfort, there is probably no cause for concern.

Overall, compared to all other sports, the frequency of injury in tennis is quite low. Nonetheless, a well-rounded and conscientious program of fitness training will greatly reduce the potential that does exist.

CHAPTER FOURTEEN

The Equipment Revolution

Tennis gear has evolved. Today a player can look frighteningly good in clothing that is flexible in all the right places and has enough aesthetic appeal to be worn at the lawn party after the match. Orthopedic shoes have eliminated the plight of skidding around the court in discount sneakers, inviting self-inflicted hotfoot. Even headbands have style. But in all the world of sport, perhaps no single item of equipment has been as drastically modified as the tennis racket.

Prior to the mid-1970s, all rackets had the same configuration and were made of either wood or steel. Today the head of the racket is available in different sizes and can be round, oval, rectangular, triangular, teardrop-shaped, egg-shaped, oblong, other geometric shapes, and even unsymmetrical. Construction might be of fiberglass, aluminum, graphite, boron, titanium, kevlar, and other space-age materials. Consequently, there is a bewildering array of well over two hundred models on the market, most of them seemingly in a constant state of metamorphosis. Whereas some racket models had previously been sold unchanged for over twenty years, today a particular model might be manufactured for only a year.

The new hybrid rackets are no mere products of fantasy. They have evolved from research which tests each racket, under controlled laboratory conditions, for stiffness, liveliness, vibration, and strength. They are also court-tested by each manufacturer's advisory staff of players for power, control mobility, and overall playability — including feel, sound, and appearance. There still is no ultimate racket, but the available variety offers something for everyone.

Indeed, for advanced levels of play, no ordinary off-the-shelf racket will be satisfactory. A better player needs a refined weapon to compliment their skill, just as an accomplished musician deserves a quality instrument. The choice can be difficult, for the options are incredibly diverse. The following general guidelines may help.

Midsize or Oversize?

Racket heads are altered in size and shape for one major reason: to manipulate the dimensions of the sweetspot (which is that area on the strings that will produce the most reliable and forceful shot).

Generally, round-headed rackets have round sweetspots, oval-headed rackets have oval sweetspots, and so on. But the important factor is that the larger the head, the larger the sweetspot will be (up to a point). For this reason alone the standard-size racket heads will probably disappear in the future.

The standard-size racket has 70 square inches of hitting surface. Midsize rackets have around 85 square inches, and oversize rackets have 100 or more square inches of hitting surface. But for actual control of the ball, there is no automatic "bigger is better" relationship for the oversize rackets. In fact, if you are a power hitter but need more control, and you are playing with an oversize racket, a step down to a midsize may be the answer. And if you are using a standard-size racket, a step up to a midsize will probably provide you with an increase in both control and power. Overall, the midsize rackets offer the best combination of strength and ball control.

What Materials Are Best?

The introduction of oversize rackets necessitated the development of frames that were lighter, stiffer, and stronger to support the dimensions of the larger heads. The first satisfactory material used was fiberglass, and it is still generally regarded as the best companion material for other fibers such as graphite, boron, or kevlar.

The better rackets are composites — a crossbreed of several materials. Composites get high marks for power, control, and maneuverability — considerably more than for wooden rackets. Price dictates their quality. For example, an inexpensive graphite racket will be made of "chopped" fibers, which are only about 25 percent as strong as the "continuous" fibers used in expensive rackets.

Stiff or Flexible?

The primary reason why rackets are made of different materials is to affect their stiffness. In general, a stiff racket will produce more power and control than a flexible racket. Therefore, if your game needs a boost in either power or control, your next racket should probably be something stiffer than what you are presently using. However, some frames are so stiff that they will vibrate considerably on impact and could be tough on sensitive elbows. Other frames are designed to be stiff in the head for control and flexible in the shaft for power.

If you are a big serve-and-volley player, the most important quality in the racket is maneuverability. This disqualifies the large-head rackets. The racket should be light and fairly stiff, with an open throat to allow it to slip through the air with ease.

If you are a baseline player, you will still want stiffness in the racket, and the frame should have good vibration damping (an ability to dissipate the vibrations caused by ball impact). The racket should also have a large sweetspot so that the ball can be hit over a bigger area of the strings and still "feel" solid.

Predictably, the better your play becomes and the more confidently you hit the ball with power, the more likely it is you will appreciate a stiff racket. A flexible racket simply will not respond with enough liveliness for your game.

Light, Medium, or Heavy Weight?

The "weight" of a racket is misleading, for what one manufacturer calls a light racket another might call a medium weight. It's all relative to the other rackets that a manufacturer makes. Some even produce an "extra light" weight, and the heavy rackets are becoming rare. Moreover, rackets can be head-heavy, head-light, or have the weight evenly distributed.

Serve-and-volley players need a light racket of around 12 ounces (strung weight), perhaps even less. Rackets of 13 ounces or more will be cumbersome for a big server, though advantageous for a baseline player. A weight of just over 12 ounces will be a comfortable weapon for groundstrokes as well as for a serve-and-volley game. Head-light frames favor the serve-and-volley player, while head-heavy rackets are better for baseliners.

What Grip Size?

There is no absolute way to measure your hand for the right grip size. The main factor is what feels comfortable. If the racket tires your arm quickly or feels like a strain to hold, the grip may be too big. If the racket twists easily in your hand on ball contact, the grip is probably too small.

What Strings To Use?

Just as you would not buy an expensive guitar and fit it with cheap strings, so should a quality tennis racket have suitable strings. Gut is still the choice of the pro players, but today a new generation of advanced synthetic strings has been developed to provide performance similar to gut. Basically, five types of strings exist.

Monofilament nylon. No longer very functional, this string is simply one strand of nylon. It is not very strong and will stretch once in the racket.

Core string. A single nylon strand wrapped by individual fibers. The most common string available.

Twisted fibers. Multiple nylon fibers twisted and bonded together.

Twisted bundles. Several bundles of twisted fibers intertwined rope-like and bonded.

Natural gut. Ribbon-like fibers of cow intestine, twisted and bonded. Expensive and wears more rapidly.

Overall, the playing quality of a string is related to its price, although this is not an absolute. While gut may be the favorite of the pros, its cost and shorter life make it of some question for most players. Some racket companies even suggest that their product will perform better with synthetic strings rather than gut.

Strings also come in, basically, 15- and 16-gauge diameters, with 16-gauge being thinner than 15-gauge. If the string is listed as 16L or 15L, it means that it is fractionally thinner than standard 16- or 15-gauge. In general, the thinner the string, the livelier the performance.

What's The Best String Tension?

If the strings of a racket are too loose, the ball will "slingshot" with less control. If the strings are tighter, they will not "give" as much on impact; thus, the ball will flatten out more as a greater surface area contacts the strings, and thereby control is enhanced. Consequently, the general rule is tight strings for control, but this is far from being dependable in all rackets and for all players.

The more important factor is the nature of the racket itself. The lighter the racket, and the larger the frame, the higher the tension should be. Light, oversize rackets may require tensions of 80 pounds or more, compared to the 55 pounds that is generically recommended for standard-size rackets. Conveniently, manufacturers have established recommended tension ranges for each of their products. If you are a power hitter, opt for the upper end of the range, and if you are a baseline player, stay more toward the middle. Don't choose the lowest recommended tension unless you are strictly a "touch" player who rarely hits strong shots. For most players, tighter stringing will provide the best combination of power and control.

Play is the Best Criterion

The characteristics of the racket are only half its story. The real test comes from how it feels in your hand. With the wide variety of rackets available today, it's more important than ever to court-test demonstration models before making your choice.

Additionally, the two most popular tennis magazines (*Tennis* and *World Tennis*) will periodically review selected new models, evaluating them for stiffness, maneuverability, control, and so on. This will provide a further guide in selecting rackets that you would like to play-test.

One final suggestion. If you're going to switch to a new racket, and especially if it's quite different in playing quality from your old one, wait if you can until the end of the season or for a break in your playing routine before making the change. That way your body will have been more divorced from the feel of your old racket, and the switch to the new one will be more readily accomplished.

CHAPTER 15

The Spirit of the Rules

What happens if you serve and ... plunk! — the ball hits the receiver before it touches the ground? Or, what should you do if you hit a shot near a line and your opponent, unsure if the ball was in or out, asks you to replay the point? And what is the right decision if your opponent inadvertently serves from the wrong side of the court and wins a point before either of you discover the mistake?

Ignorance of the law has never been an excuse, neither in civil courts nor on tennis courts. All players have the responsibilitiy to be familiar with the rules of the game. Otherwise, situations could arise where one player is unjustly penalized, even though the injustice was not intended. When all players know the rules, tennis is a faster and more enjoyable game, with no interference from debates about the resolution of any situation.

The official rules that govern tennis are a product of the International Tennis Federation, of which the United States Tennis Association (USTA) is a member. They are presented in complete form in Appendix C of this book, beginning on page 197. However, like all laws, they do not cover every conceivable event that can occur during play. Nor do they dictate the spirit that is between their lines, or the "unwritten" codes of conduct that are expected from every experienced player. These matters are the topics of this chapter.

Implied Integrity

No tradition in tennis is older than that of integrity among players. Largely, this integrity is a matter of information, primarily through having a complete knowledge of the rules, but also through understanding the ethical codes that oblige every player to do nothing which detracts from the game itself, or from an opponent's concentration on their own play. This includes giving an opponent the benefit of doubt on line calls, avoiding foot faults during serving, never intentionally distracting an opponent, never stalling in an effort to upset an opponent, and always conducting oneself in a fashion that makes the game enjoyable for everyone, including spectators. In this way, honest players will have the same approach to all situations, and the competitive ideals of tennis will remain high.

Line Calls

A dozen or more times in every set your perception gets a test as a ball lands so near a line that it's difficult to tell, accurately, if it was in or out. Here are some hypothetical situations regarding this occurrence.

1. During a rally you keep a ball in play that you realize, a bit later, was out. Can you make a delayed call of "out" and claim the point?

- No. Any call of "out" must be made as soon as possible. Otherwise, a player could see their return go out-of-bounds and then decide to make the "out" call on the opponent's previous placement.

2. Suppose your opponent's serve and your return of the serve happen so fast that you have sent the ball back over the net before you have fixed in your mind that the ball was actually out.

- The same principle applies: the ball must be called out immediately. However, there is some allowance in this instance, because it is understood that the receiver is concentrating first on returning the ball, second on making the call. But in no case can the call be made after the ball has either been sent back into play or has been hit out-of-bounds.

3. What if your opponent hits a point-ending placement that you are not sure was in or out — must you still make an immediate call?

- In this case, time permits you to have a "second look" at the placement, sometimes even finding a mark left by the ball, before making the call.

4. Can you ask for a replay of a point where you are unable to make a sure call?

- Absolutely not! The rules do not allow it. Whenever there is doubt, that doubt must be resolved in favor of your opponent; therefore, the ball is always considered as good.

5. Can you ask your opponent to make the call on a ball you did not clearly see?

- Yes, but only when you believe that your opponent was in a better position to see the ball than you were. Usually this happens when you are looking **across** a line and your opponent is looking **down** the line at the placement. The player looking down the line is much more likely to have accurately seen the ball than a player looking across a line. Otherwise, when looking across a line, a ball must not be called out unless you clearly saw part of the court between where the ball landed and the line.

6. Should you enlist the aid of a spectator to help make a line call?

- Never. It is discourteous to your opponent, an avoidance of your responsibility, and does not guarantee accuracy or impartiality on the part of the spectator anyhow.

7. Suppose you hit a point-ending placement that you clearly saw as out and your opponent calls good. Should you correct the call, and as a result lose the point?

- Yes; even if your opponent does not ask you to make the call.

8. Suppose you hit a serve you see as out, but your opponent nevertheless returns the ball without making an "out" call. Could you ask for a replay on the basis that the return was unexpected and caught you off-guard?

- It must be assumed that the receiver made the return in good faith, thinking the serve to be good; therefore, play must continue, with no allowance for a replay. However, there is a general guideline that the server (or the server's partner in doubles) should volunteer a call on a **second** serve that is clearly seen as out, since this call terminates the point.

Keep in mind that your opponent is always entitled to a prompt hand signal or an "out" call on each missed shot, particularly when the ball may be obviously out to you, but might not be so obvious to your opponent.

One rather irksome situation is when a player sees a ball which is apparently going out and then catches the ball before it lands. The rules clearly state that the player automatically loses the point, since the ball is alive as long as it's in the air and therefore cannot be touched by a player (see Rule 20; Case 7). However, sometimes a player will chase down a ball and catch it before it bounces simply to keep it from rebounding over a fence or into a neighboring court; thus, some discretion must be used in trying to enforce the exact letter of this rule. Making such a call against an opponent who caught a ball unquestionably going out-of-bounds, though lawfully correct, may be ethically unsound when that player was merely trying to conserve time by not having to collect the errant ball after its bounce.

The Let

Sometimes an event occurs which prevents a player from having full concentration on the point being played. Such is the case when, for example, a player is distracted by a ball coming from another court, or by other players walking around or behind the court. This distraction allows the hindered player to legally call a let, with the privilege of replaying the point. However, the let must be called **right away.** This prevents any player from having a "two chance" option whereby that player was, for instance, hindered by a ball from another court but continues to play the point and, having hit the ball out, then tries to exercise the let. Furthermore, a let cannot be called when there was a hindrance but the player had absolutely no chance of retrieving a good placement from their opponent even without the hindrance.

Note that a replayed point begins with the server being granted the normal two attempts. In effect, this means that if the server was hindered or otherwise interrupted during or before the **second** serve attempt, the rules allow for the server to have **both** attempts over again (see USTA comment on Rule 13). However, the concept of an "inordinate delay" should be applied in this circumstance. That is, unless there is an inordinate amount of time between serves caused by the hindrance, a let should not be allowed, and the server must carry on with the second attempt. But when the server is forced, by some reason not of their own doing, to wait an unreasonable length of time to hit the second attempt, the **receiver** should acknowledge that fact and "grant" the server the privilege to start again with the first serve. This is a prime example of the importance for all players to know the rules so that the receiver in this case not only understands what should be done, but also observes the courtesy of recognizing the event which allows the server to have both attempts.

That Bothersome Foot Fault

Everybody does it now and then, usually unknowingly. But what do you do if your opponent commits repeated and blatant foot faults?

The rules have no provision about what to do, but a USTA interpretation of the foot fault (see Rule 8) authorizes the receiver to first inform the server of the violation and then, if it continues, to make the call. However, the call should be made only when the receiver is absolutely certain of the violation.

It's irritating. When you are receiving, you do not want to be bothered with having to give some of your attention to watching for a foot fault; therefore, the only ones that you are likely to notice are the flagrant violations. But even the slightest encroachment on the line is still a foot fault, and thus compliance with this rule is very much a function of each player's personal sense of honor. Knowingly committing foot faults is cheating, just as surely as making a deliberate bad line call is, and the players who willfully fault or refuse to acknowledge that they might be doing it must be questioned as to their respect for fair play.

Other Considerations

Following are some additional matters which, when understood by all players, will make for a better and more enjoyable match.

1. Whenever a player realizes that they have committed a violation, that player should make the call immediately. This includes such things as hitting the ball after two bounces, touching the net, or hitting the ball before it has crossed over the net.

2. If a player calls a ball out, then realizes that it was good, a correction should be made.
3. The server should announce the score of the set prior to the first serve of a new game, and the score of the game prior to serving each point. Always, the server's score is announced first, the receiver's second.
4. If there is disagreement among the players as to the score and it cannot be resolved, the score shall revert back to the last score on which there was agreement, or it should be settled by the spin of a racket.
5. Although a receiver may change their position on the court as the server prepares to hit or begins the motion, this must not be done in a deliberate attempt to disrupt the server. Nor should a receiver, in a similar attempt to unnerve the server, become "unready" as the server begins the motion.
6. Sometimes a server will, having missed a first attempt, hit the second serve before the receiver has had ample time to assume a ready position. While this is a violation (of Rule 12) on the part of the server, the receiver must also recognize that even when being victimized by such a "quick serve," if any overt attempt is made to return the ball, the receiver forfeits the right to ask for a replay of the second serve.
7. Stalling in an attempt to unnerve an opponent is not permitted. The rules allow a maximum of one and a half minutes to change ends of the court and only 30 seconds between points.
8. Intentionally returning serves that are out in an effort to upset an opponent shall not be tolerated.
9. During the warm-up prior to the start of a match, it is courtesy to keep the ball within easy reach of the opponent and to refrain from returning the ball when the opponent is practicing serves.
10. All practice serves should be taken during a warm-up instead of allowing the second server of the match to practice serves prior to their first turn (but after the first game has been played). And under no circumstances is a "first ball in" allowed for any server's first attempt.

APPENDIX A

The National Tennis Rating Scale

How would you rate yourself? An experienced player who still has trouble with the backhand? A competent weekender who can hit serves, volleys, and groundstrokes with reasonable success? An all-court player who has developed power and consistency on all strokes?

The National Tennis Rating Program will give you reference points for your own self-appraisal. The scale was developed to be more specific than the standard divisions of beginner, intermediate, and advanced. And it is a valid rating tool that will help you decide which lessons or tournament you should sign up for, as well as who your most compatible social opponents will be.

To place yourself on the scale, read all the categories, and then choose the one which best describes your present ability. Make sure that you can perform all the skills in the classification you select, as well as those in the preceding levels. If you have some doubt, place yourself in the lower category, and keep in mind the number that you come up with is but a temporary classification, subject to change as you improve in skill.

THE NATIONAL TENNIS RATING PROGRAM

PRO VERIFICATION GUIDELINES

(General Characteristics of Various Playing Levels)

Rating	Forehand	Backhand	Serve	Volley	Special Shots	Other
1.0	No concept of waist-level stroke. Most often swings from elbow at eye-level.	Most likely avoids backhands or misses completely.	No knowledge of service motion or procedure.	Makes little contact with the ball at net or doesn't go to net at all.		Little knowledge of scorekeeping and basic positioning.
1.5	Late preparation; No follow through; Erratic contact; No direction.	Avoids backhands when possible. No change of grip.	Inconsistent toss and motion; Infrequent contact on center of strings; No follow through; No backscratch or full swing; Frequent double faults.	Only FH volley; Infrequent success.		Little knowledge of procedures; Difficulty with scorekeeping.
2.0	No directional intent. Infrequently in position. Can keep a rally of up to 3 hits when set up.	Grip problems; No follow through; Erratic contact; No direction; Faces net.	Mostly ½ swing; Frequently a back-forth motion; Can frequently get the ball into play; Double faults still common.	Frequently swings; Reluctant to play net; Avoids BH. No footwork; Successful on setup FH's; No depth.		Can keep play moving in singles and doubles.
2.5	Form developing. Well prepared for moderate shots. Follows through on most shots. Fairly consistent on set-ups.	Still has grip and preparation problems. Lack of confidence; No follow-through; Can compensate frequently for a ball coming to the BH side.	Starting a full motion; Can be consistent on the second serve; No directional intent; Frequently no backscratch.	Can angle FH volley when set up. Does not bend for low volleys (usually drops racket head). Still uncomfortable at the net, especially on the BH side. Grip problems.	Can lob intentionally.	Weak court coverage; Cannot return lobs; Can return serve on FH consistently; Cannot adjust to variance in serves; Usually remains in the initial doubles position.
3.0	Fairly consistent with some directional intent; Lacks depth control.	Little directional intent. Frequently prepared; Usually lacks follow-through; Can be consistent on set-ups.	Developing rhythm; Little consistency when trying for power.	Consistent FH volleys; Frequently uses FH racket face on BH volleys; Can be offensive on set-ups. Inconsistent BH volley when using BH racket face; Has trouble with low and wide balls.	Can occasionally handle balls hit at the feet (but not with a good half-volley form). Can make contact on overheads; Can lob consistently.	Can frequently cover lobs in doubles; Recognizes offensive doubles play, but weak in its execution; Can return serve on the BH, but with little directional intent. Developing match play sense.

The National Tennis Rating Scale

Rating					
3.5	Good consistency on set-ups. Still lacks depth on difficult shots; Has directional intent on moderate balls; May have good preparation, but still weak on deep shots.	Preparation problems; Starting to hit with directional intent on easy shots; Starting to follow through instead of punch.	Starting to serve with some power and control. Tries to direct serves; Usually flat serves; May be trying to learn to use spin.	More aggressive net play. Some ability to cover side shots. Using proper footwork; Can direct FH volleys; Consistent contact, but little offense on BH volleys.	Can use full overhead swing on shots within reach. Recognizes approach shots and half volleys; Can place the return of serve.	Moves up and back well. Covering court fairly well. With doubles partner, can effectively cover the net.
4.0	Dependable most of the time with consistent depth and control; Can control running FH; Starting to develop topspin. Frequently may try to hit too good a shot off the FH.	Player can direct the ball with consistency on each shot; Returns difficult shots defensively; Little control on running BHs; Still lacks depth.	Places both first and second serves; Frequent power on first serve with some control; Starting to use spin; Tends to overhit first serve.	Depth and control on FH volley; Can direct BH volleys, but usually lacks depth; Developing wide and low volleys on both sides of the body.	Can direct easy overheads; Can poach in doubles; Can hit both offensive and defensive lobs. Follows aggressive shots to the net; Hits to opponents' weaknesses.	Has more confidence, but rallies are still commonly lost due to impatience. Not yet playing good percentage tennis; Has developed teamwork in doubles.
4.5	Very dependable; Uses speed and spin effectively. Tends to overhit on difficult shots. Offensive on easy shots.	Can hit with depth. Usually not offensive; Can control direction and depth, but not under pressure.	Aggressive serving, with limited double faults; Still developing spin and offense on second serve; Frequently hits with good depth.	Can handle a mixed sequence of volleys; Good footwork; Has depth and directional control on BH; Developing touch; Most common error is still overhitting.	Approach shots with good depth and control; Can consistently hit overheads as far back as the service line; Starting to hit drop volleys; Can change pace on groundstrokes.	More intentional variety in game; Covers up weaknesses well; Plans tactics more than one shot ahead.
5.0	Strong shot with control, depth and spin; Uses FH to set up offensive situations; Has developed good touch; Consistent on passing shots.	Can use BH as an aggressive shot with good consistency; Has good direction and depth on most shots. Difficult shots are returned with-out intent of direction or depth, but can frequently hit winners off of set-ups.	Serve is placed effectively with the intent of hitting to a weakness or of developing an offensive situation; Can mix topspin, slice, and flat serves; Good depth and spin on most second serves, and few double faults.	Can hit most volleys with depth, pace and direction; Can hit either flat or under-spin volleys. Plays difficult volleys with depth; Given opportunity, volley is hit automatically for a winner.	Has added drop shot and lob volley to repertoire; Approach shots and passing shots are hit with a high degree of effectiveness.	
5.5	The 5.0 player frequently has an outstanding shot around which he can mold his game or protect weaknesses. Has sound strategy in singles and doubles and can vary game plan according to opponent. This player has become "match wise", and "beats himself" less than the 4.5 player. Covers court well, plays percentage tennis, and has good anticipation. Hits mid-court volley with consistency, but may lack depth. Serve return is consistent, and can gain offense against a weak second serve. Overhead can be hit from most any position on the court.					
6.0 to 7.0	This player can hit dependable shots in stress situations; Has developed good anticipation, and can pick up cues from such things as opponent's toss, body position, backswing, preparation, etc. First and second serves can be depended on in stress situations and can be hit offensively at any time. Can analyze and exploit opponents' weaknesses.					
	These players will generally not need NTRP ratings, as their rankings or past rankings speak for themselves. The 6.0 player frequently makes travel for competition a part of his life-style, and sometimes earns a portion of the game and often travels from city to city for competition. The 6.5 player frequently makes travel for competition a part of his life-style, and sometimes earns a portion of his income from prize-winnings. The 7.0 player is generally committed to tournament competition as a life-style and frequently depends on tournament winnings as a portion of his income.					

© USTA, NTA, USPTA, 1979

THE NATIONAL TENNIS RATING PROGRAM

1.0 This player is just starting to play tennis.

1.5 This player has limited playing experience and is still working primarily on getting the ball over the net; has some knowledge of scoring but is not familiar with basic positions and procedures for singles and doubles play.

2.0 This player may have had some lessons but needs on-court experience; has obvious stroke weaknesses but is beginning to feel comfortable with singles and doubles play.

2.5 This player has more dependable strokes and is learning to judge where the ball is going; has weak court coverage or is often caught out of position, but is starting to keep the ball in play with other players of the same ability.

3.0 This player can place shots with moderate success; can sustain a rally of slow pace but is not comfortable with all strokes; lacks control when trying for power.

3.5 This player has achieved stroke dependability and direction on shots within reach, including forehand and backhand volleys, but still lacks depth and variety; seldom double faults and occasionally forces errors on the serve.

4.0 This player has dependable strokes on both forehand and backhand sides; has the ability to use a variety of shots including lobs, overheads, approach shots and volleys; can place the first serve and force some errors; is seldom out of position in a doubles game.

4.5 This player has begun to master the use of power and spins; has sound footwork; can control depth of shots and is able to move opponent up and back; can hit first serves with power and accuracy and place the second serve; is able to rush net with some success on serve in singles as well as doubles.

5.0 This player has good shot anticipation; frequently has an outstanding shot or exceptional consistency around which a game may be structured; can regularly hit winners or force errors off of short balls; can successfully execute lobs, drop shots, half volleys and overhead smashes; has good depth and spin on most second serves.

5.5 This player can execute all strokes offensively and defensively; can hit dependable shots under pressure; is able to analyze opponents' styles and can employ patterns of play to assure the greatest possibility of winning points; can hit winners or force errors with both first and second serves. Return of serve can be an offensive weapon.

6.0 This player has mastered all the above skills; has developed power and/or consistency as a major weapon; and can vary strategies and styles of play in a competitive situation. This player typically has had intensive training for national competition at junior or collegiate levels.

6.5 This player has mastered all of the above skills and is an experienced tournament competitor who regularly travels for competition and whose income may be partially derived from prize winnings.

7.0 This is a world class player.

© 1979 USTA, NTA, USPTA — Revised 1981

APPENDIX B

A Self-Appraisal Checklist

There's a lot to remember about each stroke in tennis — **too** much, it often seems. When on the court, trying to put all the information into motion, the body is usually too busy performing to listen to all the details the brain may want to tell it. So it's better to keep the mental reminders subtle and simple — abbreviated cues that will set off the right muscle patterns.

What follows is a series of reminders about the essentials of each aspect of tennis. They are not everything that is important, but they are some of the **most** important factors.

Use the list to build your own mental cue system for performance. Keep the cues brief, so that on the court you can use a small package of information to remind your body of the things it ought to be doing.

Take the list along to the court. Check the appropriate box for each item on the list, or have someone else evaluate your performance. Then use the checklist as a reference, noting those parts of your game which are only sometimes performed, or rarely performed, and structure your practice time around those factors.

SELF-APPRAISAL

PERFORMANCE CUES	Usually performed	Sometimes performed	Rarely performed
For all strokes:			
1. Stay relaxed, yet alive, limber, alert, and responsive.			
2. Hit as if the racket is a part of you — an extension of your arm.			
3. Make every stroke fluid, free-flowing, rhythmical.			

	Usually performed	Sometimes performed	Rarely performed
4. Hit the ball with your entire body, not just your arm.			
5. Keep the racket alive — active through contact. Emphasize the follow-through.			
6. Play dynamic, lively, spontaneous tennis.			
7. Enjoy the sensory stimulus of the game itself.			
For the groundstrokes:			
1. Stay athletic, lively on your toes, cat-like on the court.			
2. Keep the grip loose to start — firm to hit.			
3. Coil and uncoil — everything back to wind up, forward to hit.			
4. Have your weight going toward the target at contact.			
5. Hit low-to-high for topspin, with a firm wrist at contact.			
6. Fling the racket into the ball for topspin, with good acceleration at contact.			
7. Hit high to low for backspin, with a firm wrist at contact.			
For the serve:			
1. Close the stance; take a Continental grip.			
2. Keep a loose, supple arm.			
3. Spiral your whole body into the backswing, racket head down.			
4. Start slow, but explode into the ball, with a whip-like action.			
5. Hit both serves with the same intensity; change only the direction of the swing.			
For the return of serve:			
1. Prime yourself to move forward.			
2. Be lively on your feet; ready to move quickly.			
3. The harder the serve, the more the swing should be compact and firm.			
4. Be a scrambler. Go to the ball. Don't retreat. Do anything to get the ball back.			
When playing the forecourt:			
1. Go to the net only on a short ball, or behind your own strong shot.			

	Usually performed	Sometimes performed	Rarely performed
2. Hit the approach shot deep.			
3. As your opponent is about to hit, come to a split-step pause.			
4. Keep the volley stroke firm, compact.			
5. For an overhead, get into position early, behind the ball.			
6. Hit the smash with flair, but only as hard as you can control.			
7. Defend the net aggressively, like a goalkeeper defending the goal.			
When hitting lobs:			
1. Hit the lob as an offensive weapon whenever you can.			
2. Hit defensive lobs with plenty of height.			
3. Keep a firm wrist for all lobs except topspin, which needs wrist.			
4. Bring the racket into the ball on the same plane as the intended loft of the shot.			
In pressure situations:			
1. When hitting on the run, shorten the backswing, give the arm whip, provide margin of safety for placement.			
2. Hit half-volleys with firm wrist; racket parallel to court, push the ball back deep.			
3. Hit a high backhand like a volley; firm grasp, push racket forward.			
4. When retreating from the net to catch up to a lob, hit a lob in return.			
On touch shots:			
1. Slacken the grip for drop shots. Bunt the ball over the net.			
2. Use drop shots, or dink the ball, only when you know that you can end the point with the shot.			
As strategy for singles:			
1. Keep the ball deep, and up the middle, especially against a strong groundstroke player.			
2. Use angled shots when you're shallow and/or off to one side.			

	Usually performed	Sometimes performed	Rarely performed
3. Beat a slugger with changes of pace, and lots of off-speed shots.			
4. Go to the forecourt often; finish the point early; hit the ball where your opponent isn't.			
5. Make things happen. Try to win points rather than trying to avoid losing them.			
6. Get the first serve in at least half the time; slow its pace if necessary.			
7. Hit second serves to the weaker side of the receiver.			
8. Do what you do best, and play it against what your opponent does worst.			

As strategy for doubles:

1. Go to the net at every opportunity.			
2. Sacrifice pace for placement.			
3. Get first serves in more often. Send them to receiver's weaker side.			
4. When at the net, as partner of server or receiver, take every ball you can get.			
5. Return serves past net player, low in front of server.			
6. Lob more often, and exploit the middle.			

As states of mind:

1. Self-talk optimism into your mind; believe in your own ability.			
2. Maintain a state of calm, even during stressful points of a match.			
3. Focus on each point, as if it were the last of the match.			
4. Believe that every serve will go in. See the ball good before hitting it.			
5. Do not let a poor shot affect your performance on the next shot.			
6. Keep an upbeat attitude, and competitive spirit, for the entire match.			
7. Use visualization, both off the court and during breaks in a match.			

APPENDIX C

Rules of Tennis and Cases and Decisions

RULES OF TENNIS

Explanatory Note

The following Rules and Cases and Decisions are the official Code of the International Tennis Federation, of which the United States Tennis Association is a member. USTA Comments and USTA Cases and Decisions have the same weight and force in USTA tournaments as do ITF Cases and Decisions.

When a match is played without officials the principles and guidelines set forth in the USTA Publication, The Code, shall apply in any situation not covered by the rules.

Except where otherwise stated, every reference in these Rules to the masculine includes the feminine gender.

THE SINGLES GAME

RULE 1

The Court

The Court shall be a rectangle 78 feet (23.77m.) long and 27 feet (8.23m.) wide.
USTA Comment: See Rule 34 for a doubles court.

It shall be divided across the middle by a net suspended from a cord or metal cable of a maximum diameter of one-third of an inch (0.8cm.), the ends of which shall be attached to, or pass over, the tops of two posts, which shall be not more than 6 inches (15cm.) square or 6 inches (15cm.) in diameter. The centres of the posts shall be 3 feet (0.914m.) outside the court on each side and the height of the posts shall be such that the top of the cord or metal cable shall be 3 feet 6 inches (1.07cm.) above the ground.

When a combined doubles (see Rule 34) and singles court with a doubles net is used for singles, the net must be supported to a height of 3 feet 6 inches (1.07m.) by means of two posts, called "singles sticks", which shall be not more than 3 inches (7.5cm.) square or 3 inches (7.5cm.) in diameter. The centres of the singles sticks shall be 3 feet (0.914m.) outside the singles court on each side.

The net shall be extended fully so that it fills completely the space between the two posts and shall be of sufficiently small mesh to prevent the ball passing through. The height of the net shall be 3 feet (0.914m.) at the centre, where it shall be held down taut by a strap not more than 2 inches (5cm.) wide and completely white in colour. There shall be a band covering the cord or metal cable and the top of the net of not less than 2 inches (5cm.) nor more than two and a half inches (6.3cm.) in depth on each side and completely white in colour.

There shall be no advertisement on the net, strap, band or singles sticks.

The lines bounding the ends and sides of the Court shall respectively be called the base-lines and the side-lines. On each side of the net, at a distance of 21 feet (6.40m.) from it and parallel with it, shall be drawn the service-lines. The space on each side of the net between the service-line and the side-lines shall be divided into two equal parts called the service-courts by the centre service-line, which must be 2 inches (5cm.) in width, drawn half-way between, and parallel with, the side-lines. Each base-line shall be bisected by an imaginary continuation of the centre service-line to a line 4 inches (10cm.) in length and 2 inches (5cm.) in width called the centre mark drawn inside the Court, at right angles to and in contact with such base-lines. All other lines shall be not less than 1 inch (2.5cm.) nor more than 2 inches (5cm.) in width, except the base-line, which may be 4 inches (10cm.) in width and all measurements shall be made to the outside of the lines. All lines shall be of uniform colour.

If advertising or any other material is placed at the back of the Court, it may not contain white or yellow, or any other light colour.

If advertisements are placed on the chairs of the Linesmen sitting at the back of the Court, they may not contain white or yellow.

Note: In the case of the International Tennis Championship (Davis Cup) or other Official Championships of the International Tennis Federation, there shall be a space behind each baseline of not less than 21 feet (6.4m.), and at the sides of not less than 12 feet (3.66m.).

USTA Comment: *It is important to have a stick 3 feet, 6 inches long, with a notch cut in at the 3-foot mark for the purpose of measuring the height of the net at the posts and in the center. These measurements always should be made before starting to play a match.*

RULE 2

Permanent Fixtures

The permanent fixtures of the Court shall include not only the net, posts, singles sticks, cord or metal cable, strap and band, but also, where there are any such, the back and side stops, the stands, fixed or movable seats and chairs round the Court, and their occupants, all other fixtures around and above the Court, and the Umpire, Net-cord Judge, Foot-fault Judge, Linesmen and Ball Boys when in their respective places.

Note: For the purpose of this Rule, the word "Umpire" comprehends the Umpire, the persons entitled to a seat on the Court, and all those persons designated to assist the Umpire in the conduct of a match.

RULE 3

The Ball

The ball shall have a uniform outer surface and shall be white or yellow in colour. If there are any seams, they shall be stitchless.

The ball shall be more than two and a half inches (6.35cm.) and less than two and five-eighths inches (6.67cm.) in diameter, and more than two ounces (56.7 grams) and less than two and one-sixteenth ounces (58.5 grams) in weight.

The ball shall have a bound of more than 53 inches (135cm.) and less than 58 inches (147cm.) when dropped 100 inches (254cm.) upon a concrete base.

The ball shall have a forward deformation of more than .220 of an inch (.56cm.) and less than .290 of an inch (.74cm.) and a return deformation of more than .350 of an inch (.89cm.) and less than .425 of an inch (1.08cm.) at 18 lb. (8.165kg.) load. The two deformation figures shall be the averages of three individual readings along three axes of the ball and no two individual readings shall differ by more than .030 of an inch (.08cm.) in each case.

RULE 4

The Racket

Rackets failing to comply with the following specifications are not approved for play under the Rules of Tennis:

(a) The hitting surface of the racket shall be flat and consist of a pattern of crossed strings connected to a frame and alternately interlaced or bonded where they cross; and the stringing pattern shall be generally uniform, and in particular not less dense in the centre than in any other area.

(b) The frame of the racket shall not exceed 32 inches (81.28cm.) in overall length, including the handle and 12½ inches (31.75cm.) in overall width. The strung surface shall not exceed 15½ inches (39.37cm.) in overall length, and 11½ inches (29.21cm.) in overall width.

(c) The frame, including the handle, and the strings:

(i) shall be free of attached objects and protrusions, other than those utilised solely and specifically to limit or prevent wear and tear or vibration, or to distribute weight, and which are reasonable in size and placement for such purposes; and

(ii) shall be free of any device which makes it possible for a player to change materially the shape of the racket.

The International Tennis Federation shall rule on the question of whether any racket or prototype complies with the above specifications or is otherwise approved, or not approved, for play. Such ruling may be undertaken on its own initiative, or upon application by any party with a bona fide interest therein, including any player, equipment manufacturer or National Association or members thereof. Such rulings and applications shall be made in accordance with the applicable Review and Hearing Procedures of the International Tennis Federation, copies of which may be obtained from the office of the Secretary.

RULE 5

Server and Receiver

The players shall stand on opposite sides of the net; the player who first delivers the ball shall be called the Server, and the other the Receiver.

Case 1. Does a player, attempting a stroke, lose the point if he crosses an imaginary line in the extension of the net,

(a) before striking the ball,

(b) after striking the ball?

Decision. He does not lose the point in either case by crossing the imaginary line and provided he does not enter the lines bounding his opponent's Court (Rule 20(e)). In regard to hindrance, his opponent may ask for the decision of the Umpire under Rules 21 and 25.

Case 2. The Server claims that the Receiver must stand within the lines bounding his Court. Is this necessary?

Decision. No. The Receiver may stand wherever he pleases on his own side of the net.

RULE 6

Choice of Ends and Service

The choice of ends and the right to be Server or Receiver in the first game shall be decided by toss. The player winning the toss may choose or require his opponent to choose:

(a) The right to be Server or Receiver, in which case the other player shall choose the end; or

(b) The end, in which case the other player shall choose the right to be Server or Receiver.

USTA Comment: *These choices should be made promptly and are irrevocable.*

RULE 7

The Service

The service shall be delivered in the following manner. Immediately before commencing to serve, the Server shall stand with both feet at rest behind (i.e., further from the net than) the base-line, and within the imaginary continuations of the centre-mark and side-line. The Server shall then project the ball by hand into the air in any direction and before it hits the ground strike it with his racket, and the delivery shall be deemed to have been completed at the moment of the impact of the racket and the ball. A player with the use of only one arm may utilize his racket for the projection.

USTA Comment: *The service begins when the Server takes a ready position and ends when his racket makes contact with the ball, or when he misses the ball in attempting to serve it.*

Case 1. May the Server in a singles game take his stand behind the portion of the base-line between the side-lines of the Singles Court and the Doubles Court?

Decision. No.

Case 2. If a player, when serving, throws up two or more balls instead of one, does he lose that service?

Decision. No. A let should be called, but if the Umpire regards the action as deliberate he may take action under Rule 21.

USTA Case 3. May a player serve underhand?

Decision. Yes. There is no restriction regarding the kind of service which may be used; that is, the player may use an underhand or overhand service at his discretion.

RULE 8

Foot Fault

The Server shall throughout the delivery of the service:

(a) Not change his position by walking or running.

(b) Not touch, with either foot, any area other than that behind the base-line within the imaginary extensions of the centre mark and side-lines.

Note: The following interpretation of Rule 8 was approved by the International Tennis Federation on 9th July, 1958:

(a) The Server shall not, by slight movements of the feet which do not materially affect the location originally taken up by him, be deemed "to change his position by walking or running".

(b) The word "foot" means the extremity of the leg below the ankle.

USTA Comment: *This rule covers the most decisive stroke in the game, and there is no justification for its not being obeyed by players and enforced by officials. No official has the right to instruct any umpire to disregard violations of it. In a non-officiated match, it is the prerogative of the Receiver, or his partner, to call foot faults, but only after all efforts (appeal to the server, requests for an umpire, etc.) have failed, and the foot faulting is so flagrant as to be clearly perceptible from the Receiver's side.*

RULE 9

Delivery of Service

(a) In delivering the service, the Server shall stand alternately behind the right and left Courts beginning from the right in every game. If service from a wrong half of the Court occurs and is undetected, all play resulting from such wrong service or services shall stand, but the inaccuracy of station shall be corrected immediately it is discovered.

(b) The ball served shall pass over the net and hit the ground within the Service Court which is diagonally opposite, or upon any line bounding such Court, before the Receiver returns it.

RULE 10

Service Fault

The Service is a fault:
(a) If the Server commits any breach of Rules 7, 8 or 9;
(b) If he misses the ball in attempting to strike it;
(c) If the ball served touches a permanent fixture (other than the net, strap or band) before it hits the ground.

Case 1. After throwing a ball up preparatry to serving, the Server decides not to strike at it and catches it instead. Is it a fault?

Decision. No.

USTA Comment: *As long as the Server makes no attempt to strike the ball, it is immaterial whether he catches it in his hand or racket or lets it drop to the ground.*

Case 2. In serving in a singles game played on a Doubles Court with doubles posts and singles sticks, the ball hits a singles stick and then hits the ground within the lines of the correct Service Court. Is this a fault or a let?

Decision. In serving it is a fault, because the singles stick, the doubles post, and that portion of the net, or band between them are permanent fixtures. (Rules 2 and 10, and note to Rule 24.).

USTA Comment: *The significant point governing Case 2 is that the part of the net and band "outside" the singles sticks is not part of the net over which this singles match is being played. Thus such a serve is a fault under the provisions of Article (c) above... By the same token, this would be a fault also if it were a singles game played with permanent posts in the singles position. (See Case 1 under Rule 24 for difference between "service" and "good return" with respect to a ball's hitting a net post.)*

USTA Comment: *In matches played without umpires each player makes calls for all balls hit to his side of the net. In doubles, normally the Receiver's partner makes the calls with respect to the service line, with the Receiver calling the side and center lines, but either partner may make the call on any ball he clearly sees out.*

RULE 11

Second Service

After a fault (if it is the first fault) the Server shall serve again from behind the same half of the Court from which he served that fault, unless the service was from the wrong half, when, in accordance with Rule 9, the Server shall be entitled to one service only from behind the other half.

Case 1. A player serves from a wrong Court. He loses the point and then claims it was a fault because of his wrong station.

Decision. The point stands as played and the next service should be from the correct station according to the score.

Case 2. The point score being 15 all, the Server, by mistake, serves from the left-hand Court. He wins the point. He then serves again from the right-hand Court, delivering a fault. This mistake in station is then discovered. Is he entitled to the previous point? From which Court should he next serve?

Decision. The previous point stands. The next service should be from the left-hand Court, the score being 30/15, and the Server has served one fault.

RULE 12

When To Serve

The Server shall not serve until the Receiver is ready. If the latter attempts to return the service, he shall be deemed ready. If, however, the Receiver signifies that he is not ready, he may not claim a fault because the ball does not hit the ground within the limits fixed for the service.

USTA Comment: *The Server must wait until the Receiver is ready for the second service as well as the first, and if the Receiver claims to be not ready and does not make any effort to return a service, the Server may not claim the point, even though the service was good.*

RULE 13

The Let

In all cases where a let has to be called under the rules, or to provide for an interruption to play, it shall have the following interpretations:

(a) When called solely in respect of a service that one service only shall be replayed.

(b) When called under any other circumstance, the point shall be replayed.

USTA Comment: *A service that touches the net in passing yet falls into the proper court (or touches the receiver) is a let. This word is used also when, because of an interruption while the ball is in play, or for any other reason, a point is to be replayed. A spectator's outcry (of "out", "fault" or other) is not a valid basis for replay of a point, but action should be taken to prevent a recurrence.*

Case 1. A service is interrupted by some cause outside those defined in Rule 14. Should the service only be replayed?

Decision. No, the whole point must be replayed.

USTA Comment: *The phrase "in respect of a service" in (a) means a let because a served ball has touched the net before landing in the proper court, OR because the Receiver was not ready... Case 1 refers to a second serve, and the decision means that if the interruption occurs during delivery of the second service, the Server gets* two serves. Example: On a second service a linesman calls "fault" and imediately correcrs it (the Receiver meanwhile having let the ball go by). The Server is entitled to two serves, on this ground: The corrected call means that the Server has put the ball into play with a good service, and once the ball is in play and a let is called, the point must be replayed . . Note, however, that if the serve is an unmistakable ace — that is, the Umpire is sure the erroneous call had no part in the Receiver's inability to play the ball — the point should be declared for the Server.

Case 2. If a ball in play becomes broken, should a let be called?

Decision. Yes.

USTA Comment: *A ball shall be regarded as having become "broken" if, in the opinion of the Chair Umpire, it is found to have lost compression to the point of being unfit for further play, or unfit for any reason, and it is clear the defective ball was the one in play.*

RULE 14

The "Let" in Service

The service is a let:

(a) If the ball served touches the net, strap or band, and is otherwise good, or, after touching the net, strap or band, touches the Receiver or anything which he wears or carries before hitting the ground.

(b) If a service or a fault is delivered when the Receiver is not ready (see Rule 12).

In case of a let, that particular service shall not count, and the Server shall serve again, but a service let does not annul a previous fault.

RULE 15

Order of Service

At the end of the first game the Receiver shall become Server, and the Server Receiver; and so on alternately in all the subsequent games of a match. If a player serves out of turn, the player who ought to have served shall serve as soon as the mistake is discovered, but all points scored before such discovery shall be reckoned. If a game shall have been completed before such discovery, the order of service remains as altered. A fault served before such discovery shall not be reckoned.

RULE 16

When Players Change Ends

The players shall change ends at the end of the first, third and every subsequent alternate game of each set, and at the end of each set unless the total number of games in such set is even, in which case the change is not made until the end of the first game of the next set.

If a mistake is made and the correct sequence is not followed the players must take up their correct station as soon as the discovery is made and follow their original sequence.

RULE 17

The Ball in Play

A ball is in play from the moment at which it is delivered in service. Unless a fault or a let is called it remains in play until the point is decided.

USTA Comment: *A point is not "decided" simply when, or because, a good shot has clearly passed a player, or when an apparently bad shot passes over a baseline or sideline. An outgoing ball is still definitely "in play" until it actually strikes the ground, backstop or a permanent fixture, or a player. The same applies to a good ball, bounding after it has landed in the proper court. A ball that becomes imbedded in the net is out of play.*

Case 1. A player fails to make a good return. No call is made and the ball remains in play. May his opponent later claim the point after the rally has ended?

Decision. No. The point may not be claimed if the players continue to play after the error has been made, provided the opponent was not hindered.

USTA Comment: *To be valid, an out call on A's shot to B's court, that B plays, must be made before B's return has either gone out of play or has been hit by A. See Case 3 under Rule 29.*

USTA Case 2. A ball is played into the net; the player on the other side, thinking that the ball is coming over, strikes at it and hits the net. Who loses the point?

Decision. If the player touched the net while the ball was still in play, he loses the point.

RULE 18

Server Wins Point

The Server wins the point:

(a) If the ball served, not being a let under Rule 14, touches the Receiver or anything which he wears or carries, before it hits the ground;

(b) If the Receiver otherwise loses the point as provided by Rule 20.

RULE 19

Receiver Wins Point

The Receiver wins the point:

(a) If the Server serves two consecutive faults;

RULE 20

Player Loses Point

A player loses the point if:

(a) He fails, before the ball in play has hit the ground twice consecutively, to return it directly over the net (except as provided in Rule 24(a) or (c); or

(b) He returns the ball in play so that it hits the ground, a permanent fixture, or other object, outside any of the lines which bound his opponent's Court (except as provided in Rule 24(a) or (c)); or

USTA Comment: *A ball hitting a scoring device or other object attached to a net post results in loss of point to the striker.*

(c) He volleys the ball and fails to make a good return even when standing outside the Court; or

(d) In playing the ball he deliberately carries or catches it on his racket or deliberately touches it with his racket more than once; or

USTA Comment: *Only when there is a definite "second push" by the player does his shot become illegal, with consequent loss of point. It should be noted that the word "deliberately" is the key word in this Rule and that two hits occurring in the course of a single continuous stroke would not be deemed a double hit.*

(e) He or his racket (in his hand or otherwise) or anything which he wears or carries touches the net, posts, singles sticks, cord or metal cable, strap or band, or the ground within his opponent's Court at any time while the ball is in play; or

USTA Comment: *Touching a pipe support that runs across the court at the bottom of the net is interpreted as touching the net; See USTA Comment under Rule 23.*

(f) He volleys the ball before it has passed the net; or

(g) The ball in play touches him or anything that he wears or carries, except his racket in his hand or hands; or

USTA Comment: *This loss of point occurs regardless of whether the player is inside or outside the bounds of his court when the ball touches him. Except for a ball used in a first service fault, a player is considered to be "wearing or carrying" anything that he was wearing or carrying at the beginning of the point during which the touch occurred. Exception: If an object worn or carried by a player falls to the ground and a ball hit by his opponent hits that object, then (1) if the ball falls outside the court, the opponent loses the point; (2) if the ball falls inside the court, a let is to be called.*

(h) He throws his racket at and hits the ball; or

(i) He deliberately and materially changes the shape of his racket during the playing of the point.

Case 1. In delivering a first service which falls outside the proper Court, the Server's racket slips out of his hand and flies into the net. Does he lose the point?

Decision. If his racket touches the net whilst the ball is in play, the Server loses the point (Rule 20*(e)*).

Case 2. In serving, the racket flies from the Server's hand and touches the net before the ball has touched the ground. Is this a fault, or does the player lose the point?

Decision. The Server loses the point because his racket touches the net whilst the ball is in play (Rule 20*(e)*).

Case 3. A and B are playing against C and D, A is serving to D, C touches the net before the ball touches the ground. A fault is then called because the service falls outside the Service Court. Do C and D lose the point?

Decision. The call "fault" is an erroneous one. C and D had already lost the point before "fault" could be called, because C touched the net whilst the ball was in play (Rule 20*(e)*).

Case 4. May a player jump over the net into his opponent's Court while the ball is in play and not suffer penalty?

Decision. No. He loses the point (Rule 20*(e)*).

Case 5. A cuts the ball just over the net, and it returns to A's side. B, unable to reach the ball, throws his racket and hits the ball. Both racket and ball fall over the net on A's Court. A returns the ball outside of B's Court. Does B win or lose the point?

Decision. B loses the point (Rule 20*(e)* and *(h)*).

Case 6. A player standing outside the service Court is struck by a service ball before it has touched the ground. Does he win or lose the point?

Decision. The player struck loses the point (Rule 20*(g)*), except as provided under Rule 14*(a)*.

Case 7. A player standing outside the Court volleys the ball or catches it in his hand and claims the point because the ball was certainly going out of court.

Decision. In no circumstances can he claim the point:

(1) If he catches the ball he loses the point under Rule 20*(g)*.

(2) If he volleys it and makes a bad return he loses the point under Rule 20*(c)*.

(3) If he volleys it and makes a good return, the rally continues.

RULE 21

Player Hinders Opponent

If a player commits any act which hinders his opponent in making a stroke, then, if this is deliberate, he shall lose the point or if involuntary, the point shall be replayed.

USTA Comment: *'Deliberate' means a player did what he intended to do, although the resulting effect on his opponent might* or might not have been what he intended. Example: a player, after his return is in the air, gives advice to his partner in such a loud voice that his opponent is hindered. 'Involuntary' means a non-intentional act such as a hat blowing off or a scream resulting from a sudden wasp sting.

Case 1. Is a player liable to a penalty if in making a stroke he touches his opponent?

Decision. No, unless the Umpire deems it necessary to take action under Rule 21.

Case 2. When a ball bounds back over the net, the player concerned may reach over the net in order to play the ball. What is the ruling if the player is hindered from doing this by his opponent?

Decision. In accordance with Rule 21, the Umpire may either award the point to the player hindered, or order the point to be replayed. (See also Rule 25).

Case 3. Does an involuntary double hit constitute an act which hinders an opponent within Rule 21?

Decision. No.

USTA Comment: *Upon appeal by a competitor that an opponent's action in discarding a "second ball" after a rally has started constitutes a distraction (hindrance), the Umpire, if he deems the claim valid, shall require the opponent to make some other nd satisfactory disposition of the ball. Failure to comply with this instruction may result in loss of point(s) or disqualification.*

RULE 22

Ball Falls on Line

A ball falling on a line is regarded as falling in the Court bounded by that line.

USTA Comment: *In matches played without officials, it is customary for each player to make the calls on all balls hit to his side of the net, and if a player cannot call a ball out with surety he should regard it as good. See The Code.*

RULE 23

Ball Touches Permanent Fixture

If the ball in play touches a permanent fixture (other than the net, posts, singles sticks, cord or metal cable, strap or band) after it has hit the ground, the player who struck it wins the point; if before it hits the ground, his opponent wins the point.

Case 1. A return hits the Umpire or his chair or stand. The player claims that the ball was going into Court.

Decision. He loses the point.

USTA Comment: *A ball in play that after passing the net strikes a pipe support running across the court at the base of the net is regarded the same as a ball landing on clear ground. See also Rule 20(e).*

RULE 24

A Good Return

It is a good return:

(a) If the ball touches the net, posts, singles sticks, cord or metal cable, strap or band, provided that it passes over any of them and hits the ground within the Court; or

(b) If the ball, served or returned, hits the ground within the proper Court and rebounds or is blown back over the net, and the player whose turn it is to strike reaches over the net and plays the ball, provided that neither he nor any part of his clothes or racket touches the net, posts, singles sticks, cord or metal cable, strap or band or the ground within his opponent's Court, and that the stroke is otherwise good; or

(c) If the ball is returned outside the posts, or singles sticks, either above or below the level of the top of the net, even though it touches the posts or singles sticks, provided that it hits the ground within the proper Court; or

(d) If a player's racket passes over the net after he has returned the ball, provided the ball passes the net before being played and is properly returned; or

(e) If a player succeeds in returning the ball, served or in play, which strikes a ball lying in the Court.

USTA Comment: *i.e., on his court when the point started; if the ball in play strikes a ball, rolling or stationary on the court, that has come from elsewhere after the point started, a let should be called. See USTA Comment under Rule 20g.*

Note to Rule 24: In a singles match, if, for the sake of convenience, a doubles Court is equipped with singles sticks for the purpose of a singles game, then the doubles posts and those portions of the net, cord or metal cable and the band outside such singles sticks shall at all times be permanent fixtures, and are not regarded as posts or parts of the net of a singles game.

A return that passes under the net cord between the singles stick and adjacent doubles post without touching either net cord, net or doubles post and falls within the area of play, is a good return.

USTA Comment: *But in doubles this would be a "through" — loss of point.*

Case 1. A ball going out of Court hits a net post or singles stick and falls within the lines of the opponent's Court. Is the stroke good?

Decision. If a service: no, under Rule 10(c). If other than a service: yes, under Rule 24(a).

Case 2. Is it a good return if a player returns the ball holding his racket in both hands?

Decision. Yes.

Case 3. The service, or ball in play, strikes a ball lying in the Court. Is the point won or lost thereby?

USTA Comment: *A ball that is touching a boundary line is considered to be "lying in the court".*

Decision. No. Play must continue. If it is not clear to the Umpire that the right ball is returned a let should be called.

Case 4. May a player use more than one racket at any time during play?

Decision. No; the whole implication of the Rules is singular.

Case 5. May a player request that a ball or balls lying in his opponent's Court be removed?

Decision. Yes, but not while a ball is in play.

USTA Comment: *The request must be honored.*

RULE 25

Hindrance of a Player

In case a player is hindered in making a stroke by anything not within his control, except a permanent fixture of the Court, or except as provided for in Rule 21, a let shall be called.

Case 1. A spectator gets into the way of a player, who fails to return the ball. May the player then claim a let?

Decision. Yes, if in the Umpire's opinion he was obstructed by circumstances beyond his control, but not if due to permanent fixtures of the Court or the arrangements of the ground.

Case 2. A player is interfered with as in Case No. 1, and the Umpire calls a let. The Server had previously served a fault. Has he the right to two services?

Decision. Yes: as the ball is in play, the point, not merely the stroke, must be replayed as the Rule provides.

Case 3. May a player claim a let under Rule 25 because he thought his opponent was being hindered, and consequently did not expect the ball to be returned?

Decision. No.

Case 4. Is a stroke good when a ball in play hits another ball in the air?

Decision. A let should be called unless the other ball is in the air by the act of one of the players, in which case the Umpire will decide under Rule 21.

Case 5. If an Umpire or other judge erroneously calls "fault" or "out", and then corrects himself, which of the calls shall prevail?

Decision. A let must be called unless, in the opinion of the Umpire, neither player is hindered in his game, in which case the corrected call shall prevail.

Case 6. If the first ball served — a fault — rebounds, interfering with the Receiver at the time of the second service, may the Receiver claim a let?

Decision. Yes. But if he had an opportunity to remove the ball from the Court and negligently failed to do so, he may not claim a let.

Case 7. Is it a good stroke if the ball touches a stationary or moving object on the Court?

Decision. It is a good stroke unless the stationary object came into Court after the ball was put into play in which case a let must be called. If the ball in play strikes an object moving along or above the surface of the Court a let must be called.

Case 8. What is the ruling if the first service is a fault, the second service correct, and it becomes necessary to call a let either under the provision of Rule 25 or if the Umpire is unable to decide the point?

Decision. The fault shall be annulled and the whole point replayed.

USTA Comment: *See Rule 13 and Explanation thereto.*

RULE 26

Score in a Game

If a player wins his first point, the score is called 15 for that player; on winning his second point, the score is called 30 for that player; on winning his third point, the score is called 40 for that player, and the fourth point won by a player is scored game for that player except as below:

If both players have won three points, the score is called deuce; and the next point won by a player is scored advantage for that player. If the same player wins the next point, he wins the game; if the other player wins the next point the score is again called deuce; and so on, until a player wins the two points immediately following the score at deuce, when the game is scored for that player.

USTA Comment: *In matches played without an umpire the Server should announce, in a voice audible to his opponent and spectators, the set score at the beginning of each game, and (audible at least to his opponent) point scores as the game goes on. Misunderstandings will be avoided if this practice is followed.*

RULE 27

Score in a Set

(a) A player (or players) who first wins six games wins a set; except that he must win by a margin of two games over his opponent and where necessary a set is extended until this margin is achieved.

(b) The tie-break system of scoring may be adopted as an alternative to the advantage set system in paragraph (a) of this Rule provided the decision is announced in advance of the match.

USTA Comment: *See the Tie-Break System in the appendix of this book.*

In this case, the following Rules shall be effective:

The tie-break shall operate when the score reaches six games all in any set except in the third or fifth set of a three set or five set match respectively when an ordinary advantage set shall be played, unless otherwise decided and announced in advance of the match.

The following system shall be used in a tie-break game.

Singles

(i) A player who first wins seven points shall win the game and the set provided he leads by a margin of two points. If the score reaches six points all the game shall be extended until this margin has been achieved. Numerical scoring shall be used throughout the tie-break game.

(ii) The player whose turn it is to serve shall be the server for the first point. His opponent shall be the server for the second and third points and thereafter each player shall serve alternately for two consecutive points until the winner of the game and set has been decided.

(iii) From the first point, each service shall be delivered alternately from the right and left courts, beginning from the right court. If service from a wrong half of the court occurs and is undetected, all play resulting from such wrong service or services shall stand, but the inaccuracy of station shall be corrected immediately it is discovered.

(iv) Players shall change ends after every six points and at the conclusion of the tie-break game.

(v) The tie-break game shall count as one game for the ball change, except that, if the balls are due to be changed at the beginning of the tie-break, the change shall be delayed until the second game of the following set.

Doubles

In doubles the procedure for singles shall apply. The player whose turn it is to serve shall be the server for the first point. Thereafter each player shall serve in rotation for two points, in the same order as previously in that set, until the winners of the game and set have been decided.

Rotation of Service

The player (or pair in the case of doubles) who served first in the tie-break game shall receive service in the first game of the following set.

Case 1. At six all the tie-break is played, although it has been decided and announced in advance of the match that an advantage set will be played. Are the points already played counted?

Decision. If the error is discovered before the ball is put in play for the second point, the first point shall count but the error shall be corrected immediately. If the error is discovered after the ball is put in play for the second point the game shall continue as a tie-break game.

Case 2. At six all, an advantage game is played, although it has been decided and announced in advance of the match that a tie-break will be played. Are the points already played counted?

Decision. If the error is discovered before the ball is put in play for the second point, the first point shall be counted but the error shall be corrected immediately. If the error is discovered after the ball is put in play for the second point an advantage set shall be played.

Case 3. If during the tie-break in a doubles game a partner receives out of turn, or a player serves out of rotation, shall the order of receiving, or serving as the case may be, remain as altered until the end of the game?

Decision. Yes.

RULE 28

Maximum Number of Sets

The maximum number of sets in a match shall be 5, or, where women take part, 3.

RULE 29

Role of Court Officials

In matches where an Umpire is appointed, his decision shall be final; but where a Referee is appointed, an appeal shall lie to him from the decision of an Umpire on a question of law, and in all such cases the decision of the Referee shall be final.

In matches where assistants to the Umpire are appointed (Linesmen, Net-cord Judges, Foot-fault Judges) their decisions shall be final on questions of fact except that if in the opinion of an Umpire a clear mistake has been made he shall have the right to change the decision of an assistant or order a let to be played. When such an assistant is unable to give a decision he shall indicate this immediately to the Umpire who shall give a decision. When an Umpire is unable to give a decision on a question of fact he shall order a let to be played.

In Davis Cup matches or other team competitions where a Referee is on Court, any decision can be changed by the Referee, who may also instruct an Umpire to order a let to be played.

The Referee, in his discretion, may at any time postpone a match on account of darkness or the condition of the ground or the weather. In any case of postponement the previous score and previous occupancy of Courts shall hold good, unless the Referee and the players unanimously agree otherwise.

Case 1. The Umpire orders a let, but a player claims that the point should not be replayed. May the Referee be requested to give a decision?

Decision. Yes. A question of tennis law, that is an issue relating to the application of specific facts, shall first be determined by the Umpire. However, if the Umpire is uncertain or if a player appeals from his determination, then the Referee shall be requested to give a decision, and his decision is final.

Case 2. A ball is called out, but a player claims that the ball was good. May the Referee give a ruling?

Decision. No. This is a question of fact, that is an issue relating to what actually occurred during a specific incident, and the decision of the on-court officials is therefore final.

Case 3. May an Umpire overrule a Linesman at the end of a rally if, in his opinion, a clear mistake has been made during the course of a rally?

Decision. No, unless in his opinion the opponent was hindered. Otherwise an Umpire may only overrule a Linesman if he does so immediately after the mistake has been made.

USTA Comment: *See Rule 17, Case 1.*

Case 4. A Linesman calls a ball out. The Umpire was unable to see clearly, although he thought the ball was in. May he overrule the Linesman?

Decision. No. An Umpire may only overrule if he considers that a call was incorrect beyond all reasonable doubt. He may only overrule a ball determined good by a Linesman if he has been able to see a space between the ball and the line; and he may only overrule a ball determined out, or a fault, by a Linesman if he has seen the ball hit the line, or fall inside the line.

Case 5. May a Linesman change his call after the Umpire has given the score?

Decision. No. If a Linesman realises he has made an error, he must call "correction" immediately so that the Umpire and players are aware of his error before the score is given.

Case 6. A player claims his return shot was good after a Linesman called "out". May the Umpire overrule the Linesman?

Decision. No. An Umpire may never overrule as a result of a protest or an appeal by a player.

RULE 30

Continuous Play and Rest Periods

Play shall be continuous from the first service till the match be concluded.

(a) Notwithstanding the above, after the third set, or when women take part the second set, either player is entitled to a rest, which shall not exceed 10 minutes, or in countries situated between Latitude 15 degrees North and Latitude 15 degrees South, 45 minutes and furthermore, when necessitated by circumstances not within the control of the players, the Umpire may suspend play for such a period as he may consider necessary.

If play is suspended and is not resumed until a later day the rest may be taken only after the third set (or when women take part the second set) of play on such later day, completion of an unfinished set being counted as one set.

If play is suspended and is not resumed until 10 minutes have elapsed in the same day the rest may be taken only after three consecutive sets have been played without interruption (or when women take part two sets), completion of an unfinished set being counted as one set.

Any national and/or committee organising a tournament, match or competition, other than the International Tennis Championships (Davis Cup and Federation Cup), is at liberty to modify this provision or omit it from its regulations provided this is announced before play commences.

USTA Rules Regarding Rest Periods

Regular MEN's and WOMEN's, and MEN's and WOMEN's Amateur — Paragraph (a) of Rule 30 applies, except that a tournament using tie-breaks may eliminate rest periods provided advance notice is given.

BOYS' 18 — All matches in this division shall be best of three sets with NO REST PERIOD, except that in interscholastic, state, sectional and national championships the FINAL ROUND may be best-of-five sets. If such a final requires more than three sets to decide it, a rest of 10 minutes after the third set is mandatory. Special Note: In severe temperature-humidity conditions the the Referee may rule that a 10-minute rest may be taken in a Boys' 18 best-of-three before the third set. However, to be valid this must be done before the match is started, and as a matter of the Referee's independent judgment.

BOYS' 16, 14 and 12, and GIRLS' 18, 16, 14 and 12 — All matches in these categories shall be best of three sets. A 10-minute rest before the third set is MANDATORY in Girls' 12, 14 and 16, and BOYS' 12 and 14. The rest period is OPTIONAL in GIRLS' 18 and. BOYS' 16. (Optional means at the option of any competitor).

All SENIOR divisions (35 and over), Mother-Daughter, Father-Son and similar combinations: Under conventional scoring, all matches best of three sets, with rest period at any player's option.

When 'NO-AD' scoring is used in a tournament the committee may stipulate that there will be no rest periods. Two conditions of this stipulation are: (1) Advance notice must be given on entry blanks for the event, and (2) The Referee is empowered to reinstate the normal rest periods for matches played under unusually severe temperature-humidity conditions; to be valid, such reinstatement must be announced before a given match or series of matches is started, and be a matter of the Referee's independent judgment.

USTA Comment: *When a player competes in an event designated as for players of a bracket whose rules as to intermissions and length of match are geared to a different physical status, the player cannot* ask for allowances based on his or her age, or her sex. For example, a female competing in an intercollegiate (men's) varsity team match would not be entitled to claim a rest period in a best-of-three-sets match unless that were the condition under which the team competition was normally held.

(b) Play shall never be suspended, delayed or interfered with for the purpose of enabling a player to recover his strength or his breath.

(c) A maximum of 30 seconds shall elapse from the moment the ball goes out of play at the end of one point to the time the ball is struck for the next point. In the event such first serve is a fault, then the second serve must be struck by the Server without delay.

The Receiver must play to the reasonable pace of the Server and must be ready to receive when the Server is ready to serve within the permitted time.

When changing ends a maximum of one minute thirty seconds shall elapse from the moment the ball goes out of play at the end of the game to the time the ball is struck for the first point of the next game.

The Umpire shall use his discretion when there is interference which makes it impossible for the server to serve within that time.

These provisions shall be strictly construed. The Umpire shall be the sole judge of any suspension, delay or interference, and after giving due warning he may disqualify the offender.

Note: A Tournament Committee has discretion to decide the time allowed for a warm-up period prior to a match. It is recommended that this does not exceed five minutes.

Case 1. A player's clothing, footwear, or equipment (excluding racket) becomes out of adjustment in such a way that it is impossible or undesirable for him to play on. May play be suspended while the maladjustment is rectified?

Decision. If this occurs in circumstances outside the control of the player, a suspension may be allowed. The Umpire shall be the sole judge of whether a suspension is justified and the period of the suspension.

Case 2. If, owing to an accident, a player is unable to continue immediately, is there any limit to the time during which play may be suspended?

Decision. No allowance may be made for natural loss of physical condition. In the case of accidental injury the Umpire may allow a one-time, three minute suspension for that injury. Play must resume in three minutes. However, the organizers of international circuits and team events recognized by the ITF may extend this if treatment is necessary.

USTA Comment: Case 2 refers to an important distinction that should be made between a disability caused by an accident during the match, and disability attributable to fatigue, illness or exertion (examples: cramps, muscle pull, vertigo, strained back). Accidental loss embodies a sprained ankle or actual injury from such mishaps as collision with netpost or net, a cut from a fall, contact with chair or backstop, or being hit with a ball, racket or other object. An injured player shall not be permitted to leave the playing area. If, in the opinion of the Umpire, there is a genuine toilet emergency, a bona fide toilet visit by a player is permissible and is not to be considered natural loss of condition.

Case 3. During a doubles game, may one of the partners leave the Court while the ball is in play?

Decision. Yes, so long as the Umpire is satisfied that play is continuous within the meaning of the Rules, and that there is no conflict with Rules 35 and 36.

USTA Comment: When a match is resumed following an interruption exceeding 10 minutes necessitated by weather or other unusual conditions, it is allowable for the players to engage in a "re-warm-up," using the balls that were in play at the time of the interruption, with the time for the next ball change not being affected. The duration of the re-warm-up will be as follows: 0-10 minutes delay, no warm-up; 11-20 minutes delay, 3 minutes warm-up; more than 20 minutes delay, 5 minutes warm-up.

RULE 31

Coaching

During the playing of a match in a team competition, a player may receive coaching from a captain who is sitting on the Court only when he changes ends at the end of a game, but not when he changes ends during a tie-break game.

A player may not receive coaching during the playing of any other match.

The provisions of this rule must be strictly construed. After due warning an offending player may be disqualified.

Case 1. Should a warning be given, or the player be disqualified, if the coaching is given by signals in an unobtrusive manner?

Decision. The Umpire must take action as soon as he becomes aware that coaching is being given verbally or by signals. If the Umpire is unaware that coaching is being given, a player may draw his attention to the fact that advice is being given.

Case 2. Can a player receive coaching during the ten minute rest in a five set match, or when play is interrupted and he leaves the court?

Decision. Yes. In these circumstances, when the player is not on the Court, there is no restriction on coaching.

Note: The word "coaching" includes any advice or instruction.

RULE 32

Changing Balls

In cases where balls are changed after an agreed number of games, if the balls are not changed in the correct sequence the mistake shall be corrected when the player, or pair in the case of doubles, who should have served with new balls is next due to serve.

THE DOUBLES GAME

RULE 33

The above Rules shall apply to the Doubles Games except as below.

RULE 34

The Doubles Court

For the Doubles Game, the Court shall be 36 feet (10.97m.) in width, i.e., 4½ feet (1.37m.) wider on each side than the Court for the Singles Game, and those portions of the singles side-lines which lie between the two service-lines shall be called the service side-lines. In other respects, the Court shall be similar to that described in Rule 1, but the portions of the singles side-lines between the base-line and service-line on each side of the net may be omitted if desired.

USTA Case 1. In doubles the Server claims the right to stand at the corner of the Court as marked by the doubles sideline. Is the foregoing correct or is it necessary that the Server stand within the limits of the center mark and the singles sideline?

Decision. The Server has the right to stand anywhere back of the baseline between the center mark extension and the double sideline extension.

RULE 35

Order of Service in Doubles

The order of serving shall be decided at the beginning of each set as follows:

The pair who have to serve in the first game of each set shall decide which partner shall do so and the opposing pair shall decide similarly for the second game. The partner of the player who served in the first game shall serve in the third; the partner of the player who served in the second game shall serve in the fourth, and so on in the same order in all the subsequent games of a set.

Case 1. In doubles, one player does not appear in time to play, and his partner claims to be allowed to play single-handed against the opposing player. May he do so?

Decision. No.

RULE 36

Order of Receiving in Doubles

The order of receiving the service shall be decided at the beginning of each set as follows:

The pair who have to receive the service in the first game shall decide which partner shall receive the first service, and that partner shall continue to receive the first service in every odd game throughout that set. The opposing pair shall likewise decide which partner shall receive the first service in the second game and that partner shall continue to receive the first service in every even game throughout that set. Partners shall receive the service alternately throughout each game.

Case 1. Is it allowable in doubles for the Server's partner to stand in a position that obstructs the view of the Receiver?

Decision. Yes. The Server's partner may take any position on his side of the net in or out of the Court that he wishes.

USTA Comment: *The same is true of the Receiver's partner.*

RULE 37

Service Out of Turn in Doubles

If a partner serves out of his turn, the partner who ought to have served shall serve as soon as the mistake is discovered, but all points scored, and any faults served before such discovery, shall be reckoned. If a game shall have been completed before such discovery, the order of service remains as altered.

USTA Comment: *For an exception to Rule 37 see Case 3 under Rule 27.*

RULE 38

Error in Order of Receiving in Doubles

If during a game the order of receiving the service is changed by the Receivers it shall remain as altered until the end of the game in which the mistake is discovered, but the partners shall resume their original order of receiving in the next game of that set in which they are Receivers of the service.

RULE 39

Service Fault in Doubles

The service is a fault as provided for by Rule 10, or if the ball touches the Server's partner or anything which he wears or carries; but if the ball served touches the partner of the Receiver, or anything which he wears or carries, not being a let under Rule 14(a) before it hits the ground, the Server wins the point.

RULE 40

Playing the Ball in Doubles

The ball shall be struck alternately by one or other player of the opposing pairs, and if a player touches the ball in play with his racket in contravention of this Rule, his opponents win the point.

USTA Comment: *This means that, in the course of making one return, only one member of a doubles team may hit the ball. If both of them hit the ball, either simultaneously or consecutively, it is an illegal return. The partners themselves do not have to "alternate" in making returns. Mere clashing of rackets does not make a return illegal, if it is clear that only one racket touched the ball.*

APPENDIX

THE TIE-BREAK SYSTEM

A tournament committee must announce before the start of its tournament the details concerning its use of tie-breaks. A tournament that has been authorized by the USTA or by a USTA Section to use VASSS No-Ad scoring may use the 9-point tie-break in any set played under No-Ad; it may change to the 12-point tie-break in its later rounds. No-Ad scoring is authorized for tournaments held at the Sectional Championship level and below, and for consolation matches in any tournament (excluding any USTA National Junior Championship). Other than the foregoing exceptions, all sanctioned tournaments using tie-breaks will use only the 12-point tie-break. Rule 27 establishes the procedure for the 12-point tie-break game. For a more detailed explanation see below.

If a ball change is due on a tie-break game it will be deferred until the second game of the next set. A tie-break game counts as one game in reckoning ball changes. The score of the tie-break set will be written 7-6(x) or 6-7(x), with the score of the winner of the match entered first, followed by the score of the tie-break game in parentheses, such as (10-8) or (8-10), with the score of the winner of the match again entered first. Changes of ends during a tie-break game are to be made within the normal 30 seconds allowed between points.

THE 12-POINT TIE-BREAK

Singles

A, having served the first game of the set, serves the first point from the right court; B serves points 2 and 3 (left and right), A serves points 4 and 5 (left and right); B serves point 6 (left) and after they change ends, point 7 (right); A serves points 8 and 9 (left and right); B serves points 10 and 11 (left and right), and A serves point 12 (left). A player who reaches 7 points during these first 12 points wins the game and set. If the score has reached 6 points all, the players change ends and continue in the same pattern until one player establishes a margin of two points, which gives him the game and set. Note that the players change ends every six points, and that the player who serves the last point of one of these 6-point segments also serves the first point of the next one (from right court). For a following set the players change ends, and B serves the first game.

Doubles

Doubles follows the same pattern, with partners preserving their serving sequence. Assume A-B versus C-D, with A having served the first game of the set. A serves the first point (right); C serves points 2 and 3 (left and right); B serves points 4 and 5 (left and right); D serves point 6 (left) and the teams change ends. D serves point 7 (right); A serves points 8 and 9 (left and right); C serves points 10 and 11 (left and right); B serves point 12 (left). A team that wins 7 points during these first 12 points wins the game and set. If the score has reached 6 points all, the teams change ends. B then serves point 13 (right), and they continue until one team establishes a two-point margin and thus wins the game and set. As in singles, they change ends for one game to start a following set, with team C-D to serve first.

THE 9-POINT TIE-BREAK

Singles

With A having served the first game of the set, he serves points 1 and 2, right court and left; then B serves points 3 and 4, right and left. Players change ends. A serves points 5 and 6, right and left, and B serves points 7 and 8, right and left. If the score reaches 4 points all B serves point 9, right or left at the election of A. The first player to win 5 points wins the game and set. The players stay for one game to start the next set, and B is the first server.

Doubles

The same format as in singles applies, with each player serving from the same end of the court in the tie-break game that he served from during the set. (Note that this operates to alter the sequence of serving by the partners on the *second*-serving team. With A-B versus C-D, if the serving sequence during the set was A-C-B-D the sequence becomes A-D-B-C in the tie-break.

VASSS NO-AD SCORING

The No-Ad procedure is simply what the name implies: the first player to win four points wins the game, the 7th point of a game becoming a game point for each player. The receiver has the choice of advantage court or deuce court to which the service is to be delivered on the 7th point. If a No-Ad set reaches 6-games all a tie-break shall be used which is normally the 9-point tie-break.

Note: The score-calling may be either in the conventional terms or in simple numbers, i.e., "zero, one, two, three, game."

Glossary

Ace — A point-winning serve that is hit beyond the reach of the receiver.

Ad — See ADVANTAGE.

Ad court — The left service court; also that court into which the serve is hit when the total number of points played in a game is an odd number.

Ad in — When the server has a score of advantage.

Ad out — When the receiver has a score of advantage.

Advantage — The next point after a deuce score. The player who wins the point is said to have the "advantage," and if that player also wins the following point, the player will have won the game; if not, the score returns to deuce. Often abbreviated to "ad."

Age-group tennis — Competition for males and females of all ages, starting at age 12, with players of like age playing against each other.

All — A tie score, as in 30-all, or four games all.

Alley — The area on either side of the singles court which is included as inbounds for doubles play.

American twist — A serve hit with exaggerated topspin.

Approach shot — A groundstroke hit by a player to prepare the way for an approach to the net.

Australian doubles — When both players of a doubles team take up a position, during the serve, on the same half of the court.

Backcourt — An undefined area in the vicinity of the baseline.

Backhand — A stroke used to play a ball on the left side of a right-handed player, and vice-versa.

Backhand court — Same as ad court; the left service court.

Backspin — Backward spin on the ball, with the top of the ball rotating away from the direction of its flight.

Baseline — The line marking the end of the court.

Baseline game — A manner of play whereby the player remains near the baseline and advances only infrequently to the net.

Break (or service break) — To win a game that the opponent serves.

Cannonball — A very fast, flat serve.

Center mark — A short line extended inward from the baseline as a continuation of the center service line, marking the two halves of the court and indicating the sides of the court in which the server must stand.

Center service line — The line dividing the service area into right (deuce) and left (ad) service courts.

Change of pace — The strategy of varying the speed of the ball from stroke to stroke.

Chip shot — A softly hit shot, usually with a great deal of backspin, intended to be dropped just over the net in front of a deep opponent.

Chop — To bring the racket into the ball with a downward motion, imparting backspin.

Closed stance — When a player has the forward foot closer to the sideline than the back foot.

Cross-court shot — Hitting the ball from one side of the court across the net to the side diagonally opposite.

Davis Cup — A series of men's team matches, with teams representing their home nation, played in an elimination-type tournament over several months, with the finals usually held in December.

Deuce — An even score in a game after six or more points have been played. Or, an even score in games after ten or more games have been played.

Deuce court — The right service court; also that court into which the serve is hit when the total points played in a game is an even number.

Dink — A term referring to any softly hit shot which is intended to be placed out of the reach of an opponent.

Double fault — Failure of a player to get either of the two service attempts into the proper service court.

Doubles — Match play between two teams of two players each.

Down-the-line shot — A ball hit across the net parallel to a sideline.

Drive — A firm groundstroke hit with the intent of being an outright winner or to force a weak return from the opponent.

Drop shot — A ball hit softly, from a groundstroke, so that it just clears the net and lands very close to it.

Drop volley — A ball hit softly from a volley stroke, with the same intent as a drop shot.

Fault — A served ball that does not land within the proper service court. Or, any other violation of the rules of service.

Flat serve — A serve hit with no attempt to spin the ball.

Forecourt — That area of the court between the net and the service line.

Foot fault — A service delivery that is illegal because the server stepped on the baseline or into the court before the racket contacted the ball.

Forehand — A stroke used to play a ball on the right side of a right-handed player, or vice-versa.

Game — A unit of a set completed when one side wins four points before the other side wins three, or, if both sides have won three points, when one side thereafter gains a two-point margin.

Groundstroke — A forehand or backhand stroke used to hit the ball after it has bounced.

Half-volley — A "pickup" stroke, usually defensive, in which the ball is contacted just as it begins to rise after it has bounced.

Hitting zone — An area behind the ball where the racket passes through just prior to contact.

Hold service — A term used when a game is won by a server.

ITF — The International Tennis Federation; the organization that governs tennis throughout the world.

Let — Any point that must be replayed. Most often, it refers to a serve that hits the top of the net, then lands in the proper service court.

Lob — A high, arching shot that lands near the opponent's baseline.

Love — A score of zero. In a love game, one side wins no points; in a love set, one side wins no games.

Match — A contest between two or four players in which one side must win a predetermined number of games or sets to be declared the winner.

Match point — Term used when a side needs but one more point to win the match.

Mixed doubles — Doubles teams composed of male and female partners.

Net cord — A term for a let serve or any shot that hits the top of the net and then lands in the opposing court.

Net game — A manner of play in which a player frequently advances to the forecourt to use the volley and smash.

No-ad — A form of scoring that eliminates deuce and replaces the traditional love-15-30-40 scoring with 0-1-2-3-4. The first player to reach 4 points becomes the winner of that game.

Open stance — When a player has the forward foot further away from the sideline than the back foot.

Overhead (smash) — A free-swinging stroke used for a ball that is over a player's head. Its motion resembles the serve.

Passing shot — To send the ball across the net to either side of an opponent beyond their reach.

Poach — Applies to a net player in doubles when that player leaves their half of the court to intercept a ball in their partner's territory.

Rally — The exchange of shots between opponents after the serve, usually referring to prolonged play.

Serve — The stroke used to put the ball into play at the start of each point. The more inclusive term **service** applies to the right to be the server and to the served ball itself.

Service break — Term used when a game is won by the receiver.

Service line — The line that defines the back boundary of the service courts.

Set — A unit of a match completed when one side wins six games, or when one side gains a lead of two games after both sides have won at least five games. In tie-breaker sets, it is the winner of the tie-breaker game.

Set point — Term used when a side needs only one more point to win the set.

Sideline — The line that marks the outside edge of either the singles or the doubles court.

Singles — Match play between two players.

Slice serve — A serve imparting sidespin to the ball.

Smash — Same as **overhead.**

Straight sets — To win a match without losing a set.

Tie-breaker — A scoring system designed to eliminate prolonged sets. If any set becomes tied at six games each, players may play a best 5-of-9 or, more commonly, a best 7-of-12-point tie-breaking game to determine the winner of the set.

Topspin — Forward spin on the ball; that is, with the top of the ball rotating in the direction of its flight.

USTA — The United States Tennis Association; the organization that governs tennis in America.

VASSS — The Van Alen Simplified Scoring System, more commonly known as no-ad scoring, where scores of 1-2-3-4 replace the traditional scoring, and the first player to reach 4 points wins the game.

Volley — A short punch stroke used to hit the ball before it bounces.

WCT — World Championship Tennis. A professional organization that arranges tournaments throughout the world, for pro players, with extraordinary prize money often being awarded.

Index

NOTE: Page numbers in italics refer to illustrations.

A

anaerobic activity, 169
angles, 115-116, *116*
"anything-goes" shot, 109
attack, 82-83, *83*
attitude, mental, 4, 48, 113-14, 133, 143-157
Australian formation, 140-142, *141*

B

backhand, 8, 12, 23-24, 25-29, *25, 28, 29*, 36-37, *36*, 41, 93, *93*, 105-106, *105*
behavior on-court, 3
biofeedback, 4
"bounce", 6, 18

C

chop, 38, 72
circle maneuver, 10, *10, 11*
circuit training, 168, *168, 169*
coil, 16
competition, 113-114
composite materials, 179
concentration, 148-149
contact points, 12-13, *12*
court surface, 126-127
cross-court shot, 116, *116*, 120

D

defense, 161-162
deformation, 19
deltoid muscles, 166
dink, 111, *111*
drift, 133-135
drop shot, 109, *110, 111*, 124
drop volley, 109-110, *110, 111*

E

endurance, 166
eye on the ball, 15-16, *16*

F

fake, 135
follow-through, 14, *14*, 15, *25*, 55, 93, *93*
foot fault, 187
footwork, 83-85, *85*
forecourt, 119-120
forehand, 12, 23, 39, 40, *40, 41*, 41
forward impact, 10-12, *11*

G

grip, 20, 39-42, *40*, 180
   Continental, *40*, 41-42, 50-51, *51, 89*
   Eastern, 39, *40*, 42
   forehand, 40, *40, 41*, 50, 51, *51*
   Western, 39, 40, *40, 41*
groundstroke, 14, 15, 19-46, 104-105, 117, *117*

H

half-volley, 103-105, *104*
hamstrings, 166

I

inordinate delay, 186
integrity, 183-184

K

K.I.S.S., 2-3
"killer instinct", 152
knees, 15, 37

L

"laws" of play, 114-115
let, 186-187
line calls, 184-186
lob, 86-87, 91-100, 146
   backspin, 97, *97*
   defensive, 91, 93-95, *94-95*

doubles, 137-139, *137, 138*
offensive, 91, 92-93, *92, 93,* 98-99, *98*
return of, 106-108, *107, 108*
topspin, 95-97, *96*
lunge, 85, *85*

M

mental practice, 155-157
middle court, 139
mixed doubles, 142
momentum, 21, *22,* 22, 23
muscle memory, 160-161

N

net play, 130-131
Newton's Law, 19

O

offense, 161-162
overhead, 86-88, *87*
overload principle, 165

P

pectoral muscles, 166
physics, 1-2
pivot, 7-9, *8, 9*
player types
　groundstroke, 117, *117*
　human backboard, 118-119
　net rusher, 120-121, *121*
　slugger, 118
poaching, 133-135, *134*
psychology, 67

Q

quadriceps muscles, 166

R

racket, 50, 177-182, *178*
　acceleration, 21
　deformation, 19
　grip, 20, 39-42, *40*
　power, 21-22
ready position, 6, *7*
relaxation, 5, 6, 56
rhythm, 6
rise, 13
rope, imaginary, 139, 140

S

sequence of shots, 121-123, *122*
serve, 16, *16,* 47-76, 150-151
　Australian formation, 140-142, *141*
　first, 58-59, *59,* 124

flat, 49, *49,* 50, *51,* 53, 55
placement, 125, *126*
practice, 188
power, 56-58
quick, 188
return of, 67-76, *68, 70-71, 72-73*
　doubles play, 135, *136*
　second, 58-59, *59,* 124, 125, *126*
slice, 60-63, *60, 61-62,* 125
strategy
　doubles, 131
　singles, 124-125, *126*
topspin, 48-50, *49, 51,* 52, 53, 55, 57, *59,* 125
service court, 47
slump, 153-154
smash, 88, 90, *90,* 105-106, *106*
spin, 31-39, *32, 33, 34,* 42-43, 47-66
　backspin, 33, *33,* 34, *34,* 37-39, *38-39,* 43
　Bernouilli principle, 31-32
　chop, 38
　topspin, 32, 33, *33,* 34-37, *34, 35, 36,* 39, 40, 41, 42-43, 48-50, *49*
　underspin, 37. *See* backspin.
stalling, 188
stance, 22-24, *23, 24,* 51-52, *51*
strength, 166
stress, 144-146
string, 180-181
　tension, 181-182
superstition, 153
sweetspot, 178
swing, 24, *25. See also* backhand *and* forehand.
　looped, 35, *35-36*

T

tension, 2, 5, 144-146
timing, 6
toss, 52-53, *52, 57, 59*
touch, 109-112
trapezius muscles, 166
triceps muscles, 166

V

visualization, 155-157
volley, 16, 81-83, *81, 82. See also* half-volley

W

warm-up, 146-148, *167,* 188
weight transfer, 21, 22, 23, 37, 57
windup, 16, 53-54, *54*
wrist snap, 54-58